Yii2 By Example

Develop complete web applications from scratch
through practical examples and tips for beginners
and more advanced users

Fabrizio Caldarelli

[PACKT] open source

PUBLISHING

community experience distilled

BIRMINGHAM - MUMBAI

Yii2 By Example

Copyright © 2015 Packt Publishing

First published: September 2015

Production reference: 1230915

Published by Packt Publishing Ltd.
Livery Place
35 Livery Street
Birmingham B3 2PB, UK.

ISBN 978-1-78528-741-1

www.packtpub.com

Credits

Author
Fabrizio Caldarelli

Reviewers
Tristan Bendixen

Samuel Liew

Acquisition Editor
Vivek Anantharaman

Content Development Editor
Anand Singh

Technical Editor
Vivek Arora

Copy Editors
Ameesha Smith-Green

Laxmi Subramanian

Project Coordinator
Mary Alex

Proofreader
Safis Editing

Indexer
Tejal Soni

Production Coordinator
Manu Joseph

Cover Work
Manu Joseph

About the Author

Fabrizio Caldarelli is an Italian programmer who started his professional career in his youth by programming with desktop-oriented languages, the first being Visual Basic. From the year 2000 onward, he spent 5 years developing software to manage radio broadcasts. During that period, he studied C#.NET to make porting of all software versus this new platform.

During the same period, he learned web programming, HTML, and ASP, and in 2003, he began to develop software using PHP as the default programming language for web pages. During those years, he collaborated as a teacher for PHP programming courses with `http://www.html.it/`, an important online reference for developers in Italy.

In 2008, he added new skills to his experience by starting to develop mobile projects for Nokia devices with Symbian C++, and a few years later, he started working on projects for iOS, Android, and naturally Windows phone.

After many PHP-based web projects, in late 2012, he moved on to the Yii framework as his primary framework for developing web applications.

Since then, he has built many important projects based on Yii 1 and later on Yii 2, day by day discovering the powerful improvement that Yii provides to getting work done.

Now he lives in Sacrofano, a small town near Rome, with his wife, Serena.

I want to thank Erika Accili for supporting me during the writing and organization of this book. I also want to thank my wife, Serena, for sustaining me during all the work, and for the rest of her life indeed!

About the Reviewers

Tristan Bendixen is currently pursuing a master's degree as a software engineer, having been passionate about programming for most of his life. He has worked as a developer on diverse projects, ranging from commercial and corporate websites to mobile phone apps and desktop applications.

He continues to work as a software developer alongside his studies, on paid projects, as well as some open source ones, which he helps with when time permits.

> I would like to thank my beloved mother and younger brother for their love and support in my constant endeavors to become a better developer, and my friends at Aalborg University for being awesome sparring partners on projects and classes alike.

Samuel Liew is a full-stack web developer who enjoys producing solutions with interesting and challenging requirements. He has experience of developing a diverse range of websites, such as governmental sites, public utilities, real estate, investor relations, contests, touchscreen kiosks, iPad feedback apps, blogs and magazines, and media news. He has also been involved with creating two proprietary content management systems using C#.NET/MongoDB and PHP/Yii/MySQL. His latest accomplishment is the development of a microstock photography website (http://vivistock.com) using the Yii Framework, which involves e-commerce transactions and implements heavy business logic.

www.PacktPub.com

Support files, eBooks, discount offers, and more

For support files and downloads related to your book, please visit www.PacktPub.com.

Did you know that Packt offers eBook versions of every book published, with PDF and ePub files available? You can upgrade to the eBook version at www.PacktPub.com and as a print book customer, you are entitled to a discount on the eBook copy. Get in touch with us at service@packtpub.com for more details.

At www.PacktPub.com, you can also read a collection of free technical articles, sign up for a range of free newsletters and receive exclusive discounts and offers on Packt books and eBooks.

https://www2.packtpub.com/books/subscription/packtlib

Do you need instant solutions to your IT questions? PacktLib is Packt's online digital book library. Here, you can search, access, and read Packt's entire library of books.

Why subscribe?

- Fully searchable across every book published by Packt
- Copy and paste, print, and bookmark content
- On demand and accessible via a web browser

Free access for Packt account holders

If you have an account with Packt at www.PacktPub.com, you can use this to access PacktLib today and view 9 entirely free books. Simply use your login credentials for immediate access.

Table of Contents

Preface

This book covers the use of the Yii2 framework from scratch up to build a complete web application.

Yii is a high-performance PHP framework that is best for developing Web 2.0 applications that provide fast, secure, and professional features to rapidly create robust projects. However, this rapid development requires the ability to organize common tasks together to build a complete application. It's all too easy to get confused about the use of these technologies.

So, walking through practical examples will help you understand how these concepts must be used and realize a successful application.

What this book covers

Chapter 1, Starting with Yii2, provides basic knowledge about the Yii2 framework, starting from requirements to explain every single functionality. Then, we will use debugging and logging tools to trace our code and provides find errors. Finally, we will write our first project based on the basic template.

Chapter 2, Creating a Simple News Reader, creates our first controllers and relative views. We will explore static and dynamic views, learn how to render views in layout and pass data from controller to view, and then look at reusing views through partial views and blocks.

Chapter 3, Making Pretty URLs, shows how to implement pretty URLs, which is useful for search engine optimization. We will also create examples where we used custom rules to parse and create the URL. Finally, we will learn how to build more customized URL rules through Rule classes.

Chapter 4, Creating a Room through Forms, shows how to build a Model class from scratch and send data from view to controller using form, which is created using the Yii2 ActiveForm widget. We will also look at commonly used methods to format data and send files from the form.

Chapter 5, Developing a Reservation System, explains how to configure a database connection and execute SQL queries from scratch with DAO support for the framework. Next, we will find out how to use Gii and get to know about the advantages it has in creating models from the database table structure. Gii creates models that extend the ActiveRecord class, and, through its use, we will finally learn how to manipulate data.

Chapter 6, Using a Grid for Data and Relations, presents the GridView widget for displaying data, directly or relationed. A fundamental topic inside GridView is Data Provider, the way to provide data to GridView. We will learn how to get Data Provider from ActiveRecord, Array, or SQL, based on the available sources.

Chapter 7, Working on the User Interface, discusses the User Interface and how Yii helps us with its core functionalities.

Chapter 8, Log in to the App, shows how to apply user authentication and authorization to an app. The first step is to create authenticated access to the application. For this purpose, we will create a database table to manage users and associate it to the Yii user component through a user model that extends IdentityInterface.

Chapter 9, Frontend to Display Rooms to Everyone, explains how to use Yii to build a modern web project based on frontend and backend applications. We will find out the differences between basic and advanced templates, installing our first advanced project based on advanced templates.

Chapter 10, Localize the App, shows how to configure multiple languages in our app. We will discover that there are two storage options to handle internationalization: files and databases.

Chapter 11, Creating an API for Use in a Mobile App, creates an API for use in mobile apps through the use of powerful tools provided by Yii. We will adopt the approach of creating a new application in order to distribute RESTful Web Services, instead of mixing web and API controllers.

Chapter 12, Create a Console Application to Automate the Periodic Task, explains how to write a console application and allows you to discover the main differences between web and console apps.

Chapter 13, Final Refactoring, helps you to reuse code using widgets and components. We will create some practical examples on how to use them.

What you need for this book

The minimum requirements for this book are: a host on the Web, local or remote, based on the PHP 5.4 environment and having a MySQL database server installed (no specific version for it).

For writing code, it is enough to have a simple highlighted syntax editor, such as block notes, TextEdit, Notepad++, PSPad, Aptana, and so on.

Who this book is for

This book is intended for anyone who wants to discover the Yii Framework or master its practical concepts. Beginner-level users will find some introductive theory in every chapter that explains the topics treated, with a lot of code showing all their practical aspects. Advanced users will find many examples with special cases illustrated and common mistakes solved.

Basic programming experience with PHP and object-oriented programming is required.

Conventions

In this book, you will find a number of text styles that distinguish between different kinds of information. Here are some examples of these styles and an explanation of their meaning.

Code words in text, database table names, folder names, filenames, file extensions, pathnames, dummy URLs, user input, and Twitter handles are shown as follows: "Now, create the view with this content in basic/views/my-authentication/ login.php."

A block of code is set as follows:

```php
<?php
return [
    2 => [
        'operator',
    ],
    1 => [
        'admin',
    ],
];
```

Any command-line input or output is written as follows:

```
$ curl -H "Accept: application/json" http://hostname/yiiadv/api/web/test-
rest/index
```

```
[{"id":1,"name":"Albert","surname":"Einstein"},{"id":2,"name":"Enzo","sur
name":"Ferrari"},{"id":4,"name":"Mario","surname":"Bros"}]
```

 Warnings or important notes appear in a box like this.

 Tips and tricks appear like this.

Reader feedback

Feedback from our readers is always welcome. Let us know what you think about this book—what you liked or disliked. Reader feedback is important for us as it helps us develop titles that you will really get the most out of.

To send us general feedback, simply e-mail feedback@packtpub.com, and mention the book's title in the subject of your message.

If there is a topic that you have expertise in and you are interested in either writing or contributing to a book, see our author guide at www.packtpub.com/authors.

Customer support

Now that you are the proud owner of a Packt book, we have a number of things to help you to get the most from your purchase.

Downloading the example code

You can download the example code files from your account at http://www.packtpub.com for all the Packt Publishing books you have purchased. If you purchased this book elsewhere, you can visit http://www.packtpub.com/support and register to have the files e-mailed directly to you.

Errata

Although we have taken every care to ensure the accuracy of our content, mistakes do happen. If you find a mistake in one of our books—maybe a mistake in the text or the code—we would be grateful if you could report this to us. By doing so, you can save other readers from frustration and help us improve subsequent versions of this book. If you find any errata, please report them by visiting http://www.packtpub.com/submit-errata, selecting your book, clicking on the **Errata Submission Form** link, and entering the details of your errata. Once your errata are verified, your submission will be accepted and the errata will be uploaded to our website or added to any list of existing errata under the Errata section of that title.

To view the previously submitted errata, go to https://www.packtpub.com/books/content/support and enter the name of the book in the search field. The required information will appear under the **Errata** section.

Piracy

Piracy of copyrighted material on the Internet is an ongoing problem across all media. At Packt, we take the protection of our copyright and licenses very seriously. If you come across any illegal copies of our works in any form on the Internet, please provide us with the location address or website name immediately so that we can pursue a remedy.

Please contact us at copyright@packtpub.com with a link to the suspected pirated material.

We appreciate your help in protecting our authors and our ability to bring you valuable content.

Questions

If you have a problem with any aspect of this book, you can contact us at questions@packtpub.com, and we will do our best to address the problem.

1
Starting with Yii2

Yii2 is a complete rewrite of the first version of one of the most famous PHP frameworks. It is a well-documented framework with a very active community.

Officially, we can find three types of support: a guide, for a complete navigation through framework topics at `http://www.yiiframework.com/doc-2.0/guide-index.html`, a reference to explore all classes that compose the framework at `http://www.yiiframework.com/doc-2.0/index.html`, and finally forum support at `http://www.yiiframework.com/forum/`.

In this chapter, we will go through the following:

- Requirements and tools
- Installing Yii2 with Composer
- Application structure
- Application properties
    - Common application components
    - Handling application events
    - Pattern MVC in Yii2
- Naming convention
    - Configuring debug toolbar
    - Using logger
    - Example – hello world from scratch with the Yii basic template and bootstrap template

Requirements and tools

The basic requirements for Yii2 are a web server (local or remote) and PHP v.5.4 (or newer). It is recommended to have a shell (or command line) access to the machine (local or remote) where we store the code, as there are scripts that it will be very beneficial to use in the development of complex applications. We can also develop the application locally and upload it to the web server when we wish to test it.

For remote hosting, there are multiple options. We can use a simple web hosting service (with PHP v.5.4 support) or we can opt for virtual or dedicated server hosting. Keep in mind that with the former option, if the server doesn't meet the PHP requirements, it can be difficult to change whatever is wrong.

Yii2 has a script, `requirements.php`, which checks whether our hosting meets the requirements to run Yii2 application.

Installing Yii2 with Composer

Composer is a tool for dependency management in PHP. Yii2 uses it to install itself and other vendors' modules (for example, bootstrap).

It is also possible to install Yii2 in the old way, by downloading the complete package and transferring it to the host, local or remote, where the framework will be installed. However, Composer will give us many benefits, like the ability to easily update the framework and ensure that all package dependencies are satisfied. Composer is de facto the new way to install and maintain projects, so I recommend using it from the start. If you are unsure about using Composer, it's worth mentioning that most users will need to learn two or three commands at most, so it's not a steep learning curve.

Yii2 has two available templates to start with: basic and advanced. We will start with the basic template, but we will also see in the next chapters how to use advanced templates.

So, let's look at how to install Yii2 with Composer. We need to access the folder through the console, where the web server's httpdocs point to and launch these commands:

```
curl -s http://getcomposer.org/installer | php
php composer.phar global require "fxp/composer-asset-plugin:1.0.0"
php composer.phar create-project --prefer-dist yiisoft/yii2-app-basic
basic
```

These commands are useful if we are in the Linux or Mac environment. On Windows, you need to download `Composer-Setup.exe` from Composer's official website and run it.

The first command gets the `http://getcomposer.org/installer` URL and passes it to PHP to create the `composer.phar` file.

The second command installs the Composer asset plugin, which allows us to manage bower and npm package dependencies through Composer.

The third and final command installs Yii2 in a directory named `basic`. If you want, you can choose a different directory name.

> During the installation, Composer may ask for our GitHub login credentials and this is normal because Composer needs to get enough API rate limit to retrieve the dependent package information from GitHub. If you don't have a GitHub account, this is the right moment to create a new one!

If we are using Windows, we need to download it from `https://getcomposer.org` and run it. The last two commands will be the same.

We have installed Yii2!

To test it, point to `http://hostname/basic/web` and we should see the *My Yii Application* page.

Application structure

Yii2's application structure is very clear, precise, and redundant (for advanced applications).

The contents of the `basic` folder should be as follows:

Folder names	Description
assets	This includes the files (`.js` and `.css`) referenced in the web page and dependencies of the app.
commands	This includes the controllers used from the command line.
config	This includes the controllers used from web.
mail	This is the mail layout repository.
models	This includes the models used in the whole application.

Folder names	Description
runtime	This is used from Yii2 to store runtime data as logs.
tests	This includes all the test's repositories (unit, functional, fixtures, and so on).
vendor	This includes the third-party module repositories managed by Composer.
views	This contains PHP files, divided into folders that refer to controller names, used to render the main content of the page template. It is mainly called from the controller's actions to render the display output. A folder named layout contains the page template's PHP files.
web	This is the entry point from web

Open web/index.php to view content:

```php
<?php
// comment out the following two lines when deployed to production
defined('YII_DEBUG') or define('YII_DEBUG', true);
defined('YII_ENV') or define('YII_ENV', 'dev');

require(__DIR__ . '/../vendor/autoload.php');
require(__DIR__ . '/../vendor/yiisoft/yii2/Yii.php');

$config = require(__DIR__ . '/../config/web.php');

(new yii\web\Application($config))->run();
```

Here, the first two constant definitions are very important.

YII_DEBUG defines whether you are in debug mode or not. If we set this, we will have more log information and will see the detail error call stack.

YII_ENV defines the environment mode we are working in, and its default value is prod. The available values are test, dev, and prod. These values are used in configuration files to define, for example, a different DB connection (local database different from remote database) or other values, always in configuration files.

Since we are at the start of our project, it is recommended to set YII_DEBUG to true, in order to have more detailed information in case we make a mistake in our code, instead of the unhelpful, blank.

The following table contains a list of all Yii2's objects:

Objects	Description
Models, Views, and Controllers	These are the common objects to apply the MVC pattern to: • Models are data representation and manipulation, usually from the database • Views are used to present data to the end user • Controllers are objects that process requests and generate responses
Components	These are objects that contain logic. The user can write his own components to create reusable functionalities. For example, a component could be a currency converter object, which can be used at many instances in our application.
Application Components	They are singletons that can be called at any point in the app. Singleton means an object instanced just one time in the entire application (so the object will always be the same). The difference between Application Components and Components is that the first can have just one instance in the whole application.
Widgets	These view reusable objects, containing both logic and rendering code. A widget could be, for example, a box displaying today's weather info.
Filters	These are objects that run before or after the execution of Controller actions. A filter can be used to change the format response output of the page, for example, from HTML to JSON.
Modules	This contains all the objects of an app, such as Models, Views, Controller, Components, and so on; we can consider them as subapp, containing reusable sections (for example, user management).
Extensions	Extensions are modules packaged, that we can easily manage using Composer.

Application properties

A Yii2 application can be configured through several properties.

The properties that need to be configured in any application are listed in the following table:

Properties	Description
id	This indicates a unique ID to distinguish this application from others. It is mainly used programmatically. An example of this property is basic.
basePath	This specifies the root directory of the application. This path is the starting point for all the other types of application objects, such as models, controllers, and views. An example of this property is dirname(__DIR__).

The other common properties are listed in the following table:

Properties	Description
aliases	This indicates an alias name for path definitions. They are defined using a key/value array and they are very useful when we need to set a path as a constant that live in the whole application. We type an alias preceded by an @ character. An example of this property is '@fileupload' => 'path/to/files/uploaded'.
bootstrap	This property allows you to configure an array of components to be run during the application bootstrap process. A common usage is to load the log or profile component, gii, or any other component. Be careful not to load too many components, otherwise the response performance of your pages may degrade. An example of this property is 'log', 'gii'.
catchAll	This property captures every request and it is used in the maintenance mode of the site.
components	This property points out a list of application components that you can use in the whole application.
language	This property specifies the language used to display the content. An example of this property is 'language' => 'en'.
modules	This property points out a list of application modules that can be used in the application.

Properties	Description
name	This property indicates the name of your app. An example of this property is 'name' => 'My App'.
params	This property specifies an array of parameters, through key/value pairs. This is a container for global params, such as the administrator's e-mail address.
timeZone	This property indicates the time zone that should be used in the application. An example of this property is 'timeZone' => 'Europe/Rome'.
charset	This property points out the charset used in the application. The default value is UTF-8.
defaultRoute	This property contains a route to be used when a request does not a specify one. This property has different default values according to the environment we are using.
	For web applications, this value will be site, so that SiteController could be used to handle these requests.
	For console applications, this value will be help, so that yii\console\controllers\HelpController can be used invoking its index action that will display help information.

Common application components

Here's a list of the most-used application components:

- request: This component handles all client requests and provides methods to easily get parameters from server global variables, such as $_SERVER, $_POST, $_GET, and $_COOKIES.

  The default state has enableCookieValidation set to true, so you need to set cookieValidationKey parameter as shown in this example:

```
'request' => [
'cookieValidationKey' => 'hPpnJs7tvs0T4N2OGAY',
],
```

- cache: This component helps you handle cache data. Yii2 defaults to the FileCache instance for the cache, but we can also configure an ApcCache, DbCache, MemCache, and so on.

  The following is a standard installation of Yii2:

```
'cache' => [
'class' => 'yii\caching\FileCache',
],
```

- user: This component deals with user authentication in the app. The most important parameter is the identityClass parameter, which defines the class that contains the user's model data, in order to have a specific method to log in or log out a user from the app.

Consider the following example:

```
'user' => [
'identityClass' => 'app\models\User',
        'enableAutoLogin' => true,
 ],
```

- errorHandler: This component provides functionalities to handle uncaught errors and exceptions. It can be configured by specifying the action to run.

Consider the following example:

```
'errorHandler' => [
'errorAction' => 'site/error',
 ],
```

- mailer: This component configures mailer connection parameters to the system that will send an e-mail. Usually, it is the same machine hosting our website, so the default values are probably correct.

Consider the following example:

```
'mailer' => [
  'class' => 'yii\swiftmailer\Mailer',
  // send all mails to a file by default. You have to set
  // 'useFileTransport' to false and configure a transport
    // for the mailer to send real emails.
    'useFileTransport' => true,
 ],
```

- log: This component is mainly used in the debug environment to log the app execution. We can set the debug level and destination.

Consider the following example:

```
'log' => [
        'traceLevel' => YII_DEBUG ? 3 : 0,
        'targets' => [
            [
                'class' => 'yii\log\FileTarget',
                'levels' => ['error', 'warning'],
            ],
        ],
    ],
```

- db: This component handles a database connection. We can have several db configuration in our app; in this case, we can define more components with the Connection class located at yii\db\.

Consider the following example:

```
db => [
    'class' => 'yii\db\Connection',
    'dsn' => 'mysql:host=localhost;dbname=yii2basic',
    'username' => 'dbuser'',
    'password' => 'dbpassword',
    'charset' => 'utf8',
],
```

Handling application events

During its lifecycle, an application can trigger many events. These events can be declared in application configuration or programmatically. Common triggers are beforeRequest, afterRequest, beforeAction, and afterAction, but every object can have its own events.

For example, a common use of events is to set mysql db timezone.

To set the time zone to UTC in db component configuration, we must define a handler for the afterOpen event:

```
'db' => [
  'class' => 'yii\db\Connection',
  'dsn' => 'mysql:host=localhost;dbname=mydb',
  'username' => 'dbuser',
  'password' => 'dbpassword',
  'charset' => 'utf8',

  'on afterOpen' => function($event) {
    $event->sender->createCommand("SET time_zone = '+00:00'")-
    >execute();
      }
],
```

An anonymous function, attached to on afterOpen event handlers, has an $event parameter, which is an instance of the yii\base\ActionEvent class. This class has a $sender object that refers to the sender of the event. In this case, $sender refers to the instance of database components (db). This property may also be null when this event is a class-level event.

The MVC pattern in Yii2

Yii2 is built according to the **Model-View-Controller** (**MVC**) design pattern.

Models, representing logic, are objects extended from \yii\base\Model, which offer many features such as attribute, attribute labels, massive assignment (to fill object attributes directly for an array), validation rules, and data exporting.

Normally, in common apps, a Model will be generated from the database, extending yii\db\ActiveRecord that implements the Active Record design pattern, with many methods to manipulate data. Yii2 provides Gii, a tool used to generate Model classes directly from the database's table structure.

Controllers, the bridge between view and model, are class instances extending from yii\base\Controller, used to process requests and generate responses.

Controllers mainly contain functions whose name starts with the action prefix that allows the framework to recognize those functions as routes, which can be requested.

Finally, we will look at views that deal with displaying data to end users that are mainly rendered in the page layout from controllers.

Naming convention

In order to allow auto-loading, Yii2 uses a simple standard to set names.

Routes that refer respectively to module, controller, and the action requested take the following format:

```
ModuleID/ControllerID/ActionID
```

We will look at each element in detail as follows:

- The ModuleID is optional, so often the format is ControllerID/ActionID
- The ModuleID must be specified in the module's configuration property, under the same name
- The ControllerID and ActionID should contain only English characters in lowercase, digits, underscores, dashes, and forward slashes

An example of route is http://hostname/index.php?r=site/index, where site is the ControllerID and index is the ActionID.

Starting from ControllerID, it is very easy to create the Controller class name. Just turn into uppercase the first letter of each word separated by dashes, then remove dashes and append the suffix Controller. If ControllerID contains slashes, just apply the rules to the part after the last slash in the ID. This is possible because controllers can be collected in subfolders, starting from `app\controllers`.

The following are some examples:

- Shop points to `app\controllers\ShopController`
- Preferred number points to `app\controllers\PreferredNumberController`
- Admin/users account points to `app\controllers\admin\UsersAccountController`

© My Company 2015   Powered by Yii Framework

Routes are passed to entry script `basic/web/index.php` through the `r` parameter.

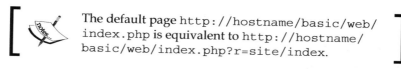

> The default page `http://hostname/basic/web/index.php` is equivalent to `http://hostname/basic/web/index.php?r=site/index`.

Configuring the debug toolbar

It is important to have a rich collection of tools to make development easier in displaying some useful information about requests and responses.

For this purpose, Yii2 provides a toolbar that displays several types of info.

A common way to activate the debug toolbar is to set in `config/web.php`:

```
'bootstrap' => ['debug'],
'modules' => [
  'debug' => 'yii\debug\Module',
]
```

Now you can set the following values:

- debug to `bootstrap` config node
- debug to `modules` config node, using the `Module` class under `yii\debug\`

The default installation of the Yii2 basic template already enables the debug toolbar, as we can see at the bottom of the `config/web.php` configuration file. The Gii module is also enabled as well, but we will work with it later.

```
if (YII_ENV_DEV) {
    // configuration adjustments for 'dev' environment
    $config['bootstrap'][] = 'debug';
    $config['modules']['debug'] = 'yii\debug\Module';
    $config['bootstrap'][] = 'gii';
    $config['modules']['gii'] = 'yii\gii\Module';
}
```

This config entry is only valid in the `YII_ENV_DEV` mode. So, we must check whether the `web/index.php` `YII_ENV` variable has the `dev` value (as shown in the default installation).

Debug toolbar closed

If we try to reload the web page at `basic/web/index.php` after these checks, we should see the following screenshot:

Debug toolbar opened

The right arrow reports that the debug toolbar is active but closed. If we click on it, the complete toolbar will open. Now, click on any item, the debug panel will be displayed.

By default, the debug toolbar can be used only in localhost. However, if we are using Yii2 in the remote hosting environment, we set the `allowedIPs` property of the `debug` module.

```
$config['modules']['debug'] = [
    'class' => 'yii\debug\Module',
    'allowedIPs' => [ '127.0.0.1', '::1']
];
```

In `allowedIPs` there is only localhost (in the IPv4 and IPv6 forms). We need to put our Internet connection and IP source address here, which can be easily found using any my IP service on the Internet, such as `http://www.whatismyip.com/`.

If our IP source is, for example, 1.2.3.4, we must add this entry to allowedIPs, in this way:

```
$config['modules']['debug'] = [
    'class' => 'yii\debug\Module',
    'allowedIPs' => [ '127.0.0.1', '::1', '1.2.3.4']
];
```

Remember that if we do not have an Internet connection with a static IP, this IP might change. So we need to check whether allowedIPs contains our current IP.

You could also use an asterisk * to allow all IP addresses, so you do not have to deal with dynamic IP issues. If you do this, you need to remember to remove the asterisk before deployment. Finally, at the bottom of our current configuration config/web.php, you will see the following code:

```
if (YII_ENV_DEV) {
    // configuration adjustments for 'dev' environment
    $config['bootstrap'][] = 'debug';
    $config['modules']['debug'] = [
        'class' => 'yii\debug\Module',
            'allowedIPs' => [ '127.0.0.1', '::1', '1.2.3.4']
    ];
    $config['bootstrap'][] = 'gii';
    $config['modules']['gii'] = 'yii\gii\Module';
}
```

Let's return to the basic/web/index.php webpage and take a look at the debug info panel.

The debug information is distributed in the menu:

- **Configuration**: This is the installed PHP version and configuration and also the installed Yii2 framework version.

- **Request**: This is the info about the request just sent, displaying parameters of the request, headers of the request and other useful data as response and session data.

- **Logs**: This involves the actions performed by Yii2 during the execution. There are additional filters in this section to select the types of logs to be displayed.

- **Performance Profiling**: This includes info about timing and duration of process.

- **Database**: This includes info about all database query occurred; we can filter for type of query to locate a specific query.

It is possible to filter all data using internal grid filter or to filter for all, latest or selecting among the last 10 rows of the log on top of the content pane.

Using the logger

In the Yii2 application, the debug info is stored using the log component. We can use this tool both in the development and production environment, but for reasons of performance and security in production, we should log only the important messages.

The default configuration file of the Yii2 basic template provides log entry in the components property of config/web.php:

```
'log' => [
  'traceLevel' => YII_DEBUG ? 3 : 0,
    'targets' => [
    [
            'class' => 'yii\log\FileTarget',
            'levels' => ['error', 'warning'],
    ],
    ],
],
```

Example – Hello world from scratch with the Yii basic template and bootstrap template

It is now time to code our first project using Yii2.

If we have not installed Yii2 yet, we will to do it now using Composer as follows:

1. Open Command Prompt to the web server.

2. Go to the document root of the web server (/var/www in a Linux machine).

3. Launch these commands (as described in the *Installing Yii with Composer* section):

   ```
   curl -s http://getcomposer.org/installer | php

   php composer.phar global require "fxp/composer-asset-
   plugin:1.0.0"

   php composer.phar create-project --prefer-dist yiisoft/yii2-
   app-basic basic
   ```

Now, we need a fresh installation of Yii2 in the basic folder of the web server document root. Point the browser to `http:/hostname/basic/web` and we should see Yii2's congratulations page:

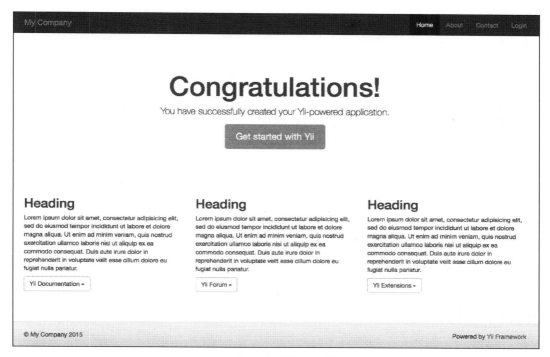

An example of the Hello world page

We will create our first action to display a memorable `hello world` on the screen.

We know from the *Application properties* section, in the defaultRoute entry, that the `SiteController` controller will be called when no route is specified in request.

So, we enter `basic/controllers` and open `SiteController.php`, which is the default controller.

In the `SiteController` class definition, we add a new method at the top, called `actionHelloWorld`, without parameters.

```
public function actionHelloWorld()
{
    echo 'hello world'
}
```

Let's save the file and point to `http://hostname/basic/web/index.php?r=site/hello-world`.

You should see a blank page with `hello world`.

 Pay attention when using the name route convention. Uppercase letters are translated to lowercase and dashes.

This is fantastic, but now we just want to put `hello world` within the page template.

We must now create a view with the content of response hello world!. In order to do this, we need to create a file named `helloWorld.php` as the name of the action under `views/site`. The naming convention need not necessarily be the same here because the view file is not automatically called from the framework.

This file only contains the `hello world` text.

We update `SiteController` with the following code:

```
public function actionHelloWorld()
{
    return $this->render('helloWorld');
}
```

In the `actionHelloWorld()` method, `$this` refers to the SiteController's instance, and `render()` will insert the `views/helloWorld.php` file content in the main content layout page.

The extension of the view file, `.php`, is automatically added from the framework to view the name parameter passed to the render method.

What if we want to pass a parameter, such as name, to `actionHelloWorld()`? Formally, we need to add just one parameter to `actionHelloWorld()` in SiteController as follows:

```
public function actionHelloWorld($nameToDisplay)
{
    return $this->render('helloWorld',
  [ 'nameToDisplay' => $nameToDisplay ]
    );
}
```

Then, under `view/site/helloWorld.php` add the following code:

```
Hello World <?php echo $nameToDisplay ?>
```

With the update of `actionHelloWorld()`, we will pass as a second parameter, an array of variables, that will be visible and used in View.

When we use parameters in the action function, we must remember that they will be mandatory and we must respect the order when passing it to the request.

To avoid this obligation, we can use the old method, parsing parameters into the function:

```php
public function actionHelloWorld()
{
    $nameToDisplay = Yii::$app->request->get('nameToDisplay');
    // Equivalent to
// $nameToDisplay =
isset($_GET['nameToDisplay'])?$_GET['nameToDisplay']:null;

    return $this->render('helloWorld',
    [ 'nameToDisplay' => $nameToDisplay ]
    );
}
```

With this solution, we can decide whether to pass the `nameToDisplay` parameter to request. The default value of the `nameToDisplay` parameter will be null, but we can decide to assign a different value.

The following is a URL example passing the `nameToDisplay` parameter `Foo`:

```
http://hostname/basic/web/index.php?r=site/hello-
world&nameToDisplay=Foo
```

Summary

In this chapter, we looked at a basic understanding of the Yii2 framework, starting from requirements to explain the main features. Then we used debugging and logging tools to trace our code and were able to find errors. Finally, we wrote our first project based on the basic template.

Next, you will learn how to create our controllers and views, to create custom interaction with frontend users.

2
Creating a Simple News Reader

This chapter explains how to write your first controller in order to display news items list and details, make interactions between controllers and views, and then customize the view's layout.

In this chapter, we will go through the following:

- Creating controller and action
- Creating a view to display the news list
- How the controller sends the data to view
    - Example – create a controller to display the static news items list and details

- Split the common view content into reusable views
    - Example – render partial in view

- Creating static pages
- Share data between views and layout
    - Example – change layout background based on the URL parameter

- Layout with dynamic blocks
    - Example – add dynamic box to display advertising info

- Using multiple layouts
    - Example – using different layout to create responsive and not responsive layout for the same view

Creating Controller and Action

In order to handle a request, the first thing to do is to create a new controller.

The things you must remember while creating a file controller are as follows:

- The namespace at the top (in basic application usually app\controllers)
- The use path for used class
- The controller class must extend the yii\web\Controller class
- The actions are handled from controller functions whose name starts with action and the first letter of each word is in uppercase

Let's point to basic/controllers and create a file named NewsController.php.

Then, create a class with the same name as the file and extend it from controller; finally, create an action named index to manage request for news/index:

```php
<?php

// 1. specify namespace at the top (in basic application usually
app\controllers);
namespace app\controllers;

// 2. specify 'use' path for used class;
use Yii;
use yii\web\Controller;

// 3. controller class must extend yii\web\Controller class;
// This line is equivalent to
// class NewsController extends yii\web\Controller
class NewsController extends Controller
{
// 4. actions are handled from controller functions whose name
starts with 'action' and the first letter of each word is
uppercase;
    public function actionIndex()
    {
            echo "this is my first controller";
    }
}
```

If we try to point the browser to `http://hostname/basic/web/index.php?r=news/index`, we will see a blank page with the notice **this is my first controller**.

Now, let's see which common errors can occur when we ignore those four things to remember mentioned at the top of this chapter.

The namespace defines the hierarchical organization for names used in our application. If we forget to declare a namespace, Yii2 with `YII_DEBUG` set to true in `web/index.php`, will display the following error message:

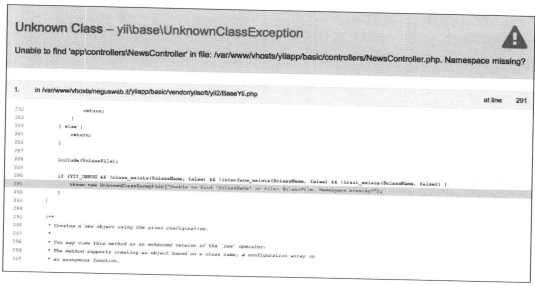

The missing Controller namespace

Yii2 reports an error in an excellent way, giving us the possibility to solve it by checking if we are missing the namespace.

Then, the `Use` keyword is employed to specify the complete path of a class in the application. A class that has a `path/to/class/ClassName` complete path, can be referenced in the app using only `ClassName` if we put an `use   path/to/class/ClassName` just after namespace declaration.

However, if we use just `ClassName` without defining the `use` declaration at the top of the file, an error such as the following can occur:

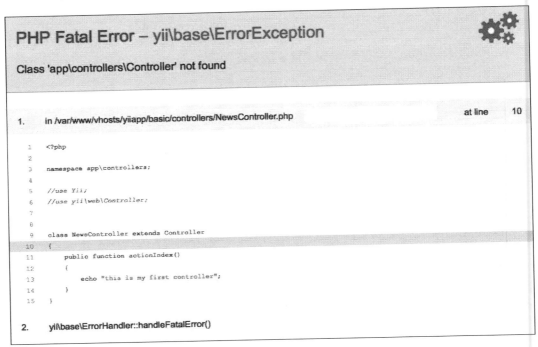

This error is simple to explain, but harder to find, especially for beginners.

In this case, the screenshot shows that it has been used the `Controller` name (after the `extends` keyword) at row 9. Since there is no complete path for the `Controller` class name, Yii2 will try to look for the `Controller` class under `app\controllers`, without finding it.

To solve this problem, we must change `Controller` with `yii\web\Controller` at row 9 and for all the next rows that will use the `Controller` class name without defining a complete class path, or that insert a `use` declaration at the top of the file, we must employ `yii\web\Controller`.

A controller is always a subclass of `yii\web\Controller` or simply, if we have used the keyword `use`, a subclass of `Controller`. Action names follow the rules described in the previous chapter.

Creating a view to display a news list

Now, we will create a simple news list in a view named `itemsList`. We will point to this view from `NewsController`, so we have to:

- Create a `news` folder under `basic/views`, that `NewsController` will use as the base folder to search for the views to be rendered (according to the view names' rules explained in the previous chapter)
- Create an `itemsList.php` file under `basic/views/news`

Now, open `basic/views/news/itemsList.php`, create an array with a list of data and display the output with a simple table of items:

```php
<?php
    $newsList = [
        [ 'title' => 'First World War', 'date' => '1914-07-28' ],
        [ 'title' => 'Second World War', 'date' => '1939-09-01' ],
        [ 'title' => 'First man on the moon', 'date' => '1969-07-
        20' ]
    ];
?>

<table>
    <tr>
        <th>Title</th>
        <th>Date</th>
    </tr>
    <?php foreach($newsList as $item) { ?>
    <tr>
        <td><?php echo $item['title'] ?></td>
        <td><?php echo $item['date'] ?></td>
    </tr>
    <?php } ?>
</table>
```

Then, we need to create an action provided by a function named `actionItemsList` that will be rendered by `http://hostname/basic/web/index.php?r=news/items-list`.

Pay attention to names for routes, controllers, and actions:

- The route for this action is news/items-list (lowercase and words separated by dashes);
- The controller class name is NewsController (uppercase with the word Controller in the end);
- The action function name in NewsController is actionItemsList (the function name has action word as prefix, dashes in the route are removed, and the first letter of each word is in uppercase);

The function to append in the NewsController class is as follows:

```
public function actionItemsList()
{
        return $this->render('itemsList');
}
```

The render() method that belongs to \yii\web\Controller, displays in the layout content of the view passed as the first parameter. When the framework is looking for the view, it will append .php extension to the name passed as the first parameter of the render() method and it will look for it in basic/view/news. The last member of the path is the name that is calling the render() method.

Now, we can point to http://hostname/basic/web/index.php?r=news/items-list, to see our beautiful table!

How the controller sends data to view

In the previous paragraph, we have seen how to display the content view. However, the view should only be responsible for displaying data, and not for manipulation. Consequently, any work on data should be done in controller action and then passed to view.

The render() method in the action of the controller has a second parameter, which is an array whose keys are names of variables, and values are the content of these variables available in view context.

Now, let's move all data manipulation of our itemsList example in controller, leaving out just the code to format the output (such as HTML).

The following is the content of the actionItemsList() controller:

```
public function actionItemsList()
{
```

```
$newsList = [
    [ 'title' => 'First World War', 'date' => '1914-07-28' ],
    [ 'title' => 'Second World War', 'date' => '1939-09-01' ],
    [ 'title' => 'First man on the moon', 'date' => '1969-07-20' ]
];


return $this->render('itemsList', ['newsList' => $newsList]);
}
```

In `views/news/itemsList.php`, we only have the following code:

```
<?php // $newsList is from actionItemsList ?>
<table>
    <tr>
        <th>Title</th>
        <th>Date</th>
    </tr>
    <?php foreach($newsList as $item) { ?>
    <tr>
        <th><?php echo $item['title'] ?></th>
        <th><?php echo $item['date'] ?></th>
    </tr>
    <?php } ?>
</table>
```

Thus, we have correctly split the working of controller and view.

Example – create a controller to display the static news items list and details using the bootstrap template

Our next goal is to complete the news reader displaying details of single news in another page.

Since we are going to use the same data for list and detail, we will extract the $newsList data from action to a function, in order to be reused for more actions.

In NewsController, we will have the following code:

```
public function dataItems()
{
  $newsList = [
    [ 'title' => 'First World War', 'date' => '1914-07-28' ],
    [ 'title' => 'Second World War', 'date' => '1939-09-01' ],
```

```
        [ 'title' => 'First man on the moon', 'date' => '1969-07-20' ]
    ];

    return $newsList;
}

public function actionItemsList()
{
    $newsList = $this->dataItems();

    return $this->render('itemsList', ['newsList' => $newsList]);
}
```

After this, we will create a new function in NewsController, actionItemDetail, that is used to handle requests of detail of a news item. This function will expect a parameter, which will allow to filter the correct items from $newsList, for example, the title.

The following is the content of actionItemDetail:

```
public function actionItemDetail($title)
{
    $newsList = $this->dataItems();

    $item = null;
    foreach($newsList as $n)
    {
        if($title == $n['title']) $item = $n;
    }

    return $this->render('itemDetail', ['item' => $item]);
}
```

Next we have to create a new view file in views/news named itemDetail.php.

The following is the content of itemDetail.php located under views/news/:

```
<?php // $item is from actionItemDetail ?>

<h2>News Item Detail<h2>
<br />
Title: <b><?php echo $item['title'] ?></b>
<br />
Date: <b><?php echo $item['date'] ?></b>
```

If we point to `http://hostname/basic/web/index.php?r=news/item-detail` without passing the title parameter, we will see the following screenshot:

It displays an error that tells us that the title parameter is missing.

Try to pass `First%20%World%20War` as the title parameter to the URL, like this `http://hostname/basic/web/index.php?r=news/item-detail&title=First%20 World%20War`; the following will be the output:

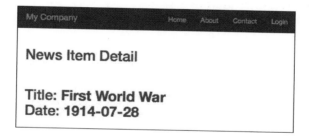

That is what we are expecting!

Finally, we want to connect together `itemsList` and `itemDetail`. In `views/news/itemsList.php`, we must change the title content into an anchor element, as follows:

```php
<?php // $newsList is from actionItemsList ?>
<table>
  <tr>
    <th>Title</th>
    <th>Date</th>
  </tr>
  <?php foreach($newsList as $item) { ?>
  <tr>
```

```
      <th><a href="<?php echo Yii::$app->urlManager-
      >createUrl(['news/item-detail' , 'title' => $item['title']])
      ?>"><?php echo $item['title'] ?></a></th>
      <th><?php echo $item['date'] ?></th>
    </tr>
    <?php } ?>
  </table>
```

To build a link, there is an available component, `urlManager`, which allows us to create links through the `createUrl()` method. The parameter in `createUrl()` is an array that contains the route path and variable to pass to the URL. To learn more about this method, just refer to the link http://www.yiiframework.com/doc-2.0/yii-web-urlmanager.html#createUrl%28%29-detail.

In our case, we have `news/item-detail` as the route to be called and the `title` parameter to be passed to the URL.

> The date can be formatted using the built-in formatter component. For example, to to display a date in the d/m/Y format, `d/m/Y : Yii::$app->formatter->asDatetime($item['date'], "php:d/m/Y");`.

It is advisable to use a unique identifier to pass data between routes. For this purpose, we add a third parameter, named `id`, to identify a record univocally.

The following is the content of `NewsController`:

```php
public function dataItems()
{
  $newsList = [
    [ 'id' => 1, 'title' => 'First World War', 'date' => '1914-07-
    28' ],
    [ 'id' => 2, 'title' => 'Second World War', 'date' => '1939-
    09-01' ],
    [ 'id' => 3, 'title' => 'First man on the moon', 'date' =>
    '1969-07-20' ]
  ];
  return $newsList;
}

public function actionItemsList()
{
  $newsList = $this->dataItems();
  return $this->render('itemsList', ['newsList' => $newsList]);
}
```

```php
public function actionItemDetail($id)
{
    $newsList = $this->dataItems();

    $item = null;
    foreach($newsList as $n)
    {
        if($id == $n['id']) $item = $n;
    }

    return $this->render('itemDetail', ['item' => $item]);
}
```

Then, change the parameter in the `createUrl` parameter in `views/news/itemsList.php`:

```php
<table>
  <tr>
    <th>Title</th>
     <th>Date</th>
  </tr>
  <?php foreach($newsList as $item) { ?>
  <tr>
    <th><a href="<?php echo Yii::$app->urlManager-
    >createUrl(['news/item-detail' , 'id' => $item['id']])
    ?>"><?php echo $item['title'] ?></a></th>
    <th><?php echo Yii::$app->formatter->asDatetime($item['date'],
    "php:d/m/Y"); ?></th>
  </tr>
  <?php } ?>
</table>
```

Splitting the common view content into reusable views

Sometimes, views share the same common portion of content. In the examples made until now, we have seen that a common area for `itemsList` and `itemDetail` could be copyright data, which displays a disclaimer about copyright info.

In order to make this, we must put the common content in a separate view and call it using the `renderPartial()` method of controller (http://www.yiiframework.com/doc-2.0/yii-base-controller.html#renderPartial%28%29-detail). It has the same types of parameters of the `render()` method; the main difference between the `render()` and `renderPartial()` methods is that `render()` writes a view content in layout and `renderPartial()` writes only view contents to output.

Example – render partial in view

In this example, we create a common view for both `itemsList` and `itemDetail` about copyright data.

Create a view file named `_copyright.php` in `views/news`.

 Usually, in Yii2's app, a view name that starts with underscore stands for common reusable view.

In this file, put only a text for copyright into `views/news/_copyright.php`:

```
<div>
     This is text about copyright data for news items
</div>
```

Now, we want to display this view inside the `itemsList` and `itemDetail` views.

Change the content in `itemsList.php` located at `views/news/` as follows:

```
<?php echo $this->context->renderPartial('_copyright'); ?>
<table>
  <tr>
    <th>Title</th>
    <th>Date</th>
  </tr>
  <?php foreach($newsList as $item) { ?>
  <tr>
    <th><a href="<?php echo Yii::$app->urlManager-
    >createUrl(['news/item-detail' , 'id' => $item['id']]) ?>">
    <?php echo $item['title'] ?> </a></th>
    <th><?php echo Yii::$app->formatter->asDatetime($item['date'],
    'php:d/m/Y'); ?></th>
  </tr>
  <?php } ?>
</table>
```

Then, change the content in `itemDetail.php` located at `views/news/` as follows:

```
<?php // $item is from actionItemDetail ?>
<?php echo $this->context->renderPartial('_copyright'); ?>
<h2>News Item Detail<h2>
<br />
Title: <b><?php echo $item['title'] ?></b>
<br />
Date: <b><?php echo $item['date'] ?></b>
```

We have put a common code at the top of the file in both views:

```php
<?php echo $this->context->renderPartial('_copyright'); ?>
```

This will render the content of the _copyright.php view without layout.

 Pay attention! Since renderPartial() is a method of the Controller class and $this refers to the View class in the view file, to access from $this to renderPartial() we will use the context member, which represents the Controller object in the View object.

Creating static pages

All websites contain static pages, whose content is static.

To create a static page in a common way, we need to:

- Create a function (action) to execute action in Controller
- Create a view for static content

Append the following action to Controller:

```php
public function actionInfo()
{
    return $this->render('info');
}
```

Then, create a view in views/controller/action-name.php. This procedure is simple but too long and redundant.

Yii2 provides a quick alternative, adding static pages to the actions() method of Controller as follows:

```php
public function actions()
{
  return [
    'pages' => [
    'class' => 'yii\web\ViewAction',
    ],
  ];
}
```

With this simple declaration, we can put all static content under views/controllerName/pages.

Finally, we can point to the URL with route `controller_name/page` and the `view` parameter with the name of a view file such as `http://hostname/basic/web/index.php?r=controllerName/pages&view=name_of_view`.

Example – add a contact page

After we have learned how to create a static page, it is time to write a contact page.

Let's put a short static content in `views/site/pages/contact.php` as follows:

```
To contact us, please write to info@example.com
```

Then, let's add a `page` attribute in the return array from the `actions()` method of `Controller`. To simplify, we will use `SiteController` that has this default implementation of the `actions()` method:

```
public function actions()
{
  return [
  'error' => [
     'class' => 'yii\web\ErrorAction',
  ],
  'captcha' => [
     'class' => 'yii\captcha\CaptchaAction',
     'fixedVerifyCode' => YII_ENV_TEST ? 'testme' : null,
  ],
 ];
}
```

After the last attribute, we will append the `page` attribute, and the following will be the result:

```
public function actions()
{
  return [
  'error' => [
    'class' => 'yii\web\ErrorAction',
  ],
  'captcha' => [
    'class' => 'yii\captcha\CaptchaAction',
    'fixedVerifyCode' => YII_ENV_TEST ? 'testme' : null,
  ],
  'pages' => [
    'class' => 'yii\web\ViewAction',
  ],
 ];
}
```

Now, every request to `site/pages/` is routed using the `ViewAction` class, which handles it simply by rendering static content of relative view.

Test it by clicking on `http://hostname/basic/web/index.php?r=site/pages&view=contact`, and we should see this:

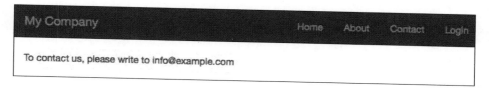

We can customize the last part of the route with these changes:

- The attribute name of array returned from the `actions()` method of `Controller`
- Set the `viewPrefix` attribute of the `ViewAction` class declaration with the first part of the URL that we want to use to reach the pages
- Change the name of the subfolder under `views/controllerName`

For example, we want to use `static` as the last part of the URL to reach static pages in `SiteController`.

We want to point to `http://hostname/basic/web/index.php?r=site/static&view=contact` to display the contact view.

This will be the `ViewAction` node in the array from the `actions()` method of `SiteController`:

```
'static' => [
'class' => 'yii\web\ViewAction',
'viewPrefix' => 'static'
],
```

We must also change the name of the static pages subfolder, renaming it from `views/site/pages` to `views/site/static`, and we can point to `http://hostname/basic/web/index.php?r=site/static&view=contact`.

Sharing data between views and layout

Yii2 provides a standard solution to share data between views and layout, through the `params` property of the View component that you can use to share data among views.

 This is a standard solution since the `params` property exists in all views and it is attached to the View component.

This property, `params`, is an array that we can use without any restriction.

Imagine that we want to fill the breadcrumb element in the layout to track the path of navigation.

Open the main layout at `views/layouts/main.php`; you should find the default implementation of breadcrumb just before declaring the footer:

```
<div class="container">
    <?= Breadcrumbs::widget([
        'links' => isset($this->params['breadcrumbs']) ?
        $this->params['breadcrumbs'] : [],
    ]) ?>
</div>
```

We need to fill the breadcrumbs property of `params` in view to display from any view to the layout custom path. For example, we want to display breadcrumbs in the `SiteController` index.

Go to `views/site/index.php` and add the following code at the top of the file:

```
$this->params['breadcrumbs'][] = 'My website';
```

 Since we are in view file, `$this` refers to View component.

Go to `http://hostname/basic/web/index.php?r=site/index` to see the breadcrumb bar appearing at the top of the page:

Example – change the layout background based on a URL parameter

Another example of communication between view and layout is, for instance, to change the layout background color based on a URL parameter.

We need to change the background of route `site/index` passing the `bckg` parameter in URL.

Therefore, we must open `views/site/index.php` and put this code at the top:

```php
<?php
$backgroundColor =
isset($_REQUEST['bckg'])?$_REQUEST['bckg']:'#FFFFFF';
$this->params['background_color'] = $backgroundColor;
```

This code will set $backgroundColor to #FFFFFF (white color), if it is not passed to the `bckg` parameter, otherwise it will be passed a value.

Then, set the `params` attribute of View component in order to write its content in layout.

Open `views/layout/main.php`, and, in the `body` tag, apply the style based on `params['background_color']` passed from view.

Then, let's change the layout of the body tag with the following:

```php
<?php
$backgroundColor = isset($this->params['background_color'])?$this-
>params['background_color']:'#FFFFFF'; ?>
<body style="background-color:<?php echo $backgroundColor ?>">
```

Finally, go to `http://hostname/basic/web/index.php?r=site/index&bckg=yellow` to have a yellow background or to `http://hostname/basic/web/index.php?r=site/index&bckg=#FF0000` to have a red one.

In this example, we are setting the `background` property of `params` only in `views/site/index.php`. Other views do not set this property, so if we have not checked whether `background_color` property exists in the layout file, we will receive an error of missing the attribute from the framework, which means:

```php
$backgroundColor = isset($this-
>params['background_color'])?$this-
>params['background_color']:'#FFFFFF';
```

Layout with dynamic block

The use of the `params` property to allow communication between view and layout, is advisable for simple cases, but there are some more complex cases where we must share the block of HTML.

For example, think about the advertising box in layout (usually left or right column of the template), that could change according to the view that is being displayed.

In this case, we need to pass the entire block of HTML code from view to layout.

For this purpose, this framework provides Block statements, where we can define entire blocks of data to send from view to layout.

Using Blocks means to define the `Block` statement in view and display it in another view, usually layout.

We define the `Block` statement in view as follows:

```php
<?php $this->beginBlock('block1'); ?>
...content of block1...
$this->endBlock(); ?>
```

Here, `beginBlock` and `endBlock` define the beginning and the end of the `block1` named statement. This content is saved into the `blocks` property of the view component with the `block1` attribute.

We can access this block through `$view>blocks[$blockID]` in every view, including layout.

To render a block in layout view, if available, use the following code:

```php
<?php if(isset($this->blocks['block1']) { ?>
    <?php echo $this->blocks['block1'] ?>
<?php } else { ?>
    ... default content if missing block1 attribute
<?php } ?>
```

Obviously, we can define all the blocks that we want.

Example – add a dynamic box to display advertising info

In this example, we will see how to display, when available, a box with advertising info that displays data sent from view.

The first thing to do is to add a block in layout displaying data.

Enter in `views/layouts/main.php` and change `div` with container class as follows:

```
<div class="container">
    <?= Breadcrumbs::widget([
      'links' => isset($this->params['breadcrumbs']) ? $this-
      >params['breadcrumbs'] : [],
    ]) ?>

    <div class="well">
        This is content for blockADV from view
        <br />
        <?php if(isset($this->blocks['blockADV'])) { ?>
            <?php echo $this->blocks['blockADV']; ?>
        <?php } else { ?>
            <i>No content available</i>
        <?php } ?>
    </div>

    <?= $content ?>
</div>
```

We have added a div with the `well` class to display the content of `blockADV`, if available. If `blockADV` is available in `$this->blocks`, it will display its content; otherwise, it will display `no content available`, as a courtesy message.

Now, we will create a new action in `NewsController`, called `advTest`, and then will create a brand new view.

Let's start off by creating a file in `views/news/advTest.php` with the following content:

```
<span>
This is a test where we display an adv box in layout view
</span>
<?php $this->beginBlock('blockADV'); ?>

    <b>Buy this fantastic book!</b>

<?php $this->endBlock(); ?>
```

We can insert any content in a block; in this case, we have put in text.

 The position where block is defined in view is not important.

Then, open `NewsController` and add a new action `advTest`:

```
public function actionAdvTest()
{
        return $this->render('advTest');
}
```

Now, point the browser to `http://hostname/basic/web/index.php?r=news/adv-test` and we will see the following screenshot:

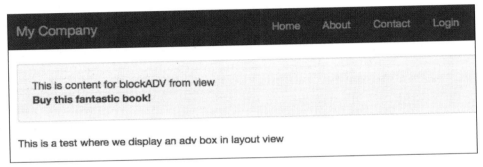

All other pages will only show `no content available` in the screenshot.

Using multiple layouts

During the building of a website or a web application, usually it could be required to render different views with different layouts. Think about, for example, the lists and details of news made in this chapter.

The layout is managed by the `$layout` property of `Controller`; `main` is the default value for this property.

Just set this property to change the layout file where to render the content of the view.

There are some important rules to write the value of the `$layout` property:

- A path alias (for example, `@app/views/layouts/main`).
- An absolute path (for example, `/main`) is where the layout value starts with a slash. The actual layout file will be looked for under the application layout path, which defaults to `@app/views/layouts`.
- A relative path (for example, `main`) is where the actual layout file will be looked for under the context module's layout path, which defaults to the `views/layouts` directory under the module directory.
- The Boolean value false is where no layout will be applied.

 If the layout value does not contain a file extension, it will use the default `.php`.

Example – using different layouts to create responsive and nonresponsive content layout for the same view

In this example, we will create a new action in `NewsController` that will change its layout depending on a value passed in the URL.

First, add a new action in `NewsController` called `actionResponsiveContentTest`:

```
public function actionResponsiveContentTest()
{
  $responsive = Yii::$app->request->get('responsive', 0);

  if($responsive)
  {
    $this->layout = 'responsive';
  }
  else
  {
    $this->layout = 'main';
  }

  return $this->render('responsiveContentTest', ['responsive' =>
  $responsive]);
}
```

In this action, we get a responsive parameter from the URL and set the $responsive variable to this value or 0 if not passed.

Then, set the $layout property of Controller to responsive or not according to the $responsive value, and pass this variable to view.

Then, create a new view in views/news/responsiveContentTest.php:

```
<?php if ($responsive) { ?>
    This layout contains responsive content
<?php } else { ?>
    This layout does not contain responsive content
<?php } ?>
```

This displays a different text block according to the $responsive value.

Finally, make a clone of main layout copying views/layouts/main.php in views/layouts/responsive.php and change in a new file views/layouts/responsive.php:

```
<div class="container"> in <div class="container-fluid"
style="padding-top:60px">
```

This change makes the div container fluid (responsive), in other words, its content is resized with respect to percentage available in the horizontal space (instead the fixed value).

If we point to http://hostname/basic/web/index.php?r=news/responsive-content-test, we will see content in a fixed layout. Instead, if we pass the responsive parameter with value 1, http://hostname/basic/web/index.php?r=news/responsive-content-test&responsive=1, we will see the content in a full width screen.

Summary

In this chapter, after understanding how a Yii2 app is structured, we have created our first Controllers and relative views. We have seen static and dynamic views, we have learned how to render views in layout and pass data from Controller to View and then we have looked at reusing Views through partial views and blocks.

Finally, we have manipulated layouts, changing them conditionally.

In the next chapter, we will display URLs in a pretty format, which is very important for all **search engine optimization (SEO)** activities on the website. Then, we will learn how to create a custom URL handler to manage any required URL customizations.

Making Pretty URLs

3

This chapter explains how to configure URL rules and make URLs pretty, in particular for search engines. We will cover the following topics in this chapter:

- Using Pretty URLs
- Custom URL rules
  - Example – news items list by year or category
- The default parameters in rules
  - Example – the index page to display list links
- Complete URL rule parameters
- The URL pattern to support a multilanguage view
- Creating the rule class

Using pretty URLs

The URL format is very important for SEO. People do not pay attention to URLs (some browsers does not display them at all), but search engines make correspondences between text in the page and the URL.

Until now, we have used this type of URL `index.php?r=site/index` or `index.php?r=site/about`, where `r` indicates the parameter route to follow. Now, we will see how to change these formats in `site/index` and `site/about`, that are more easily readable and useful for search engines.

In order to use pretty URLs, we need to configure Yii2 to handle them, and this can be done in a couple of minutes.

First of all, we must ensure that all requests are rewritten to `web/index.php`. In Linux, we can change web server configuration using Apache and insert the `.htaccess` file in Yii2's app root folder, if this file does not exist. The `.htaccess` file allows us to override some default configuration of the web server.

> In the Linux environment, the filename starting with dot indicates that this file is hidden.

The content of `.htaccess` is the same as Yii1:

```
RewriteEngine on

# If a directory or a file exists, use it directly
RewriteCond %{REQUEST_FILENAME} !-f
RewriteCond %{REQUEST_FILENAME} !-d
# Otherwise forward it to index.php
RewriteRule . web/index.php
```

If the app root is `/var/www/vhosts/yiiapp/basic`, we will insert `.htaccess` in `/var/www/vhosts/yiiapp/basic`.

The first row activates `RewriteEngine` of the web server; then, in the second and third rows, the script checks whether the request is not in an existing file or folder; and finally the request is rewritten to `web/index.php`. With these changes, all the requests that are not existing files or path folders will be rewritten to `web/index.php`.

> We can also configure rewrite rules in Apache configuration instead of the `.htaccess` file, if we have access to this level of Apache configuration.
>
> If the `.htaccess` configuration has been ignored, check whether `AllowOverride` is set to `All` as follows:
>
> ```
> <Directory /var/www/path/to/folder>
>     AllowOverride All
> </Directory>
> ```
>
> And that is not set to `None`.

The last thing to do now is to configure Yii2 in order to handle a pretty URL.

Let's open `config/web.php` and add these contents in the `components` attribute:

```
'urlManager' => [
  'enablePrettyUrl' => true,
],
```

Adding the `enablePrettyUrl` property, we have just configured `urlManager` to enable the pretty URL, toggling the pretty URL format.

The previous URL `index.php?r=site/index` becomes `/index.php/site/index` and `index.php?r=site/about` becomes `/index.php/site/about`.

Using the `enablePrettyUrl` property, we will have the prefix `index.php` again. We can choose whether to keep it or not; however, to limit the URL length, it is advisable to remove it.

In order to control the presence of the `index.php` prefix, we use another property called `showScriptName`.

If we set this property to `false`, we will remove the first part of the URL. This is our updated configuration:

```
'urlManager' => [
    'enablePrettyUrl' => true,
    'showScriptName' => false,
],
```

Now, point the browser to `http://hostname/basic/web/site/index` to view the first page of the Yii2 application and check whether the other links are in the pretty format.

Finally, there is another property for the `urlManager` component, used to enable URL parsing based only on given URL rules, named `enableStrictParsing`. If this property is true, only the rules defined in `urlManager` will be executed; if there is no URL that matches the request, an error will be displayed.

Custom URL rules

Yii2 give us the opportunity to customize URL rules as we want. This can be done using the `rules` property in `urlManager`, an array where keys are patterns and values are corresponding routes. Patterns are common regular expression patterns, so it is necessary to have some familiarity with regular expression.

Patterns can contain parameters that will be passed to the route. In the next example, we will display a list of news that can be filtered through year or category parameter, based on parameters passed to the URL.

Example – list news items by year or category

In this example, we will create a new Controller named `News` in `controllers/NewsController.php`. In this new controller, we will insert a `data()` function containing an array with test data, and a function named `actionItemsList`.

The first thing to do is to configure the `rules` property under the `urlManager` component under `config/web.php`:

```
'rules' => [
    news/<year:\d{4}>/items-list' => ' news/items-list',
    'news/<category:\w+>/items-list' => 'test-rules/items-list',
],
```

Here, we have two patterns:

- `news/<year:\d{4}>/items-list`
- `news/<category:\w+>/items-list`

The first pattern catches requests with a numeric parameter with four digits, passed to the `news /items-list` route as the `year` GET parameter. We can request 'news/2014/items-list' or 'news/2015/items-list'.

The second pattern catches requests with the word parameter, passed to the `news/items-list` route as the `category` GET parameter. We can request news/business/items-list or news/shopping/items-list.

Then, we create `NewsController` where to define the `data()` function, to return static data to be used as data source, and the `actionItemsList()` function to handle requests to news/year/or/category/itemsList:

```php
<?php

namespace app\controllers;

use Yii;
use yii\web\Controller;

class NewsController extends Controller
{
  public function data()
  {
    return [
    [ "id" => 1, "date" => "2015-04-19", "category" => "business",
    "title" => "Test news of 2015-04-19" ],
```

```
  [ "id" => 2, "date" => "2015-05-20", "category" => "shopping",
  "title" => "Test news of 2015-05-20" ],
  [ "id" => 3, "date" => "2015-06-21", "category" => "business",
  "title" => "Test news of 2015-06-21" ],
  [ "id" => 4, "date" => "2016-04-19", "category" => "shopping",
  "title" => "Test news of 2016-04-19" ],
  [ "id" => 5, "date" => "2017-05-19", "category" => "business",
  "title" => "Test news of 2017-05-19" ],
  [ "id" => 6, "date" => "2018-06-19", "category" => "shopping",
  "title" => "Test news of 2018-06-19" ]
  ];
}

public function actionItemsList()
{
  // if missing, value will be null
  $year = Yii::$app->request->get('year');
  // if missing, value will be null
  $category = Yii::$app->request->get('category');

  $data = $this->data();
  $filteredData = [];

  foreach($data as $d)
  {
    if(($year != null)&&(date('Y', strtotime($d['date'])) ==
    $year)) $filteredData[] = $d;
    if(($category != null)&&($d['category'] == $category))
    $filteredData[] = $d;
  }

  return $this->render('itemsList', ['year' => $year, 'category'
  => $category, 'filteredData' => $filteredData] );
}
```

Finally, we create a view in `views/news/itemsList.php`, displaying the parameter used, year or category, and a list of results:

```
<?php if($year != null) { ?>
<b>List for year <?php echo $year ?></b>
<?php } ?>
<?php if($category != null) { ?>
<b>List for category <?php echo $category ?></b>
<?php } ?>
```

```
<br /><br />


<table border="1">
    <tr>
        <th>Date</th>
        <th>Category</th>
        <th>Title</th>
    </tr>
<?php foreach($filteredData as $fd) { ?>
    <tr>
        <td><?php echo $fd['date'] ?></td>
        <td><?php echo $fd['category'] ?></td>
        <td><?php echo $fd['title'] ?></td>
    </tr>
<?php } ?>
</table>
```

Now, let's point to `http://hostname/basic/web/news/2015/items-list` to display the items list filtered out by year:

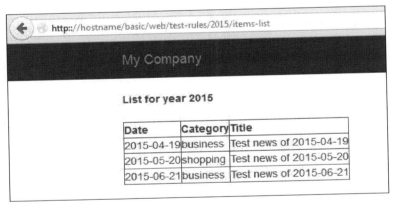

List items filtered by year

Try to change the year between news and items list to see how the data result changes in the list. The rules that are created allow us to display the items list filtered by category. Point to `http://hostname/basic/web/news/business/items-list` to see the list filtered by business category:

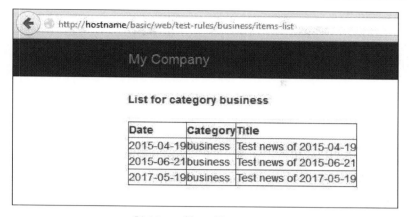

List items filtered by category

We can also point to `http://hostname/basic/web/news/shopping/items-list` to see the list filtered by shopping category.

Default parameters in rules

In rules, all the parameters that are declared are required; if the URL misses some parameter, the rule will not be applied. This problem can be solved using the default property of rule.

The URL rule structure has a parameter, named defaults, containing default parameters to be passed as default. Parameter defaults is an array, where keys are names of parameters and values are their corresponding values.

For example, change the second rule to a complete array and add `['category' => 'shopping']` as the default property rule:

```
'rules' => [
    'news/<year:\d{4}>/items-list' => 'news/items-list',
    [
        'pattern' => 'news/<category:\w+>/items-list',
        'route' => 'news/items-list',
        'defaults' => ['category' => 'shopping']
    ]
],
```

Now, if we point to `http://hostname/basic/web/news/items-list` without specifying the year or category parameter, the first rule will be skipped and the second one will be executed using shopping as the default value, because the category is missing.

Example – the index page to display the links list

Now, create an index page to see how to create these custom URLs. In this page, we will display URL links to have the data filtered by year (for the last 5 years) and links to view the data filtered by category (shopping and business).

URLs are made using `yii\helpers\Url`, along with the `to()` method, where the first parameter can be:

The first parameter can be:

- An array that will be passed to the `toRoute()` method to generate the URL. The first item of this array is the route to be rendered and the other items are the parameters to be passed to the route; for example, `Url::to(['news/items-list', 'year' => 2015])`.

- A string with a leading @; this is treated as an alias, and the corresponding aliased string will be returned

- An empty string that returns the currently requested URL.

- A normal string that will be returned as it is.

Create a simple `actionIndex` in `NewsController`:

```
public function actionIndex()
{
    return $this->render('index');
}
```

Then, create a view for the index action under `views/news/index.php`:

```
<?php

use yii\helpers\Url;
use yii\helpers\Html;

?>

<b>Filter data by year:</b>
<br />
<ul>
  <?php $currentYear = date('Y'); ?>
  <?php for($year=$currentYear;$year>($currentYear-5);$year--) {
  ?>
  <li><?php echo Html::a( 'List items by year '.$year,
  Url::to(['news/items-list', 'year' => $year]) ) ?></li>
```

```
    <?php } ?>
</ul>

<br />

<b>Filter data by category:</b>
<br />
<ul>
  <?php $categories = ['business', 'shopping']; ?>
  <?php foreach($categories as $category) { ?>
  <li><?php echo Html::a( 'List items by category '.$category,
  Url::to(['news/items-list', 'category' => $category]) ) ?></li>
  <?php } ?>
</ul>

<br /><br />
```

Point to `http://hostname/news/index` and it will display:

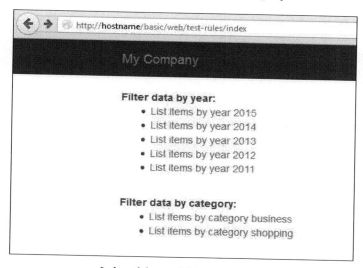

Index of the available filtered data

The complete URL rule parameters

The URL rule contains the following parameters:

- `defaults`: As we have seen, we can declare default GET parameters that this rule provides

- `encodeParams`: This value indicates whether the parameters should be encoded or not

- `host`: This is the host info part of a URL
- `mode`: This indicates whether this rule should be used for parsing the requested URL or creating a URL
- `name`: This is the name of the rule
- `pattern`: This is the pattern to be used to parse and create the path info part of a URL
- `route`: This is the route of the controller action
- `suffix`: This is the URL suffix used for this rule (`.json`, `.html`, and so on)
- `verb`: This is the HTTP verb that this rule should match with (GET, POST, DELETE, and so on)

The URL pattern to support the multilanguage view

There are different ways to display the same view in different languages. A basic approach to support multilanguage views could be to insert a language code at the start of the route. For example, the previous route `news/index` will become `en/news/index` in English language, `it/news/index` in Italian language, `fr/news/index` in French language, and so on.

Append this rule in the `rules` property of `UrlManager`:

```
[
    'pattern' => '<lang:\w+>/<controller>/<action>',
    'route' => '<controller>/<action>',
],
```

All the requests that have a language ID as the prefix in the path info, will be matched and passed to the `<controller>/<action>` route with the `$lang` parameters passed in GET.

Now, create a new action named `actionInternationalIndex` in `NewsController` to test the multilanguage support:

```
public function actionInternationalIndex()
{
    // if missing, value will be 'en'
    $lang = Yii::$app->request->get('lang', 'en');

    Yii::$app->language = $lang;

    return $this->render('internationalIndex');
}
```

In this action, `$lang` is taken from GET parameters. If the request does not contain the `$lang` parameter, the `en` value will be used as default.

Create new view in `views/news/internationalIndex.php` to check the language code passed to the URL.

```
Requested language for this page is:
<br />
<b><?php echo Yii::$app->language ?></b>
```

Verify whether this action is working correctly by visiting `http://hostname/news/international-index`:

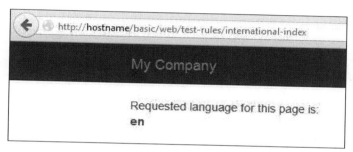

Setting the English language

We are visualizing this page in English because no language code was passed to the URL. Consequently, the default language code, `en`, has been used. However, if we write the language code in the URL, the result will change.

For example, pointing to `http://hostname/basic/web/it/news/international-index` will display the following:

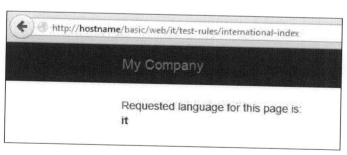

Setting the Italian language

This response gives us the confirmation that we have used `it` as the language code.

In this simple approach to support multi language, we get the $lang value from the request, as we have done in actionInternationalIndex; however, this is redundant and has to be generalized in all the requests. We could create a BaseController class as the base class for every Controller and then override the beforeAction() method, where we can set the Yii::$app->language parameter.

Creating the rule class

URL rules declared in terms of pattern-route pairs can cover the majority of projects. However, it is not flexible enough with dynamic data, where the URL could be any format and value stored in the database.

Now, we need to display item details using a URL that contains only the item title, such as http://hostname/basic/web/news/Test news of 2015-04-19

There is no way to solve this with URL rules, as we have done until now.

A more general solution to parse and create URL requests is using Rule classes.

The Rule class extends Object and implements UrlRuleInterface.

The next example will explain how to display item details, finding it from the title (defined in data() array of objects), and parsing and creating routes with a Rule class.

The route displayed in the browser will have the news/title format.

For this purpose, create a new folder components under the basic folder if it does not exist, and create components/NewsUrlRule.php with the following content:

```php
<?php

namespace app\components;

use yii\web\UrlRuleInterface;
use yii\base\Object;

class NewsUrlRule extends Object implements UrlRuleInterface
{

    public function createUrl($manager, $route, $params)
    {
```

```
    if ($route === 'news/item-detail') {
      if (isset($params['title'])) {
        return 'news/'.$params['title'];
      }
    }
    return false;   // this rule does not apply
  }

  public function parseRequest($manager, $request)
  {
    $pathInfo = $request->getPathInfo();

    if (preg_match('%^([^\/]*)\/([^\/]*)$%', $pathInfo, $matches)) {
      if($matches[1] == 'news')
      {
        $params = [ 'title' => $matches[2]];
        return ['news/item-detail', $params];
      }
      else
      {
        return false;
      }
    }
    return false;   // this rule does not apply
  }
}
```

The first method, `createUrl()` receives `$manager`, `$route`, and `$params`. With route and params, the framework builds the URL. In this case, we check whether the route passed is equivalent to `news/item-detail` and if it is so, return the corresponding URL.

The second method, `parseRequest()` receives `$manager` and `$request`. A match with a custom regular expression will be done to extract the required parts, using the `$request` data. The process will return the route, to be executed.

Now, link these components to `urlManager` of the `web.php` file located at `config/`, appending the following lines in the `rule` property of the `urlManager` component:

```
[
'class' => 'app\components\NewsUrlRule',
// ...configure other properties...
],
```

The next thing to do is to create `actionItemDetail` in `NewsController`, as follows:

```php
public function actionItemDetail()
{
    $title = Yii::$app->request->get('title');

    $data = $this->data();

    $itemFound = null;

    foreach($data as $d)
    {
        if($d['title'] == $title) $itemFound = $d;
    }

    return $this->render('itemDetail', ['title' => $title,
'itemFound' => $itemFound]);
}
```

In this action, we simply find the item starting from the title received from the route. We pass the title and `itemFound` to view.

The last file to create is `view` under `views/news/itemDetail.php`:

```php
Detail item with title <b><?php echo $title ?></b>
<br /><br />
<?php if($itemFound != null) { ?>
    <table border="1">
        <?php foreach($itemFound as $key=>$value) { ?>
        <tr>
            <th><?php echo $key ?></th>
            <td><?php echo $value ?></td>
        </tr>
        <?php } ?>
    </table>

    <br />

    Url for this items is: <?php echo yii\helpers\Url::to(['news/item-
detail', 'title' => $title]); ?>

<?php } else { ?>
    <i>No item found</i>
<?php } ?>
```

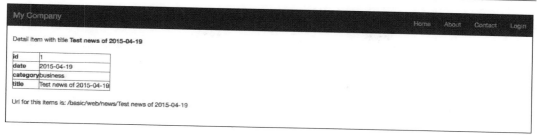

Item detail output

In this view, the item details (if the item is found) along with how to build the URL of the item detail will be displayed.

Summary

In this chapter, we saw how to implement pretty URLs, which is useful for search engine optimization. We also created examples where we used custom rules to parse and create the URL. Finally, we learned how to build more customized URL rules through Rule classes.

In the next chapter, we will cover the use of a database, which is a fundamental aspect of every web application. We will start from the configuration of a database connection through to the tools that Yii2 makes available to developers, and to build a complete reservation system based on database data, using framework widgets.

4
Creating a Room through Forms

This chapter explains how to write a model class to store data that will be sent from View to Controller using a form, with validating input, formatting data, and uploading files. In this chapter, we will cover the following topics:

- Creating a Model
    - Example – a model to store room data
- Using ActiveForm
    - Example – creating a new room from the HTML form
- Formatting date, time, and numbers
- Uploading files
    - Example – uploading an image of the room

Creating a Model

The first step to manipulate data between View and Controller is to create a Model. A **Model** is a class that extends the Model class located under yii\base\, the base used for data models.

This is a suitable class for providing simple solutions in order to encapsulate data, assign content from array (form data), and validate data using rules. The Model base class implements the following commonly used features:

- **Attribute declaration**: By default, every public class member is considered a model attribute; we can access all the members using the attributes property of Model.

- **Attribute labels**: Each attribute may be associated with a label for display purposes; we can extend the `attributeLabels()` method to return labels related to public members of Model.

- **Massive attribute assignment**: We can fill the member's content of Model by passing an entire array of values. This is convenient when we need to fill a model with data from the form.

- **Scenario-based validation**: Model provides rules to validate data. We can choose which ones apply according to the scenario, a keyword that defines the rules to apply.

While performing data validation, Model also raises the following events:

- `EVENT_BEFORE_VALIDATE`: This is an event raised at the beginning of `validate()`

- `EVENT_AFTER_VALIDATE`: This is an event raised at the end of `validate()`

You can directly use Model to store model data or extend it with customization.

Example – a Model to store room data

Now, let's create Model to store room data. To create this, we choose to name all fields with words written in lowercase characters and separated by underscores.

We can identify these fields of Model as follows:

- `floor`: In a more generic situation, we consider this as a string member

- `room_number`: This is an integer member

- `has_conditioner`: This is an integer member with two values 0 and 1

- `has_tv`: This is an integer member with two values 0 and 1

- `has_phone`: This is an integer member with two values 0 and 1

- `available_from`: This is a date member that it is represented with a string in PHP

- `price_per_day`: This is a float member

- `assistance_email`: This is a string member containing an e-mail address

- `description`: This is a string member

Now, create the `Model` class, named `Room` as the base class, in the previous field list, creating a file under `basic/models/Room.php` with the following content:

```php
<?php
namespace app\models;
use Yii;
use yii\base\Model;
class Room extends Model {
    public $floor;
    public $room_number;
    public $has_conditioner;
    public $has_tv;
    public $has_phone;
    public $available_from;
    public $price_per_day;
    public $description;
}
```

The second thing to do is to append the `attributeLabels()` method in order to give a label to every member. This is not necessary, but it is a useful method to get labels displayed in the end user frontend.

```php
public function attributeLabels()
{
    return [
        'floor' => 'Floor',
        'room_number' => 'Room number',
        'has_condition' => 'Condition available',
        'has_tv' => 'TV available',
        'has_phone' => 'Phone available',
        'available_from' => 'Available from',
        'price_per_day' => 'Price (EUR/day)',
        'description' => 'Description',
    ];
}
```

The last thing is to create rules to validate data. Rules are based on validators, whose defaults are listed as follows:

- boolean: `yii\validators\BooleanValidator`
- captcha: `yii\captcha\CaptchaValidator`
- compare: `yii\validators\CompareValidator`
- date: `yii\validators\DateValidator`

- double: `yii\validators\NumberValidator`
- email: `yii\validators\EmailValidator`
- exist: `yii\validators\ExistValidator`
- file: `yii\validators\FileValidator`
- filter: `yii\validators\FilterValidator`
- image: `yii\validators\ImageValidator`
- in: `yii\validators\RangeValidator`
- integer: `yii\validators\NumberValidator`
- match: `yii\validators\RegularExpressionValidator`
- required: `yii\validators\RequiredValidator`
- safe: `yii\validators\SafeValidator`
- string: `yii\validators\StringValidator`
- trim: `yii\validators\FilterValidator`
- unique: `yii\validators\UniqueValidator`
- url: `yii\validators\UrlValidator`

A Rule is an array whose values are in the following order:

- A string or an array to define an attribute or list of attributes to apply the rule
- The type of validator
- The on attribute to define which scenario to use
- The other parameters, depending on the validator that is used

Write the `rules()` method of the Room Model class:

```
/**
 * @return array the validation rules.
 */
public function rules()
{
    return [
        ['floor', 'integer', 'min' => 0],
        ['room_number', 'integer', 'min' => 0],
        [['has_conditioner', 'has_tv', 'has_phone'], 'integer',
        'min' => 0, 'max' => 1],
        ['available_from', 'date', 'format' => 'php:Y-m-d'],
        ['price_per_day', 'number', 'min' => 0],
        ['description', 'string', 'max' => 500]
    ];
}
```

The preceding code is explained as follows:

- The first rule establishes that floor is an integer, with 0 as the minimum value
- The second rule establishes that room_number is an integer, with 0 as the minimum value; we can put together floor and room in a single rule, melting them into an array as the first parameter of a single rule
- The third rule establishes that has_condition, has_tv, and has_phone are integers with possible values between 0 and 1 (formally a Boolean value)
- The fourth rule establishes that available_from is a date
- The fifth rule establishes that price_per_day is a number and its minimum value is 0
- The last rule establishes that description is a string with a maximum of 500 characters

These rules will be applied when the validate() method of Model is called. This method is automatically called when we attempt to call the save() method.

Using ActiveForm

Now we will create an HTML form in view to send data from view to controller. We could build a form in the standard way using the form tag and input fields, but Yii2 provides helper classes that simplify the building of a form and its content.

For this purpose, we will use ActiveForm, a widget that builds an interactive HTML form for one or multiple data models.

As for any Yii2 widget, we will indicate with the begin() static method, the moment we start using it, and with the end() static method, the moment we stop using it, from yii\widgets\ActiveForm. The code between these methods will be placed in the form:

```
$form = ActiveForm::begin();
... content here ...
ActiveForm::end();
```

The first method, begin(), returns an object that we can use inside the content to create the input fields. This method accepts an array as the parameter to indicate configuration attributes to be applied. The last method, end(), marks the end of the widget, so this can be rendered with its content.

Now, we need some input fields to insert in the code, which is done using the `field()` method of the `ActiveForm` instance that we just created. This method requires two parameters: model and field name and returns an object of type `ActiveField`. With this method, we just demand `ActiveForm` to create a new field; however, in this case, we also need to specify the type of field we want.

This operation is made calling a method from `ActiveField` relative to the kind of input to the instance. The most common are:

- `label()`: This is used to generate a label tag
- `textInput()`: This is used to generate an input field with type `text`
- `textarea()`: This is used to generate a `textarea` tag
- `radio()`: This is used to generate an input field with type `radio`
- `checkbox()`: This is used to generate an input field with type `checkbox`

Example – creating a new room from the HTML form

Firstly, create a new controller, `RoomsController`, under `basic/controllers/RoomsController.php` with an action named `create`:

```php
<?php

namespace app\controllers;

use Yii;
use yii\web\Controller;
use app\models\Room;


class RoomsController extends Controller
{
    public function actionCreate()
    {
        $model = new Room();
        $modelCanSave = false;

        if ($model->load(Yii::$app->request->post()) && $model->validate()) {
            $modelCanSave = true;
        }

        return $this->render('create', [
            'model' => $model,
```

```
            'modelSaved' => $modelCanSave
        ]);
    }
}
```

At the start of the `create()` method, we create a new instance of the `Room` class assigned to the `$model` variable. The `load()` method fills the `$model` attributes with data taken from the key position named `$model->formName()` of an array passed as parameters. By default, `$model->formName()` returns the class name of the object, as shown in the following code:

```
$model->load(Yii::$app->request->post())
```

The preceding code is equivalent to:

```
if (isset($_POST[$model->formName()])) {
   $this->setAttributes($_POST[$model->formName()]);
}
```

Going back to the `load() && validate()` condition, if `load()` returns true, `validate()` will also be executed and all rules in the `rules()` method of model will be evaluated.

In this case, `Model` is ready to be saved to the data store (in the database in the next chapters). Now, it is important to mark this condition with a simple variable named `$modelCanSave`, passed to the `create` view.

Create a file for the `create` view under `basic/views/rooms/create.php`:

```php
<?php
use yii\helpers\Html;
use yii\widgets\ActiveForm;
use yii\helpers\Url;
use yii\helpers\ArrayHelper;
?>

<?php if($modelCanSave) { ?>
<div class="alert alert-success">
    Model ready to be saved!
</div>
<?php } ?>

<?php $form = ActiveForm::begin(); ?>
<div class="row">
    <div class="col-lg-12">
        <h1>Room form</h1>
        <?= $form->field($model, 'floor')->textInput() ?>
        <?= $form->field($model, 'room_number')->textInput() ?>
```

```
                <?= $form->field($model, 'has_conditioner')->checkbox() ?>
                <?= $form->field($model, 'has_tv')->checkbox() ?>
                <?= $form->field($model, 'has_phone')->checkbox() ?>
                <?= $form->field($model, 'available_from')->textInput() ?>
                <?= $form->field($model, 'price_per_day')->textInput() ?>
                <?= $form->field($model, 'description')->textarea() ?>
        </div>
    </div>
    <div class="form-group">
        <?= Html::submitButton('Create' , ['class' => 'btn btn-
        success']) ?>
    </div>
    <?php ActiveForm::end(); ?>
```

If the $modelCanSave variable is true, an alert div with the green background
will be displayed to notify that $model is loaded and validate (ready to be saved
in database).

For the test code, point to http://hostname/basic/web/rooms/create.
The following screen should appear:

Create room HTML form

The framework automatically takes care of the validation checks on input fields, corresponding to the rules list in the `rules()` method of Model. We can check this by typing characters in the **Floor** input. We should see the following screenshot:

The validation check of the integer field

The validation informs us that **Floor** must be an integer, as required in the rules list. Once all the fields are filled with correct values (date format, yyyy-mm-dd), just click on the **Create** button and we should see a box with green background displaying **Model ready to be saved**.

Format date, time, and numbers

Now, let's see how to format the date, time, and numeric fields. Yii2 provides helpers for each of these types.

To format a value, we will use `Yii::$app->formatter`; this object belongs to the `Formatter` class located under `yii\i18n\` and supports many types of formatting. All the methods used for this purpose start with an `as` prefix. Therefore, the `asDate` method will be used to format dates, and the `asCurrency` method will be used to format currencies.

The first parameter of each formatting method is the value to be formatted and other fields refer to the format to be used and other optional parameters.

Let's change the view content by adding content of the Model that is ready to be saved:

```php
<?php if ($modelCanSave) { ?>
<div class="alert alert-success">
    Model ready to be saved!
    <br /><br />
    These are values: <br />
    Floor: <?php echo $model->floor; ?> <br />
```

```
Room Number: <?php echo $model->room_number; ?> <br />
Has conditioner: <?php echo Yii::$app->formatter-
>asBoolean($model->has_conditioner); ?> <br />
Has TV: <?php echo Yii::$app->formatter->asBoolean($model-
>has_tv); ?> <br />
Has phone: <?php echo Yii::$app->formatter->asBoolean($model-
>has_phone); ?> <br />
Available from (mm/dd/yyyy): <?php echo Yii::$app->formatter-
>asDate($model->available_from,'php:m/d/Y'); ?> <br />
Price per day: <?php echo Yii::$app->formatter-
>asCurrency($model->price_per_day,'EUR'); ?> <br />
```

```
</div>
<?php } ?>
```

If `$model` is ready to be saved, in the box with the green background, we will have the output of each of the fields of Model.

In this example, we have used:

- The `boolean` formatter for `has_condition, has_tv,` and `has_phone` members uses the default representation of false and true values; defaults are `No` for false and `Yes` for true, but we can change this behavior setting in the `$booleanFormat` member of `Yii::$app->formatter`

- The `date` formatter for `available_from member` takes the date format to be used as the second parameter; this date format can be represented with PHP date function style or ICU standard

- The `currency` formatter for the `price_per_day` member is the second parameter with three characters type of currency to be used

This is how the box with the content of Model appears:

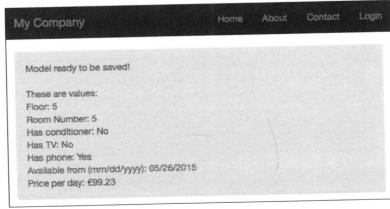

Show summary of Model content when validation is successful

Uploading files

The common task when data is sent from view to controller is uploading files. Also, in this case, Yii2 provides a convenient helper to handle this task: `yii\web\UploadedFile`. This class has two important methods: `getInstance()` (in plural form `getInstances()`) and `saveAs()`.

The first method, `getInstance()`, allows us to get the file from the form's input field, while the second method, `saveAs()`, as its name implies, allows us to save file input field content to the server filesystem.

Before we start with the example, it is important to create a folder that will contain the uploaded files. The best place to create this folder is at the root directory of the application. So create a folder named `uploadedfiles` under the `basic/` folder.

 Make sure that this folder is writable.

Next, to centralize configuration, define an alias for this new folder, so that we can change this path from app configuration. Enter in `basic/config/web.php` and append the `aliases` property, if it does not exist, to the `$config` array with these lines:

```
'aliases' =>
[
        '@uploadedfilesdir' => '@app/uploadedfiles'
],
```

 @app is a system aliases that defines the application's root directory.

Example – uploading an image of a room

In this example, we will see how to upload an image of a room.

We need to make changes in model, view, and controller. Let's start with model.

In model, we need to add a new property, named `fileImage`, with its specific rule.

This is the final version of Model:

```php
<?php
namespace app\models;
```

```
use Yii;
use yii\base\Model;
class Room extends Model
{
    public $floor;
    public $room_number;
    public $has_conditioner;
    public $has_tv;
    public $has_phone;
    public $available_from;
    public $price_per_day;
    public $description;

    public $fileImage;

    public function attributeLabels()
    {
        return [
            'floor' => 'Floor',
            'room_number' => 'Room number',
            'has_conditioner' => 'Conditioner available',
            'has_tv' => 'TV available',
            'has_phone' => 'Phone available',
            'available_from' => 'Available from',
            'price_per_day' => 'Price (Eur/day)',
            'description' => 'Description',
            'fileImage' => 'Image'
        ];
    }

    /**
     * @return array the validation rules.
     */
    public function rules()
    {
        return [
            ['floor', 'integer', 'min' => 0],
            ['room_number', 'integer', 'min' => 0],
            [['has_conditioner', 'has_tv', 'has_phone'],
            'integer', 'min' => 0, 'max' => 1],
            ['available_from', 'date', 'format' => 'php:Y-m-d'],
            ['price_per_day', 'number', 'min' => 0],
            ['description', 'string', 'max' => 500],

            ['fileImage', 'file']
        ];
    }
}
```

In rules, for the `fileImage` field, we can add many types of validation; for example, check if required, check mime type (`.gif`, `.jpeg`, and `.png`).

Next, we will use the static method `getInstance()` of the `UploadedFile` class in controller, to get the file from the input file field and then use `saveAs` to save in the specific folder. This is the final version of `RoomsController`:

```php
<?php

namespace app\controllers;

use Yii;
use yii\web\Controller;
use app\models\Room;

class RoomsController extends Controller
{
    public function actionCreate()
    {
        $model = new Room();
        $modelCanSave = false;

        if ($model->load(Yii::$app->request->post()) && $model-
            >validate()) {

            $model->fileImage = UploadedFile::getInstance($model,
            'fileImage');

            if ($model->fileImage) {
                $model->fileImage-
                >saveAs(Yii::getAlias('@uploadedfilesdir/' .
                $model->fileImage->baseName . '.' . $model-
                >fileImage->extension)));
            }

            $modelCanSave = true;
        }

        return $this->render('create', [
            'model' => $model,
            'modelSaved' => $modelCanSave
        ]);
    }
}
```

`UploadedFile::getInstance` gets the file from the `$_FILES` array to fill the `fileImage` property of Model with its data.

The last thing to do is to update the `create` view content, by appending the `fileInput` field. This is the final version:

```php
<?php
use yii\helpers\Html;
use yii\widgets\ActiveForm;
use yii\helpers\Url;
use yii\helpers\ArrayHelper;
?>

<?php if($modelCanSave) { ?>
<div class="alert alert-success">
    Model ready to be saved!
    <br /><br />
    These are values: <br />
    Floor: <?php echo $model->floor; ?> <br />
    Room Number: <?php echo $model->room_number; ?> <br />
    Has conditioner: <?php echo Yii::$app->formatter-
    >asBoolean($model->has_conditioner); ?> <br />
    Has TV: <?php echo Yii::$app->formatter->asBoolean($model-
    >has_tv); ?> <br />
    Has phone: <?php echo Yii::$app->formatter->asBoolean($model-
    >has_phone); ?> <br />
    Available from (mm/dd/yyyy): <?php echo Yii::$app->formatter-
    >asDate($model->available_from,'php:m/d/Y'); ?> <br />
    Price per day: <?php echo Yii::$app->formatter-
    >asCurrency($model->price_per_day,'EUR'); ?> <br />
    Image:
    <?php if(isset($model->fileImage)) { ?>
        <img src="<?php echo Url::to('@uploadedfilesdir/'.$model-
        >fileImage->name) ?>" />
    <?php } ?>
</div>
<?php } ?>


<?php $form = ActiveForm::begin(['options' => ['enctype' =>
'multipart/form-data']]); ?>
<div class="row">
    <div class="col-lg-12">
        <h1>Room form</h1>
        <?= $form->field($model, 'floor')->textInput() ?>
        <?= $form->field($model, 'room_number')->textInput() ?>
```

```
<?= $form->field($model, 'has_conditioner')->checkbox() ?>
<?= $form->field($model, 'has_tv')->checkbox() ?>
<?= $form->field($model, 'has_phone')->checkbox() ?>
<?= $form->field($model, 'available_from')->textInput() ?>
<?= $form->field($model, 'price_per_day')->textInput() ?>
<?= $form->field($model, 'description')->textarea() ?>


        <?= $form->field($model, 'fileImage')->fileInput() ?>
    </div>
</div>
<div class="form-group">
    <?= Html::submitButton('Create' , ['class' => 'btn btn-
    success']) ?>
</div>
<?php ActiveForm::end(); ?>
```

Take care of the last row of this example, `ActiveForm::end()` that closes the body of the `$form` widget defined at the top of the file using the `ActiveForm::begin()` method.

> In this example, the `ActiveForm` widget has been created by filling the `enctype` property of the configuration array with the `multipart/form-data` value, which allows us to send the binary data other than the form text parameters. However, this does not deal with Yii or PHP, because this is an HTML requirement for notifying the browser how to send files to the server.

In this view, if the model has been validated and the `fileImage` property is filled, the corresponding image will be displayed.

Summary

In this chapter, we saw how to build a Model class from scratch and send data from view to controller using form, created using Yii2 ActiveForm widget. We also looked at the common useful methods to format data and sent files from the form.

In the next chapter, you will learn how to work with databases and save model data from view form to database.

5
Developing a Reservation System

In this chapter, you will learn how to configure and manage databases, using SQL or ActiveRecord directly, then you will see how to solve common tasks, such as saving single and multiple models from a form, and how to create data aggregation and filtered views.

We will cover the following topics in this chapter:

- Configuring a DB connection:
    - For example, creating rooms, customers, and reservations tables
- For example, testing a connection and executing a SQL query
- Using Gii to create room, customer, and reservation models
- Using ActiveRecord to manipulate data:
    - For example, querying rooms list with ActiveRecord
- Working with relationships:
    - For example, using relationships to connect rooms, reservations, and customers
- How to save a model from a form:
    - For example, creating and updating a room from a form
- Setting up the GMT time zone
- Using multiple database connections:
    - For example, configuring a second DB connection to export data to a local SQLite DB

Configuring a DB connection

Yii2 offers a high-level layer to access databases, built on top of **PHP Data Objects** (**PDO**).

This framework allows us to manipulate a database table's content through the use of ActiveRecord objects. This encapsulates methods to access single or multiple records, as well as filtering, joining, and ordering data in an intuitive way.

Again, we can work with databases using plain SQL, but this means that we must handle dissimilarities in SQL languages passing through different databases (MySQL, SQL Server, Postgres, Oracle, and so on), which means losing Yii2 facilities.

A database object connection is an instance of yii\db\Connection:

```
$db = new yii\db\Connection([
    'dsn' => 'mysql:host=localhost;dbname=my_database',
    'username' => 'my_username',
    'password' => 'my_password',
    'charset' => 'utf8',
]);
```

In this example, we have a connection to a MySQL Server with a mysql connection string to the database my_databases, setting my_username as username and my_password as password. Moreover, we set charset to utf8 in order to guarantee standard charset use. This is a standard database connection entry.

Other common available connection strings are:

- MySQL and MariaDB: mysql:host=localhost;dbname=mydatabase
- SQLite: sqlite:/path/to/database/file
- PostgreSQL: pgsql:host=localhost;port=5432;dbname=mydatabase
- MS SQL Server (via mssql driver): mssql:host=localhost;dbname=mydata base
- Oracle: oci:dbname=//localhost:1521/mydatabase

If we do not provide a direct driver to database and we have to use ODBC, we will have a sample of the ODBC connection object as follows:

```
$db = new yii\db\Connection([
    'driverName' => 'mysql',
    'dsn' =>
    'odbc:Driver={MySQL};Server=localhost;Database=
my_database',
    'username' => 'my_username',
    'password' => 'my_password',
    'charset' => 'utf8',
]);
```

For convenience, we will set the database connection as an application component because it will be adopted in many points of the application. In `basic/config/web.php`:

```
return [
    // ...
    'components' => [
        // ...
        'db' => [
            'class' => 'yii\db\Connection',
            'dsn' => 'mysql:host=localhost;dbname=my_database',
            'username' => 'my_username',
            'password' => 'my_password',
            'charset' => 'utf8',
        ],
    ],
    // ...
];
```

In the basic template, database configuration is in a separate file, generally `basic/config/db.php`.

If we open `basic/config/web.php`, we can see that the `db.php` file fills the `db` property of the main configuration.

Example – creating rooms, customers, and reservations tables

Now, we need a MySQL database instance to work with. Open the DB administration panel as phpMyAdmin (if provided) or access the DB directly using a console and create a new database named `my_database`, associated with the username `my_username` and the password `my_password`.

In this example, we will create three database tables to manage rooms, customers, and reservations data.

A room will have the following fields:

- `id` as an integer
- `floor` as an integer
- `room_number` as an integer
- `has_conditioner` as an integer
- `has_tv` as an integer
- `has_phone` as an integer
- `available_from` as the date
- `price_per_day` as a decimal
- `description` as text

The script of the `room` table will be:

```
CREATE TABLE `room` (
    `id` int(11) NOT NULL PRIMARY KEY AUTO_INCREMENT,
    `floor` int(11) NOT NULL,
    `room_number` int(11) NOT NULL,
    `has_conditioner` int(1) NOT NULL,
    `has_tv` int(1) NOT NULL,
    `has_phone` int(1) NOT NULL,
    `available_from` date NOT NULL,
    `price_per_day` decimal(20,2) DEFAULT NULL,
    `description` text);
```

A customer will have the following fields:

- `id` as an integer
- `name` as a string
- `surname` as a string
- `phone_number` as a string

The script of the `customer` table will be

```
CREATE TABLE `customer` (
 `id` int(11) NOT NULL PRIMARY KEY AUTO_INCREMENT,
 `name` varchar(50) NOT NULL,
 `surname` varchar(50) NOT NULL,
 `phone_number` varchar(50) DEFAULT NULL
);
```

A reservation will have the following fields:

- `id` as an integer
- `room_id` as an integer that is a reference to a room table
- `customer_id` as an integer that is a reference to a customer table
- `price_per_day` as a decimal
- `date_from` as the date to specify check in
- `date_to` as the date to specify check out
- `reservation_date` as a timestamp of creation
- `days_stay` as an integer

The script of the `reservation` table will be:

```
CREATE TABLE `reservation` (
 `id` int(11) NOT NULL AUTO_INCREMENT,
 `room_id` int(11) NOT NULL,
 `customer_id` int(11) NOT NULL,
 `price_per_day` decimal(20,2) NOT NULL,
 `date_from` date NOT NULL,
 `date_to` date NOT NULL,
 `reservation_date` timestamp NOT NULL DEFAULT CURRENT_TIMESTAMP,
);
```

Finally, place `basic/config/web.php` in the `components` property:

```
$db = new yii\db\Connection([
    'dsn' => 'mysql:host=localhost;dbname=my_database',
    'username' => 'my_username',
    'password' => 'my_password',
    'charset' => 'utf8',
]);
```

Then we are ready to test the connection to the DB.

Example – test connection and executing the SQL query

Now let's see how to test the DB connection.

Put some rooms data in the database table:

```
INSERT INTO `my_database`.`room` (`id`, `floor`, `room_number`,
`has_conditioner`, `has_tv`, `has_phone`, `available_from`,
`price_per_day`, `description`)
VALUES
(NULL, '1', '101', '1', '0', '1', '2015-05-20', '120', NULL),
(NULL, '2', '202', '0', '1', '1', '2015-05-30', '118', NULL);
```

Database queries are made using the yii\db\Command object, which is created statically by the yii\db\Connection::createCommand() method.

The most important methods to retrieve data from a command are:

- queryAll(): This method returns all the rows of a query, where each array element is an array that represents a row of data; if the query returns no data, the response is an empty array

- queryOne(): This method returns the first row of the query, that is, an array, which represents a row of data; if the query returns no data, the response is a false Boolean value

- queryScalar(): This method returns the value of the first column in the first row of the query result; otherwise false will be returned if there is no value

- query(): This is the most common response that returns the yii\db\DataReader object

Now we will display the room table's content in different ways.

We will update RoomsController in basic/controllers/RoomsController.php. In this file, we will append an index action to fetch data and pass it to view:

```php
<?php

namespace app\controllers;

use Yii;
use yii\web\Controller;

class RoomsController extends Controller
{
```

```
public function actionIndex()
{
    $sql = 'SELECT * FROM room ORDER BY id ASC';

    $db = Yii::$app->db;

    $rooms = $db->createCommand($sql)->queryAll();
// same of
 // $rooms = Yii::$app->db->createCommand($sql)->queryAll();

    return $this->render('index', [ 'rooms' => $rooms ]);
}
}
```

The content of `actionIndex()` is very simple. Define the `$sql` variable with the SQL statement to be executed, then fill the `$rooms` array with the query result, and finally render the `index` view, passing the rooms variable.

In the view content, in `basic/views/rooms/index.php`, we will display the `$rooms` array in a table to exploit Bootstrap CSS's advantages, and apply the `table` class to the table HTML tag.

This is the content of `basic/views/rooms/index.php`, where we can also see the data formatter used:

```
<table class="table">
    <tr>
        <th>Floor</th>
        <th>Room number</th>
        <th>Has conditioner</th>
        <th>Has tv</th>
        <th>Has phone</th>
        <th>Available from</th>
        <th>Available from (db format)</th>
        <th>Price per day</th>
        <th>Description</th>
    </tr>
    <?php foreach($rooms as $item) { ?>
    <tr>
        <td><?php echo $item['floor'] ?></td>
        <td><?php echo $item['room_number'] ?></td>
        <td><?php echo Yii::$app->formatter-
        >asBoolean($item['has_conditioner']) ?></td>
```

```
        <td><?php echo Yii::$app->formatter-
        >asBoolean($item['has_tv']) ?></td>
        <td><?php echo ($item['has_phone'] == 1)?'Yes':'No'
        ?></td>
        <td><?php echo Yii::$app->formatter-
        >asDate($item['available_from']) ?></td>
        <td><?php echo Yii::$app->formatter-
        >asDate($item['available_from'], 'php:Y-m-d') ?></td>
        <td><?php echo Yii::$app->formatter-
        >asCurrency($item['price_per_day'], 'EUR') ?></td>
        <td><?php echo $item['description'] ?></td>
    </tr>
    <?php } ?>
</table>
```

The `floor` and `room_number` fields are directly displayed.

The next two fields `has_conditioner` and `has_tv` are shown by employing a Boolean formatter supplied by Yii2; the Boolean formatter will use the locale defined during the configuration of Yii2.

The next field `has_phone` renders its value as the previous two fields; the reason for this is to indicate how to produce the same output of a Boolean formatter in a standard PHP style.

Then, the `available_from` field is rendered using the date formatter in two different ways, directly and passing the format to be used. Or, if no parameter is passed, it adopts the default format.

Again, the `price_per_day` field is rendered through the currency formatter, passing the currency as a parameter. If no parameter is passed, the default value will be used. The last field `description` is displayed directly. Point your browser to `http://hostname/basic/web/rooms/index` to see the content as follows:

A list of rooms

Using Gii to create room, customer, and reservation models

Yii2 provides a powerful tool to generate models, controllers, and CRUD (create, read, update, and delete) actions, forms, modules, and extensions: Gii.

At the bottom of the `basic/config/web.php` file, placed in the basic standard configuration, there is a block of code that enables Gii:

```
if (YII_ENV_DEV) {
    // configuration adjustments for 'dev' environment
    $config['bootstrap'][] = 'debug';
    $config['modules']['debug'] = 'yii\debug\Module';

    $config['bootstrap'][] = 'gii';
    $config['modules']['gii'] = 'yii\gii\Module';
}
```

Verify that these lines are present, otherwise append them at the bottom of the `web.php` file before the `return $config` statement. The last check is in `basic/web/index.php`. Verify that `YII_ENV` is dev, with this line:

```
defined('YII_ENV') or define('YII_ENV', 'dev');
```

Now, we can point our browser to `http://hostname/basic/web/gii`, and we should see this error page:

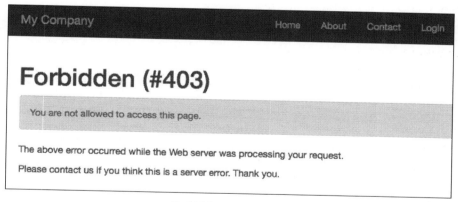

Forbidden access to Gii

This page will be displayed since access to Gii is locked by a password.

We need to add extra configuration to the `gii` module, passing other allowed IPs. Gii's configuration has an attribute named `allowedIPs`, which consents to specify which IP addresses can access the Gii page:

```
'allowedIPs' => ['127.0.0.1', '::1', '192.168.178.20']
```

In this extract, Gii will accept access from a localhost (in the IPv4 form with 127.0.0.1 and IPv6 form with ::1) and from 192.168.178.20, which should be our IP address in private network.

If the Yii2 application is running on an external hosting, we will set our IP public address in this list of allowed IPs. For example, if our IP is 66.249.64.76, this entry will be appended to existent (if we want maintain other permitted access points):

```
'allowedIPs' => ['127.0.0.1', '::1', '192.168.178.20',
'66.249.64.76']
```

To allow access from everywhere (useful in the development stage), we can add * in this list, which means that the Gii page can be accessed from every IP address:

```
'allowedIPs' => ['127.0.0.1', '::1', '192.168.178.20', '*']
```

Consequently, the content of `gii]['gii'] = 'yii\gii\Module'` is:

```
    $config['modules']['gii'] = [
        'class' => 'yii\gii\Module',
        'allowedIPs' => ['127.0.0.1', '::1', '192.168.178.20',
        '*'] ]; configuration in basic/config/web.php will be:
if (YII_ENV_DEV) {
    // configuration adjustments for 'dev' environment
    $config['bootstrap'][] = 'debug';
    $config['modules']['debug'] = 'yii\debug\Module';

    $config['bootstrap'][] = 'gii';
    //$config['modules'
}
```

Now, we are able to access to Gii from any IP.

Refresh the browser by clicking on the page `http://hostname/basic/web/gii` and we can finally see its content:

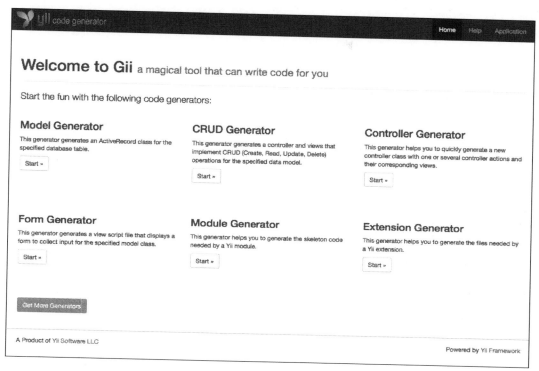

Successful access to Gii

Now, click on the **Start** button of **Model Generator**; we will have a form of **Model Generator** where **Table Name** is the unique field to fill in. When we start to type the table name, auto-suggestion will display the possible choices. After doing this, when we move to the **Model Class** field, this will be automatically filled in by a framework. The other fields can be left with the default settings.

Type `room` in **Table Name** and then click on the **Model Class** field. This field will be filled with **Room**, which is the filename in the `models` folder.

Clicking on the **Preview** button will display the path where the file will be created and the action will be applied (it should be the overwrite value because we created it in the previous chapter).

Finally, click on the **Generate** button to complete this action. A response message will give us information about the execution of this operation.

This is the form with a successful result:

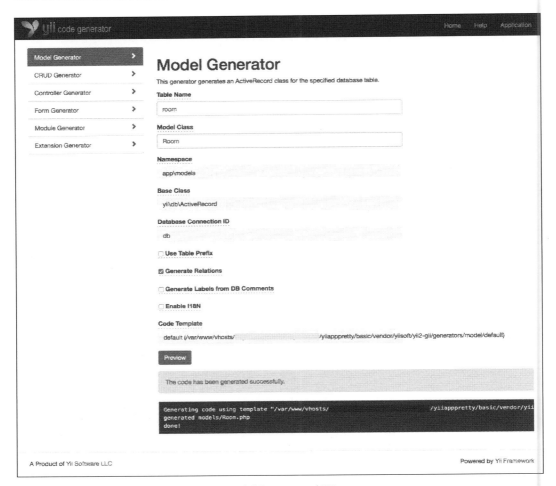

Model Generator of Gii

Repeat this operation for the other two tables: reservations and customers.

Now, we have three models in the `basic/models` folder: `Room.php`,
`Reservation.php,` and `Customer.php`.

Let's explain what Gii has done. Open the `basic/models/Room.php` file, and we
have three methods:

- `tableName()`
- `rules()`
- `attributeLabels()`

The first method, `tableName()`, simply returns the name of table to which this model is linked:

```
public static function tableName()
{
    return 'room';
}
```

The second method, `rules()`, is important because it contains rules validation to be checked when the `validate()` method is launched (it is launched automatically in the `save()` method) or a massive attributes assignment as:

```
$model->attributes = arrayWithData;
```

This is the content of the `rules()` method:

```
public function rules()
{
    return [
        [['floor', 'room_number', 'has_conditioner', 'has_tv',
        'has_phone', 'available_from'], 'required'],
        [['floor', 'room_number', 'has_conditioner', 'has_tv',
        'has_phone'], 'integer'],
        [['available_from'], 'safe'],
        [['price_per_day'], 'number'],
        [['description'], 'string']
    ];
}
```

The first rule specifies that the fields `floor`, `room_number`, `has_condition`, `has_tv`, and `avaiable_from` are mandatory because they are passed to the required validator. Moreover, they must be an integer, as required by the second rule.

 Fields that are not in rules, will be skipped in a massive assignment because they are considered unsafe (since they are not present in rules). So it is necessary that when a field that has not got a validator rule, it must have an entry in the 'safe' validator.

The fourth rule specifies that the `price_per_day` field is a number, while the last rule states that `description` is a string.

 These rules are read automatically from the database field type and constraint.

The last method `attributeLabels()` specifies the representation of fields in the display view as a form, grid, and so on.

This is the content of `attributeLabels()`:

```
public function attributeLabels()
{
    return [
        'id' => 'ID',
        'floor' => 'Floor',
        'room_number' => 'Room Number',
        'has_conditioner' => 'Has Conditioner',
        'has_tv' => 'Has Tv',
        'has_phone' => 'Has Phone',
        'available_from' => 'Available From',
        'price_per_day' => 'Price Per Day',
        'description' => 'Description',
    ];
}
```

Yii2 reports—in the model—any relationship between the tables present in a database. We have the `Reservation` model that has links to `Room` and `Customer`.

Follow these instructions to make the framework able to create a relationship in the model:

1. Check that the database tables use the InnoDB engine (which supports relationships and foreign keys).

2. In the `Reservation` table, add two indexes, respectively for the `room_id` and `customer_id` fields:

```
ALTER TABLE `reservation` ADD INDEX ( `room_id` ) ;
ALTER TABLE `reservation` ADD INDEX ( `customer_id` ) ;
```

3. In the `Reservation` table, add two constraints to the `room` and `customer` tables:

```
ALTER TABLE `reservation` ADD FOREIGN KEY ( `room_id` )
REFERENCES `room` (`id`) ON DELETE RESTRICT ON UPDATE
RESTRICT ;
ALTER TABLE `reservation` ADD FOREIGN KEY ( `customer_id` )
REFERENCES `customer` (`id`) ON DELETE RESTRICT ON UPDATE
RESTRICT ;
```

In these constraints, we used RESTRICT for DELETE and UPDATE operations. RESTRICT avoids the deletion of reservations that refer to customers or rooms that we are trying to delete. Therefore, to delete a customer or room that figures in reservations, we will be required to first delete the reservations.

This behavior ensures that important data such as reservations is never deleted automatically (in a cascade) when deleting a room or a customer. An error message will be displayed when you try to do this to a reservation linked to the customer or room.

In other contexts, a commonly used keyword is CASCADE, which removes all data that refers to linked tables.

Open Gii again and navigate to `http://hostname/basic/web/gii`, then click on the **Start** button in **Model Generator** and type `room` in **Table Name**. Click on the **Preview** button at the bottom of the page and this time you will see that `models/Room.php` exists and the action is overwrite, unflagged.

Click on the check near 'overwrite' and then on the **Generate** button. In this way, we have forced to overwrite the `Room` model with the relational data from the `Room` table.

Now, `basic/models/Room.php` contains a new method named `getReservations` at the bottom, with this content:

```
/**
 * @return \yii\db\ActiveQuery
 */
public function getReservations()
{
    return $this->hasMany(Reservation::className(),
    ['room_id' => 'id']);
}
```

This method returns an ActiveQuery instance, which is used to build a query to be dispatched to the database.

When called as a property, this method will return the list of reservations linked to the model.

You might encounter the case where $model is an instance of the Room class for example: $reservationsList = $model->reservations;

In this case, fill the $reservationsList variables with a list of reservations related to this Room model.

This is not surprising, although the hasMany method returns an ActiveQuery object.

If we explore the __get() method of BaseActiveRecord (which is the base class of ActiveRecord) that handles the property requirements, we can see these lines of code:

```
            $value = parent::__get($name);
            if ($value instanceof ActiveQueryInterface)
    {
                return $this->_related[$name] = $value-
                >findFor($name, $this);
            } else {
                return $value;
            }
```

This returns linked results when the $value content is an instance of ActiveQueryInterface (which is an interface implemented by the ActiveQuery class).

Using ActiveRecord to manipulate data

ActiveRecord offers a convenient way to access and manipulate data stored in a database. This class is linked to a database table and represents a row of the linked table. Its attributes are the fields of the table and its methods allow us to perform common actions on database, such as selecting, inserting, or updating SQL statements.

Many common databases are supported by ActiveRecord, such as:

- MySQL
- PostgreSQL
- SQLite
- Oracle
- Microsoft SQL Server

Also, some NoSQL databases are supported, such as:

- Redis
- MongoDB

ActiveRecord reads the table structure every time it is instanced and makes available table columns as its properties. Every change to the table structure is immediately available in the ActiveRecord object.

Therefore, if a table contains the fields id, floor, and room_number, and if $model is an instance of yii\db\ActiveRecord, in order to access these fields, it will be enough to type:

```
$id = $model->id;
$floor = $model->floor;
$room_number = $model->room_numer;
```

ActiveRecord handles properties request with the __get magic method and catches the respective content of a table column. In the previous paragraph, you saw how to create a model class from database tables to extend yii\db\ActiveRecord with Gii. The syntax used by ActiveRecord is simple and redundant, so it is easy to remember. Now let's look at how to query data from a database with ActiveRecord.

Data is fetched from a database through an \yii\db\ActiveQuery object to build the query, and finally calls on one() or all() methods to get an ActiveRecord object or a list of ActiveRecord objects.

An ActiveQuery object is returned from an ActiveRecord object by calling its static method ::find().

If Room is a model (and subclasses ActiveRecord), an ActiveQuery will be returned from:

```
// $query is an ActiveQuery object
$query = Room::find();
```

ActiveQuery objects provide methods to build the query with names such as in SQL expression.

The most common ones are:

- where() to add conditions
- orderBy() to apply an order
- groupBy() to make aggregations

Almost all of these methods support a parameter that can be a string or an array. If it is a string, it will be passed exactly as it is to the SQL query; if it is an array, a key will be used as the column name, and a value as the corresponding value. For example, we want to build query to find a room on the first floor:

```
$query = Room::find()->where('floor = 1');
// equivalent to
$query = Room::find()->where(['floor' => 1]);
```

For complex conditions, where() supports the operator format where the condition is an array with:

```
[operator, operand1, operand2, ...]
```

For example, we want to build a query to find a room on the first floor:

```
$query = Room::find()->where(['>=', 'floor', 1]);
// equivalent to
$query = Room::find()->where('floor >= 1';
```

Other conditions can be added using andWhere() or orWhere(), by just using the and or or logical link.

An array parameter of the where() method is preferable to a string, because we can easily split the field name from its content and set the second parameter of the where() method with an array with pair keys => values of parameters.

After creating a query object, to get data from an ActiveQuery, we will have:

- one(): This method returns an ActiveRecord object or null if not found
- all(): This method returns a list of ActiveRecord objects or an empty array if not found

So, to get rooms on the first floor, we must write:

```
$query = Room::find()->where(['floor' => 1]);
$items = $query->all();
// equivalent to
$items = Room::find()->where(['floor' => 1])->all();
```

There is a more concise syntax to fetch data from an ActiveRecord: the `findOne()` and `findAll()` methods, which return a single ActiveRecord or a list of ActiveRecords. The only difference from the previous methods is that they accept a single parameter, which can be:

- A number to filter by primary key
- An array of scalar values to filter by a list of primary key values (only for `findAll()` because `findOne()` returns a single ActiveRecord)
- An array of name-value pair to filter by a set of attribute values

Other common methods of ActiveRecord are:

- `validate()`: This method is used to apply rules validation to attributes of a model

- `save()`: This method is used to save a new model or to update one that already exists (if the `save()` method is applied to a fetched ActiveRecord object)

- `delete()`: This method is used to delete a model

Example – query rooms list with ActiveRecord

In this example, we will query the rooms list using ActiveRecord and filter through the following fields: `floor`, `room_number`, and `price_per_day` with operators (`>=`, `<=`, and `=`).

A data filter will take place using the `SearchFilter` container to encapsulate all of the filter data inside a single array.

Starting from a view, create a new file with the path `basic/views/rooms/indexFiltered.php`.

In this view, we will put the search filter on the top and then a table to display the results.

We have three fields to filter: `floor`, `room_number`, and `price_per_day`, all with an operator. The data filter will be passed to the controller and the filter selected will be kept after executing `actionIndexFiltered` in the controller.

This is the content of the view concerning the filtered form:

```php
<?php
use yii\helpers\Url;

$operators = [ '=', '<=', '>=' ];

$sf = $searchFilter;

?>

<form method="post" action="<?php echo Url::to(['rooms/index-
filtered']) ?>">
    <input type="hidden" name="<?= Yii::$app->request->csrfParam;
    ?>" value="<?= Yii::$app->request->csrfToken; ?>" />

    <div class="row">
        <?php $operator = $sf['floor']['operator']; ?>
        <?php $value = $sf['floor']['value']; ?>
        <div class="col-md-3">
            <label>Floor</label>
            <br />
            <select name="SearchFilter[floor][operator]">
                <?php foreach($operators as $op) { ?>
                    <?php $selected = ($operator ==
                    $op)?'selected':''; ?>
                    <option value="<?=$op?>"
                    <?=$selected?>><?=$op?></option>
                <?php } ?>=
            </select>
            <input type="text" name="SearchFilter[floor][value]"
            value="<?=$value?>" />
        </div>

        <?php $operator = $sf['room_number']['operator']; ?>
        <?php $value = $sf['room_number']['value']; ?>
        <div class="col-md-3">
            <label>Room Number</label>
            <br />
            <select name="SearchFilter[room_number][operator]">
                <?php foreach($operators as $op) { ?>
                    <?php $selected = ($operator ==
                    $op)?'selected':''; ?>
```

```
            <option value="<?=$op?>"
            <?=$selected?>><?=$op?></option>
        <?php } ?>
    </select>
    <input type="text"
    name="SearchFilter[room_number][value]"
    value="<?=$value?>" />
</div>

<?php $operator = $sf['price_per_day']['operator']; ?>
<?php $value = $sf['price_per_day']['value']; ?>
<div class="col-md-3">
    <label>Price per day</label>
    <br />
    <select name="SearchFilter[price_per_day][operator]">
        <?php foreach($operators as $op) { ?>
            <?php $selected = ($operator ==
            $op)?'selected':''; ?>
            <option value="<?=$op?>"
            <?=$selected?>><?=$op?></option>
        <?php } ?>
    </select>
    <input type="text"
    name="SearchFilter[price_per_day][value]"
    value="<?=$value?>" />
</div>
</div>
<br />
<div class="row">
    <div class="col-md-3">
        <input type="submit" value="filter" class="btn btn-
        primary" />
        <input type="reset" value="reset" class="btn btn-
        primary" />

    </div>
</div>
</form>
```

Pay attention:

At the beginning of the view, there is a keyword use, which explains the complete path of the Url class. If we remove it, the framework will search the Url class requested in the <form> tag in the current namespace, that is app/controllers.

After declaring the <form> tag, we inserted:

```
<input type="hidden" name="<?= Yii::$app->request-
>csrfParam; ?>" value="<?= Yii::$app->request-
>csrfToken; ?>" />
```

This is mandatory to allow the framework to verify the sender of the post data.

The $searchFilter variable is used as $sf to provide a more concise form.

Now update RoomsController in basic/controllers/RoomsController.php and add a new action named actionIndexFiltered. Create an ActiveQuery object from Room and check whether there is content in the SearchFilter keyword of the $_POST array.

For every present filter, a condition will be added to $query using the andWhere method, passing an operator, field name, and value. For a more concise form of the actioned content, we put a filtered field in the loop, because they have the same redundant structure (operator and value):

```php
public function actionIndexFiltered()
{
    $query = Room::find();

    $searchFilter = [
        'floor' => ['operator' => '', 'value' => ''],
        'room_number' => ['operator' => '', 'value' => ''],
        'price_per_day' => ['operator' => '', 'value' => ''],
    ];

    if(isset($_POST['SearchFilter']))
    {
        $fieldsList = ['floor', 'room_number',
        'price_per_day'];

        foreach($fieldsList as $field)
        {
            $fieldOperator =
            $_POST['SearchFilter'][$field]['operator'];
```

```
        $fieldValue =
        $_POST['SearchFilter'][$field]['value'];

        $searchFilter[$field] = ['operator' =>
        $fieldOperator, 'value' => $fieldValue];

        if( $fieldValue != '' )
        {
            $query->andWhere([$fieldOperator, $field,
            $fieldValue]);
        }
        }
    }

    $rooms = $query->all();

    return $this->render('indexFiltered', [ 'rooms' => $rooms,
    'searchFilter' => $searchFilter ]);

}
```

Finally, we need to display the results in a table format. So at the bottom of the view, add a table to display the content of the filtered rooms (copied from `basic/views/rooms/index.php`):

```
<table class="table">
    <tr>
        <th>Floor</th>
        <th>Room number</th>
        <th>Has conditioner</th>
        <th>Has tv</th>
        <th>Has phone</th>
        <th>Available from</th>
        <th>Available from (db format)</th>
        <th>Price per day</th>
        <th>Description</th>
    </tr>
    <?php foreach($rooms as $item) { ?>
    <tr>
        <td><?php echo $item['floor'] ?></td>
        <td><?php echo $item['room_number'] ?></td>
        <td><?php echo Yii::$app->formatter-
        >asBoolean($item['has_conditioner']) ?></td>
        <td><?php echo Yii::$app->formatter-
        >asBoolean($item['has_tv']) ?></td>
```

```
            <td><?php echo ($item['has_phone'] == 1)?'Yes':'No'
            ?></td>
            <td><?php echo Yii::$app->formatter-
            >asDate($item['available_from']) ?></td>
            <td><?php echo Yii::$app->formatter-
            >asDate($item['available_from'], 'php:Y-m-d') ?></td>
            <td><?php echo Yii::$app->formatter-
            >asCurrency($item['price_per_day'], 'EUR') ?></td>
            <td><?php echo $item['description'] ?></td>
        </tr>
        <?php } ?>
    </table>
```

Now point the browser to `http://hostname/basic/web/rooms/index-filtered` and this should be displayed:

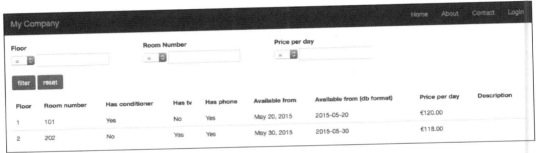

A list of rooms with filters

We can create tests by changing the filter values and operators as much as we want.

Working with relationships

ActiveRecord provides us with skills to work with relationships between database tables. Yii2 employs two methods to establish the relationship between the current and other ActiveRecord classes: `hasOne` and `hasMany`, which return an ActiveQuery based on the multiplicity of the relationship.

The first method `hasOne()` returns at most one related record that matches the criteria set by this relationship, and `hasMany()` returns multiple related records that match the criteria set by this relationship.

Both methods require that the first parameter is the class name of the related ActiveRecord and that the second parameter is the pair of primary keys that are involved in the relationship: the first key is relative to a foreign ActiveRecord and the second key is related to the current ActiveRecord.

Usually, `hasOne()` and `hasMany()` are accessed from properties that identify which object (or objects) will be returned.

The method in this example is:

```
class Room extends ActiveRecord
{
    public function getReservations()
    {
return $this->hasMany(Reservation::className(), ['room_id' =>
'id']);
    }
}
```

By calling `$room->reservations`, framework will execute this query:

```
SELECT * FROM `reservation` WHERE `room_id` = id_of_room_model
```

The use of the `hasOne()` method is similar, and as an example will look like this:

```
class Reservation extends ActiveRecord
{
    public function getRoom()
    {
return $this->hasOne(Room::className(), ['id' => 'room_id']);
    }
}
```

Calling `$reservation->room`, framework will execute this query:

```
SELECT * FROM `room` WHERE `id` = reservation_id
```

Remember that when we call a property that contains the `hasOne()` or `hasMany()` methods, a SQL query will be executed and its response will be cached. So, the next time that we call the property, a SQL query will not be executed and the last cached response will be released.

This approach to get related data is called **lazy loading**, which means that data is loaded only when it is effectively requested.

Now let's write an example to display the last reservation details about a room. Create a reservations model class using Gii if you have not done so before.

First of all, we need some data to work with. Insert this record in the `customer` table:

```
INSERT INTO `customer` (`id` ,`name` ,`surname` ,`phone_number`)
VALUES ( NULL , 'James', 'Foo', '+39-12345678');
```

In the `reservation` table, insert these records:

```
INSERT INTO `reservation` (`id`, `room_id`, `customer_id`,
`price_per_day`, `date_from`, `date_to`, `reservation_date`)
VALUES (NULL, '2', '1', '90', '2015-04-01', '2015-05-06', NULL),
(NULL, '2', '1', '48', '2019-08-27', '2019-08-31',
CURRENT_TIMESTAMP);
```

Open the room model in `basic/models/Room.php` and append this property declaration at the bottom of the file:

```
public function getLastReservation()
{
    return $this->hasOne(
      Reservation::className(),
      ['room_id' => 'id']
      )
      ->orderBy('id');
}
```

As said before, `hasOne()` and `hasMany()` return an ActiveQuery instance. We can append any methods to complete the relationship as we have done before by appending the `orderBy()` method to get the first record.

Create a new action named `actionLastReservationByRoomId($room_id)` in the `Rooms` controller, with the following content:

```
public function actionLastReservationByRoomId($room_id)
{
    $room = Room::findOne($room_id);

    // equivalent to
    // SELECT * FROM reservation WHERE room_id = $room_id
    $lastReservation = $room->lastReservation;

    // next times that we will call $room->reservation, no sql
    query will be executed.

    return $this->render('lastReservationByRoomId', ['room' =>
    $room, 'lastReservation' => $lastReservation]);
}
Finally, create the view in
basic/views/rooms/lastReservationByRoomId.php with this
content:<table class="table">
<tr>
    <th>Room Id</th>
    <td><?php echo $lastReservation['room_id'] ?></td>
</tr>
```

```
        <tr>
            <th>Customer Id</th>
            <td><?php echo $lastReservation['customer_id'] ?></td>
        </tr>
        <tr>
            <th>Price per day</th>
            <td><?php echo Yii::$app->formatter-
            >asCurrency($lastReservation['price_per_day'], 'EUR')
            ?></td>
        </tr>
        <tr>
            <th>Date from</th>
            <td><?php echo Yii::$app->formatter-
            >asDate($lastReservation['date_from'], 'php:Y-m-d')
            ?></td>
        </tr>
        <tr>
            <th>Date to</th>
            <td><?php echo Yii::$app->formatter-
            >asDate($lastReservation['date_to'], 'php:Y-m-d') ?></td>
        </tr>
        <tr>
            <th>Reservation date</th>
            <td><?php echo Yii::$app->formatter-
            >asDate($lastReservation['reservation_date'], 'php:Y-m-d
            H:i:s') ?></td>
        </tr>
    </table>
```

Point your browser to `http://hostname/basic/web/rooms/last-reservation-by-room-id?room_id=2` to visualize this frame:

A visualization of the last reservation of a room with id = 2

Only the last reservation inserted in the database will be displayed.

What about displaying all the last reservations for each room in a single table?

Here, the lazy loading approach will have performance issues because for every room, it will execute a single SQL query to get data for the last reservation. This is a code snippet in the view:

```
for($roomsList as $room)
{
    // SELECT * FROM reservation WHERE room_id = $room->id
      $lastReservation = $room->lastReservation;
}
```

In order to complete the script's execution, it will execute as many related SQL queries as the number of rooms, and when the number of rooms grows, this solution will not be efficient anymore.

The Yii2 framework provides another type of loading data, named eager loading, to solve this kind of problem.

Eager loading is applied using the `with()` method of ActiveQuery. This method's parameters can be either one or multiple strings, or a single array of relation names and the optional callbacks to customize the relationships.

When we get a rooms list, if we apply the `with()` method to the query, a second SQL query will automatically be executed and this will return the list of the last reservations for each room.

With this example, we will get a rooms list and a list of the `lastReservation` relation for each room entry. In this way, when we refer to `$room->lastReservation`, no other SQL query will be executed:

```
// SELECT * FROM `room`
// SELECT * FROM `reservation` WHERE `room_id` IN ( room_id list from
previous select ) ORDER BY `id` DESC
$rooms = Room::find()
->with('lastReservation')
->all();

// no query will be executed
$lastReservation = $rooms[0]->lastReservation;
```

Let's write a complete example to get a full list of the last reservations for each room. In `basic/controllers/RoomsController.php`, append a new action named `actionLastReservationForEveryRoom()`:

```
public function actionLastReservationForEveryRoom()
{
        $rooms = Room::find()
        ->with('lastReservation')
        ->all();

        return $this->render('lastReservationForEveryRoom',
['rooms' => $rooms]);
}
```

This action will pass a list of rooms named `lastReservationForEveryRoom` to the view, together with the `lastReservation` relation loaded using the eager loading.

Create a view named `lastReservationForEveryRoom.php` in `basic/views/rooms/lastReservationForEveryRoom.php`:

```
<table class="table">
    <tr>
        <th>Room Id</th>
        <th>Customer Id</th>
        <th>Price per day</th>
        <th>Date from</th>
        <th>Date to</th>
        <th>Reservation date</th>
    </tr>
    <?php foreach($rooms as $room) { ?>
    <?php $lastReservation = $room->lastReservation; ?>
    <tr>
        <td><?php echo $lastReservation['room_id'] ?></td>
        <td><?php echo $lastReservation['customer_id'] ?></td>
        <td><?php echo Yii::$app->formatter-
        >asCurrency($lastReservation['price_per_day'], 'EUR')
        ?></td>
        <td><?php echo Yii::$app->formatter-
        >asDate($lastReservation['date_from'], 'php:Y-m-d')
        ?></td>
        <td><?php echo Yii::$app->formatter-
        >asDate($lastReservation['date_to'], 'php:Y-m-d') ?></td>
        <td><?php echo Yii::$app->formatter-
        >asDate($lastReservation['reservation_date'], 'php:Y-m-d
        H:i:s') ?></td>
    </tr>
    <?php } ?>
</table>
```

In this view, the last reservation data will be displayed for each room. Since the first room has no reservations, an empty row will be displayed. This is the result:

Room Id	Customer Id	Price per day	Date from	Date to	Reservation date
		(not set)	*(not set)*	*(not set)*	*(not set)*
2	1	€48.00	2019-08-27	2019-08-31	2015-05-25 02:45:37

Last reservation for every room

There are two variants to the `with()` method: `joinWith()` and `innerJoinWith()`, which apply a left join or an inner join to a primary query.

For example, this is the use of `joinWith()` with:

```
$rooms = Room::find()
    ->leftJoinWith('lastReservation')
    ->all();
```

The preceding code snippet is equivalent to:

```
SELECT `room`.* FROM `room` LEFT JOIN `reservation` ON
`room`.`id` = `reservation`.`room_id` ORDER BY `id`
DESC


SELECT * FROM `reservation` WHERE `room_id` IN ( room_
id
list from previous sql respone ) ORDER BY `id` DESC
```

Remember that the inner join selects all rows from both tables as long as there is a match between the columns in both tables; instead, the left join returns all rows from the left table (room), with the matching rows in the right table (reservation). The result is NULL in the right side when there is no match.

Sometimes it happens that we need more than one level of relationship between tables. For example, we could find a customer related to a room. In this case, starting from the room, we pass through the reservation and go from the reservation to the customer.

The relationship here will be:

```
room -> reservation -> customer
```

If we want to find out the customer object from the room object, just type:

```
$customer = $room->customer;
```

Generally, we have more levels of relationship, but in this case only two (reservation and customer).

Yii2 allows us to specify a junction table using the `via()` or `viaTable()` method. The first one, `via()`, is based on an existing relationship in the model, and it supports two parameters:

- Relation name
- A PHP callback parameter to customize the associated relation

The second method, `viaTable()`, is based on direct access to a physical table in the database and supports three parameters:

- The first parameter is a relation or table name
- The second parameter is the link associated with the primary model
- The third parameter is a PHP callback to customize the associated relation

Example – using a relationship to connect rooms, reservations, and customers

In this example, we will look at how to build a single view that displays the rooms, reservations, and customers lists at the same time; when a user clicks on the **Detail** button of rooms record, the reservations list will be filtered with data linked to that room. In the same way, when a user clicks on the **Detail** button of a reservations record, the customers list will be filtered with data linked to that reservation.

If no parameter is passed (a condition that occurs when a page is called for the first time), either the rooms, reservations, or customers list contains a full record of data from the respective tables.

Start writing `actionIndexWithRelationships` in `basic/controllers/RoomsController.php`. This is the task list for this action:

- Check which parameter of detail has been passed (`room_id` identifies that the reservations list has to be filled in with the data filtered using `room_id`, while `reservation_id` identifies that the customers list has to be filled with the data filtered using `reservation_id`)
- Fill in three models: `roomSelected`, `reservationSelected`, and `customerSelected` to display the details and fill in three arrays of models: `rooms`, `reservations`, and `customers`

This is the complete content of `actionIndexWithRelationships`:

```php
public function actionIndexWithRelationships()
{
    // 1. Check what parameter of detail has been passed
    $room_id = Yii::$app->request->get('room_id', null);
    $reservation_id = Yii::$app->request-
>get('reservation_id', null);
    $customer_id = Yii::$app->request->get('customer_id',
null);

    // 2. Fill three models: roomSelected, reservationSelected
    and customerSelected and
    //     Fill three arrays of models: rooms, reservations and
    customers;
    $roomSelected = null;
    $reservationSelected = null;
    $customerSelected = null;

    if($room_id != null)
    {
        $roomSelected = Room::findOne($room_id);

        $rooms = array($roomSelected);
        $reservations = $roomSelected->reservations;
        $customers = $roomSelected->customers;
    }
    else if($reservation_id != null)
    {
        $reservationSelected =
        Reservation::findOne($reservation_id);

        $rooms = array($reservationSelected->room);
        $reservations = array($reservationSelected);
        $customers = array($reservationSelected->customer);
    }
    else if($customer_id != null)
    {
        $customerSelected = Customer::findOne($customer_id);

        $rooms = $customerSelected->rooms;
        $reservations = $customerSelected->reservations;
        $customers = array($customerSelected);
    }
```

```
else
{
    $rooms = Room::find()->all();
    $reservations = Reservation::find()->all();
    $customers = Customer::find()->all();
}

return $this->render('indexWithRelationships',
['roomSelected' => $roomSelected, 'reservationSelected' =>
$reservationSelected, 'customerSelected' =>
$customerSelected, 'rooms' => $rooms, 'reservations' =>
$reservations, 'customers' => $customers]);
}
```

> Remember to add the use keyword for Customer and Reservation
> classes at the top of the RoomsController file:
>
> ```
> use app\models\Reservation;
> use app\models\Customer;
> ```

The second part of the action body requires more attention, because there are filled in selected models and list models in this specific position.

Only one parameter at a time can be selected between $room_id, $reservation_id, and $customer_id. When one of these three parameters is selected, three arrays of the Room, Reservation, and Customer model will be filled in, using the relationships in the model. For this purpose, models must have all the relationships employed in the previous code.

Let's make sure that all the relationships exist in the models.

The Room model in basic/models/Room.php must have both getReservations() and getCustomers() defined, which both use the via() method to handle the second level of relationship:

```
public function getReservations()
{
    return $this->hasMany(Reservation::className(),
    ['room_id' => 'id']);
}
public function getCustomers()
{
    return $this->hasMany(Customer::className(), ['id' =>
    'customer_id'])->via('reservations');
}
```

The `Reservation` model in `basic/models/Reservation.php` must have `getCustomer()` and `getRoom()`, both returning a single related model:

```php
public function getRoom()
{
        return $this->hasOne(Room::className(), ['id' =>
        'room_id']);
}

public function getCustomer()
{
        return $this->hasOne(Customer::className(), ['id' =>
        'customer_id']);
}
```

Finally, the `Customer` model in `basic/models/Customer.php` must have `getReservations()` and `getRooms()`, which use the `via()` method to handle the second level of relationship:

```php
public function getReservations()
{
        return $this->hasMany(Reservation::className(),
        ['customer_id' => 'id']);
}

public function getRooms()
{
        return $this->hasMany(Room::className(), ['id' =>
        'room_id'])->via('reservations');
}
```

Now write a view file in `basic/view/rooms/indexWithRelationships.php`. We will split the HTML page into three parts (three tables), using the CSS provided by Bootstrap (which we will examine widely in the next few chapters).

The first table will be for the rooms list, the second table for the reservations list, and the last one for the customers list:

```php
<?php
use yii\helpers\Url;
?>

<a class="btn btn-danger" href="<?php echo Url::to(['index-with-
relationships']) ?>">Reset</a>

<br /><br />
```

```
<div class="row">
    <div class="col-md-4">
        <legend>Rooms</legend>
        <table class="table">
            <tr>
                <th>#</th>
                <th>Floor</th>
                <th>Room number</th>
                <th>Price per day</th>
            </tr>
            <?php foreach($rooms as $room) { ?>
            <tr>
                <td><a class="btn btn-primary btn-xs" href="<?php
                echo Url::to(['index-with-relationships',
                'room_id' => $room->id]) ?>">detail</a></td>
                <td><?php echo $room['floor'] ?></td>
                <td><?php echo $room['room_number'] ?></td>
                <td><?php echo Yii::$app->formatter-
                >asCurrency($room['price_per_day'], 'EUR') ?></td>
            </tr>
            <?php } ?>
        </table>

        <?php if($roomSelected != null) { ?>
            <div class="alert alert-info">
                <b>You have selected Room #<?php echo
                $roomSelected->id ?></b>
            </div>
        <?php } else { ?>
            <i>No room selected</i>
        <?php } ?>
    </div>

    <div class="col-md-4">
        <legend>Reservations</legend>
        <table class="table">
            <tr>
                <th>#</th>
                <th>Price per day</th>
                <th>Date from</th>
                <th>Date to</th>
            </tr>
            <?php foreach($reservations as $reservation) { ?>
            <tr>
```

```
            <td><a class="btn btn-primary btn-xs" href="<?php
            echo Url::to(['index-with-relationships',
            'reservation_id' => $reservation->id])
            ?>">detail</a></td>
            <td><?php echo Yii::$app->formatter-
            >asCurrency($reservation['price_per_day'], 'EUR')
            ?></td>
            <td><?php echo Yii::$app->formatter-
            >asDate($reservation['date_from'], 'php:Y-m-d')
            ?></td>
            <td><?php echo Yii::$app->formatter-
            >asDate($reservation['date_to'], 'php:Y-m-d')
            ?></td>
        </tr>
        <?php } ?>
    </table>

    <?php if($reservationSelected != null) { ?>
        <div class="alert alert-info">
            <b>You have selected Reservation #<?php echo
            $reservationSelected->id ?></b>
        </div>
    <?php } else { ?>
        <i>No reservation selected</i>
    <?php } ?>

</div>
<div class="col-md-4">
    <legend>Customers</legend>
    <table class="table">
        <tr>
            <th>#</th>
            <th>Name</th>
            <th>Surname</th>
            <th>Phone</th>
        </tr>
        <?php foreach($customers as $customer) { ?>
        <tr>
            <td><a class="btn btn-primary btn-xs" href="<?php
            echo Url::to(['index-with-relationships',
            'customer_id' => $customer->id])
            ?>">detail</a></td>
            <td><?php echo $customer['name'] ?></td>
            <td><?php echo $customer['surname'] ?></td>
            <td><?php echo $customer['phone_number'] ?></td>
```

```
            </tr>
            <?php } ?>
        </table>

        <?php if($customerSelected != null) { ?>
            <div class="alert alert-info">
                <b>You have selected Customer #<?php echo
                $customerSelected->id ?></b>
            </div>
        <?php } else { ?>
            <i>No customer selected</i>
        <?php } ?>
    </div>
</div>
```

Test the code by pointing your browser to `http://hostname/basic/rooms/index-with-relationships`. This should be the result of trying to filter a room on the second floor:

Rooms with relationships between reservations and customers

How to save a model from a form

Let's now look at how to save a model from a form, which could be a new or an updated model.

The steps you need to follow are:

1. In the `action` method, create a new model or get an existing model.

2. In the `action` method, check whether there is data in the `$_POST` array.

3. If there is data in `$_POST`, fill in the `attributes` property of the model with data from `$_POST` and call the `save()` method of the model; if `save()` returns true, redirect the user to another page (the details page, for example).

From now on, we will continue to use widgets and helper classes provided by the framework. In this case, the HTML form will be rendered using the `yii\widget\ActiveForm` class.

The most simple form we can write is the following:

```php
<?php
use yii\widgets\ActiveForm;

$form = ActiveForm::begin([
    'id' => 'login-form',
]) ?>
    ...
    ...
    ...
<?php ActiveForm::end() ?>
```

This code generates a form HTML tag with `login-form` as the `id` attribute and empty content; the `method` and `action` attributes are respectively, by default, the post and same action URL that generated the form. Other properties about AJAX validation and client validation can be set, as you will see further on.

The widget `$form` is created by employing a static method `ActiveForm::begin`, passing as an array that contains attributes of a form HTML tag (`id`, `action`, `method`, and so on) a configuration parameter and a key named `options` to specify all the extra options that we want to pass to form the HTML tag. Finally, the form will be completed when we call the static method `ActiveForm::end()`. Between the `begin()` and `end()` methods of the form, we can insert all the content needed.

In particular, the input fields of the form can be managed using the ActiveField widget. The ActiveField widget related to an attribute of model is created by calling the `field()` method of the `$form` object:

```php
$field = $form->field($model, 'attribute');
```

The object returned from the `field()` method is a generic field that we can specialize by simply applying other methods to generate all the common kinds of input fields: hidden, text, password, file, and so on. This returns the same ActiveField `$field` object, and consequently other methods can be applied in a cascade.

A text field input is created with:

```
$textInputField = $field->textInput();
```

Or can be created simply like this:

```
$textInputField = $form->field($model, 'attribute')->textInput();
```

This variable `$textInputField` is again an ActiveField (the same object of `$field`), so we can apply all the other methods required to complete our input field; for example, if we need to place a hint in input field, we can use:

```
$textInputField->hint('Enter value');
```

Or we can simply use:

```
$textInputField = $form->field($model, 'attribute')->textInput()-
>hint('Enter value');
```

Additional framework in addition automatically takes into account the attribute's validation rules, which are defined in the `rules()` method of the model class. For example, if an attribute is required and we click on it and pass it to another field without typing anything, an error alert will be displayed reminding us that the field is required.

When an input field is created using the ActiveField widget, the `id` and `name` properties of this input will have this format: `model-class-name_attribute-name` for `id` and `model-class-name[attribute-name]` for `name`. This means that all the attributes of the model will be passed to the controller action when we submit the form grouped in a container array named the same as the model class.

For example, if the `$model` class is `Room` and the attribute is `floor` whose content is `12`, create a text field from the `$form` object:

```
<?php echo $floorInputField = $form->field($model, 'floor')
->textInput()->hint('Enter value for floor');
```

This outputs the following HTML:

```
<input id="Room_floor" name="Room[floor]" value="12"
placeholder="Enter value for floor" />
```

Example – creating and updating a room from a form

Just from following the instructions in the previous paragraph, we will try to create and update a room from the HTML form.

We now update the previously created `actionCreate()` method in `RoomsController` with some code to instantiate a new model object, check the content of the `$_POST` array, and if it is set, we call `save()` on the model:

```php
public function actionCreate()
{
    // 1. Create a new Room instance;
    $model = new Room();

    // 2. Check if $_POST['Room'] contains data;
    if(isset($_POST['Room']))
    {
        $model->attributes = $_POST['Room'];

        // Save model
        if($model->save())
        {
         // If save() success, redirect user to action view.
         return $this->redirect(['view', 'id' => $model->id]);
        }
    }

    return $this->render('create', ['model' => $model]);
}
```

To update the view in `basic/views/rooms/create.php`, pass:

```php
<?php
use yii\widgets\ActiveForm;
use yii\helpers\Html;
?>

<div class="row">
```

```
<div class="col-lg-6">

    <h2>Create a new room</h2>

    <?php $form = ActiveForm::begin(['id' => 'room-form']) ?>

    <?php echo $form->field($model, 'floor')->textInput(); ?>
    <?php echo $form->field($model, 'room_number')-
    >textInput(); ?>
    <?php echo $form->field($model, 'has_conditioner')-
    >checkbox(); ?>
    <?php echo $form->field($model, 'has_tv')->checkbox(); ?>
    <?php echo $form->field($model, 'has_phone')->checkbox();
    ?>
    <?php echo $form->field($model, 'available_from')-
    >textInput(); ?>
    <?php echo $form->field($model, 'price_per_day')-
    >textInput(); ?>
    <?php echo $form->field($model, 'description')-
    >textArea(); ?>
    <?php echo Html::submitButton('Save', ['class' => 'btn
    btn-primary']); ?>
    <?php ActiveForm::end() ?>
</div>
</div>
```

By default, `ActiveForm::begin()` creates a form that has client validation enabled; therefore, the form will be submitted only when all the validation rules are satisfied as the `submit` button is rendered using `yii\helpers\Html`.

Pay attention to the top of view that contains the `use` keyword to define the complete path of the classes `Html` and `ActiveForm`:

```
use yii\widgets\ActiveForm;
use yii\helpers\Html;
```

Point your browser to `http://hostname/basic/rooms/create` to display the form to create a new room. The following screenshot shows what you should display, reporting in it some particular conditions:

The form to create a new room

This screenshot presents different states of fields: the floor input has a red border because it has the wrong type of content (it must be an integer!), the room number has a green border to indicate that is correct, and the **Available From** field has a red border because it is required but the user left it blank. The framework provides a more concise form to fill in attributes if `$_POST` data is available:

```
$model->load(Yii::$app->request->post());
```

This fills in the attributes of the model if the `$_POST[model-class]` content is available, and with this suggestion we can change the `actionCreate` content as follows:

```
public function actionCreate()
{
    // 1. Create a new Room instance;
    $model = new Room();

    // 2. Check if $_POST['Room'] contains data and save
    model;
    if( $model->load(Yii::$app->request->post()) && ($model-
    >save()) )
    {
        return $this->redirect(['detail', 'id' => $model-
        >id]);
    }

    return $this->render('create', ['model' => $model]);
}
```

This is extraordinarily concise! Similarly, we can handle the update action to save changes to an existing model.

We can make a reusable form by putting its content in an external. Create a new file in `basic/views/rooms/_form.php` (the first underscore indicates that this is a view that is includable in other views) and cut and paste the code about form generation from the `create` view to this new `_form` view:

```
<?php
use yii\widgets\ActiveForm;
use yii\helpers\Html;
?>
<?php $form = ActiveForm::begin(['id' => 'room-form']) ?>

<?php echo $form->field($model, 'floor')->textInput(); ?>
<?php echo $form->field($model, 'room_number')->textInput(); ?>
<?php echo $form->field($model, 'has_conditioner')->checkbox(); ?>
<?php echo $form->field($model, 'has_tv')->checkbox(); ?>
<?php echo $form->field($model, 'has_phone')->checkbox(); ?>
<?php echo $form->field($model, 'available_from')->textInput(); ?>
<?php echo $form->field($model, 'price_per_day')->textInput(); ?>
<?php echo $form->field($model, 'description')->textArea(); ?>
```

```php
<?php echo Html::submitButton('Create', ['class' => 'btn btn-
primary']); ?>

<?php ActiveForm::end() ?>
```

In the `basic/views/rooms/create.php` file, instead of the form code, just put the code to render the `_form` view in it:

```php
<?php echo $this->render('_form', ['model' => $model]); ?>
```

 When we modify the `create` view, remember to pass `$model` as the second parameter to render the `_form` view.

We are ready to build the update flow in order to update the room content from a form. Firstly, create an action in `basic/controllers/RoomsController.php` named `actionUpdate`, passing `$id` as a parameter that identifies the primary key to find the model.

In this action, we will put some code to get the model based on the `id` primary key, check whether the `$_POST` array contains data, and then save the model:

```php
public function actionUpdate($id)
{
    // 1. Create a new Room instance;
    $model = Room::findOne($id);

    // 2. Check if $_POST['Room'] contains data and save
    model;
    if( ($model!=null) && $model->load(Yii::$app->request-
    >post()) && ($model->save()) )
    {
        return $this->redirect(['detail', 'id' => $model-
        >id]);
    }

    return $this->render('update', ['model' => $model]);
}
```

This is basically equivalent to the code for the `create` action. Now, create the `update` view in `basic/views/rooms/update.php` with the following content:

```php
<div class="row">

    <div class="col-lg-6">

        <h2>Update a room</h2>
```

```php
<?php echo $this->render('_form', ['model' => $model]); ?>
        </div>

    </div>
```

From the database, check for one existing room and type the `id` value of this URL in your browser: `http://hostname/basic/rooms/update?id=id-found`.

For example, if `id` of an existing room is 1, type this URL in your browser:

`http://hostname/basic/rooms/update?id=1`

This will show a form with the filled in field based on the model attributes' content.

This example is complete, having built the `detail` view, which shows the content of model attributes. Create an action named `actionDetail`, passing `$id` as a parameter, which identifies the primary key to find the model:

```php
public function actionDetail($id)
{
    // 1. Create a new Room instance;
    $model = Room::findOne($id);

    return $this->render('detail', ['model' => $model]);
}
```

Then, create the `detail` view to display some of the model attributes' values in `basic/views/rooms/detail.php`:

```html
<table class="table">
    <tr>
        <th>ID</th>
        <td><?php echo $model['id'] ?></td>
    </tr>
    <tr>
        <th>Floor</th>
        <td><?php echo $model['floor'] ?></td>
    </tr>
    <tr>
        <th>Room number</th>
        <td><?php echo $model['room_number'] ?></td>
    </tr>
</table>
```

Now after successfully creating or updating model, the detail view will be displayed with the content of some attributes of the model.

Setting up the GMT time zone

It is important to set the default time zone for date/time management.

Usually, when we refer to date/time, do not pay attention to which time zone value is being referred to.

For example, if we live in Rome and want to spend our next holiday in New York, when we receive the check-in date/time from the hotel, we must consider which time zone time is being referred to (whether local or remote).

When we display a date/time value that could be misunderstood, it is always recommended to add a time zone reference to it. The time zone is expressed through positive or negative hours compared to a reference that is usually **GMT (Greenwich Mean Time)**.

For example, if it is 9 p.m. in Rome (GMT +1), in GMT time it will be 8 p.m. (GMT +0), 3 p.m. in New York (GMT -5), and finally 12 p.m. in Los Angeles (GMT -8).

Therefore, it is necessary to establish a common shared time value. For this purpose, it is advisable to use GMT as the time reference for all values and operations on values.

We need to configure the time zone in two environments:

- In an application, set the `timeZone` attribute of a configuration; this will set the default time zone for all functions about the date and time

- Some databases, such as MySQL, do not have internal management of time zones, so every value uses the default time zone of the database or the time zone configured during connection from the application to the database; we will set the default time zone during the connection to the database

Complete the first step. Open `basic/config/web.php` and add the `timeZone` property with the GMT value in the `config` array, for example, after the `basePath` property:

```
'timeZone' => 'GMT',
```

The second step is setting the time zone for the database connections, if the database, such as MySQL, does not provide it. This is done globally by adding this code in the `on afterOpen` event. Open `basic/config/db.php` and append it as the last attribute in an array (usually the last attribute is `charset`):

```
'on afterOpen' => function($event) {
$event->sender->createCommand("SET time_zone = '+00:00'")->execute();
}
```

This code means that once the connection with the database is opened, the SQL query SET time_zone = +00:00 will be executed for every connection that we are going to establish with the database, and every date/time field value and function related to the GMT (+00:00) time zone will be considered.

Let's make a test. Create a new controller that simply displays the current date/time and time zone, in basic/controllers/TestTimezoneController.php with an action named actionCheck():

```php
<?php

namespace app\controllers;

use Yii;
use yii\web\Controller;

class TestTimezoneController extends Controller
{
    public function actionCheck()
    {
        $dt = new \DateTime();
        echo 'Current date/time: '.$dt->format('Y-m-d H:i:s');
        echo '<br />';
        echo 'Current timezone: '.$dt->getTimezone()->getName();
        echo '<br />';
    }
}
```

Point your browser to http://hostname/basic/web/test-timezone/check. This is what my browser displayed:

```
Current date/time: 2015-05-27 19:53:35
Current timezone: GMT
```

And, the local time (in Rome) was 21:53:35, because Rome was then at +02:00 GMT due to daylight savings time.

If we comment the timeZone property in the app configuration in basic/config/web.php, we will see the default server time zone that is in my browser:

```
Current date/time: 2015-05-27 21:53:35
Current timezone: Europe/Rome
```

This confirms that we have changed the default `timezone` property for all date/time functions. The last check to perform is on the database. Create a new action named `actionCheckDatabase` to verify that the database's default time zone for the current (and every) connection is GMT:

```
public function actionCheckDatabase()
{
        $result = \Yii::$app->db->createCommand('SELECT NOW()')-
        >queryColumn();

        echo 'Database current date/time: '.$result[0];
}
```

Point your browser to `http://hostname/basic/web/test-timezone/check-database`. This is what my browser displayed:

```
Database current date/time: 2015-05-27 20:12:08
```

And the local time (in Rome) was 22:12:08, because Rome was then at +02:00 GMT.

Remember that, from now on, all date/time information displayed in a database refers to the GMT time zone, although this specification was missing (as we can see in the previous database's current date/time).

> Another strategy to handle the GMT time zone in a database's date/time column is to store the value as a timestamp, which is by definition an integer that indicates the number of seconds from 01/01/1970 at 00:00:00 in the GMT (UTC) time zone; so it is immediately understandable that field is a date/time with the GMT time zone, but remember that any database function applied to it will be executed using the database's default time zone.

Using multiple database connections

Applications can require multiple database connections so that they can send and get data from different sources.

Using other database sources is incredibly simple. The only thing to do is to add a new database entry in the main configuration and use ActiveRecord support. All the operations on records will be transparent for the developer.

Here are some examples of connection strings (dsn) to configure access to other databases:

- **MySQL and MariaDB:** `mysql:host=localhost;dbname=mydatabase`
- **SQLite:** `sqlite:/path/to/database/file`
- **PostgreSQL:** `pgsql:host=localhost;port=5432;dbname=mydatabase`
- **CUBRID:** `cubrid:dbname=demodb;host=localhost;port=33000`
- **MS SQL Server (via the `sqlsrv` driver):** `sqlsrv:Server=localhost;Database=mydatabase`
- **MS SQL Server (via the `dblib` driver):** `dblib:host=localhost;dbname=mydatabase`
- **MS SQL Server (via the `mssql` driver):** `mssql:host=localhost;dbname=mydatabase`
- **Oracle:** `oci:dbname=//localhost:1521/mydatabase`

Example – configuring a second DB connection to export data to a local SQLite DB

We now want to add a new database connection to a SQLite DB. When we use a database, we have to make sure that the PDO driver is installed in the system, otherwise PHP cannot handle it.

Open `basic/config/web.php` and the inner `components` attribute, and append a new attribute named `dbSqlite` with the following attributes:

```
'dbSqlite' => [
    'class' => 'yii\db\Connection',
    'dsn' => 'sqlite:'.dirname(__DIR__).'/../db.sqlite',
],
```

This entry will use a DB SQLite named `db.sqlite`, which we can find in the `dirname(__DIR__).'/../web/db.sqlite'` path, under the `/basic/web` folder. If this file does not exist, it will be created (if a write permission is present in the `/basic/web` folder).

 Be sure that the `/basic/web` folder is writable, otherwise it will be impossible for the framework to create a `db.sqlite` file.

Create a new controller to handle actions in this new database. This will be put in `/basic/controllers/TestSqliteController.php`.

Insert the first action named `actionCreateRoomTable` in this new controller, which will create the same structure of the `Room` table from MySQL in `dbSqlite`:

```php
<?php

namespace app\controllers;

use Yii;
use yii\web\Controller;


class TestSqliteController extends Controller
{
    public function actionCreateRoomTable()
    {
        // Create room table
        $sql = 'CREATE TABLE IF NOT EXISTS room (id int not null,
floor int not null, room_number int not null, has_conditioner int not
null, has_tv int not null, has_phone int not null, available_from date
not null, price_per_day float, description text)';
        \Yii::$app->dbSqlite->createCommand($sql)->execute();
        echo 'Room table created in dbSqlite';

    }
}
```

> Pay attention so that in `actionCreateRoomTable`, the database instance is taken from: `\Yii::$app->dbSqlite`.

Point your browser to `http://hostname/basic/web/test-sqlite/create-room-table` and create a `db.sqlite` file in `basic/web` and a `room` table in it.

As we have mentioned before, if the PDO driver is correctly installed, a blank page with the **Room table created in dbSqlite** text will be displayed.

Now we want to clone the room table from MySQL to SQLite to make a backup of this table. We need to save the records from MySQL to SQLite and verify the data stored to display it in a table.

Create a new action named `actionBackupRoomTable()` that executes these steps:

1. Create a `room` table (if it does not exist).
2. Delete all the records from the room in `dbSqlite` (alias truncate).
3. Load all the records from the room table in MySQL (using ActiveRecord).

4. Insert every single record from MySQL into SQLite.

5. Render the view to display data from SQLite with the table (to verify that the copy succeeded).

The content of the `actionBackupRoomTable()` action is:

```
use app\models\Room;

public function actionBackupRoomTable()
{
    // Create room table
    $sql = 'CREATE TABLE IF NOT EXISTS room (id int not null,
    floor int not null, room_number int not null,
    has_conditioner int not null, has_tv int not null,
    has_phone int not null, available_from date not null,
    price_per_day float, description text)';
    \Yii::$app->dbSqlite->createCommand($sql)->execute();

    // Truncate room table in dbSqlite
    $sql = 'DELETE FROM room';
    \Yii::$app->dbSqlite->createCommand($sql)->execute();

    // Load all records from MySQL and insert every single
    record in dbqlite
    $models = Room::find()->all();

    foreach($models as $m)
    {
        \Yii::$app->dbSqlite->createCommand()->insert('room',
        $m->attributes)->execute();
    }

    // Load all records from dbSqlite
    $sql = 'SELECT * FROM room';
    $sqliteModels = \Yii::$app->dbSqlite->createCommand($sql)-
    >queryAll();

    return $this->render('backupRoomTable', ['sqliteModels' =>
    $sqliteModels]);
}
```

Finally, create a view `backupRoomTable` in `basic/views/test-sqlite/backupRoomTable.php` with the following content to display data from `dbSqlite`:

```php
<h2>Rooms from dbSqlite</h2>

<table class="table">
    <tr>
        <th>Floor</th>
        <th>Room number</th>
        <th>Has conditioner</th>
        <th>Has tv</th>
        <th>Has phone</th>
        <th>Available from</th>
        <th>Available from (db format)</th>
        <th>Price per day</th>
        <th>Description</th>
    </tr>
    <?php foreach($sqliteModels as $item) { ?>
    <tr>
        <td><?php echo $item['floor'] ?></td>
        <td><?php echo $item['room_number'] ?></td>
        <td><?php echo Yii::$app->formatter-
        >asBoolean($item['has_conditioner']) ?></td>
        <td><?php echo Yii::$app->formatter-
        >asBoolean($item['has_tv']) ?></td>
        <td><?php echo ($item['has_phone'] == 1)?'Yes':'No'
        ?></td>
        <td><?php echo Yii::$app->formatter-
        >asDate($item['available_from']) ?></td>
        <td><?php echo Yii::$app->formatter-
        >asDate($item['available_from'], 'php:Y-m-d') ?></td>
        <td><?php echo Yii::$app->formatter-
        >asCurrency($item['price_per_day'], 'EUR') ?></td>
        <td><?php echo $item['description'] ?></td>
    </tr>
    <?php } ?>
</table>
```

Navigate your browser to `http://hostname/basic/web/test-sqlite/backup-room-table`, which should display a similar output to this:

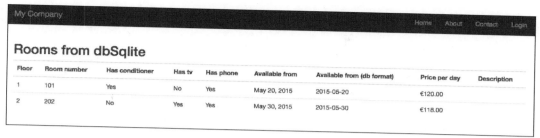

The list of rooms from the SQLite database

We can now download the `db.sqlite` file from `http://hostname/basic/web/db.sqlite` to preserve a backup copy of the room table!

Summary

In this chapter, you mastered how to configure a database connection and execute SQL queries from scratch with DAO support of the framework. Next, you found out how to use Gii and got to know about the advantages it has in creating models from the database table structure. Gii creates models that extend the ActiveRecord class and through its use, you finally learned to manipulate data. All the examples are accompanied with a visualization grid that shows data, which is graphically enhanced by Bootstrap's presence in Yii2.

We carefully analyzed the common topic of tables' relationships, which must be managed in models and then displayed in views.

At the end of the chapter, after you learned to manipulate data with ActiveRecord, you wrote a complete flow to save data from a HTML form to a database. Finally, you learned the importance of setting the GMT time zone in date/time fields and using other database sources in the same application in order to make a backup of the primary database.

In the next chapter, you will learn to use and customize the grid widget to improve data visualization.

6
Using a Grid for Data and Relations

We will cover the following topics in this chapter:

- DataProvider for grids
- Using grids
- Custom columns in grids:
    - For example: displaying a reservations list by clicking on a customer grid row
- Filters in GridView
- Displaying and filtering ActiveRecord relational data in a grid's column
- Summarizing the footer row in a grid:
    - For example: extending GridView to customize the footer row in a grid
- Multiple grids on one page:
    - For example: managing reservations and room grids in the same view

Introduction

In the previous chapter, you learned how to get data from databases. Now it is time to use a fundamental widget provided by framework: GridView. The first topic we'll cover is data input format expected by a grid. Then we will analyze the default implementation of a grid and proceed to look at customizations to display the relationship between data. Finally, you will learn to extend the grid base class to display everything we need in a grid layout.

DataProvider for grids

GridView is the widget provided by Yii2 to display data in a grid layout.

This widget requires that data used as an input source is an extension of the abstract class `yii\data\BaseDataProvider`.

To deal with a data source, DataProvider supplies some additional actions to handle pagination and sorting.

`BaseDataProvider` has a method named `getModels()` that returns a list of items for the current page. This means that we could also use DataProvider to paginate data from a source and display it as we need to.

By default, the framework has three core classes that extend `yii\data\BaseDataProvider`:

- `yii\data\ActiveDataProvider`
- `yii\data\ArrayDataProvider`
- `yii\data\SqlDataProvider`

The first one, `ActiveDataProvider`, uses a `yii\db\Query` instance from ActiveRecord as a data source. The parameter array is passed to the constructor and the `yii\db\Query` object is filled out in the `query` attribute:

```
// build an ActiveDataProvider with an empty query and a pagination
with 35 items for page
$provider = new \yii\data\ActiveDataProvider([
    'query' => Room::find(),
    'pagination' => [
        'pageSize' => 35,
    ],
]);

// get all rooms in current page
$rooms = $provider->getModels();
```

`ActiveDataProvider` is the most used DataProvider, since it depends directly on ActiveRecord, the best way to interact with databases.

The second point, `ArrayDataProvider`, uses an array of items that can be sorted or paginated as a data source. This provider is employed when data can not be represented with ActiveRecord, for example, when they are taken from another data source, such as a JSON REST service or RSS feed.

The primary difference between `ActiveDataProvider` is that all data should be immediately passed to a construct:

```
// build an ArrayDataProvider with an empty query and a pagination
with 40 items for page
$provider = new \yii\data\ArrayDataProvider([
    'allModels' => Room::find()->all(),
    'pagination' => [
        'pageSize' => 40,
    ],
]);

// get all rooms in current page
$rooms = $provider->getModels();
```

In this snippet, we took data from an ActiveRecord to show the differences between `ActiveDataProvider` and `ArrayDataProvider`. For this last provider, all the modes should be passed to the constructor.

So, if the `Room` table has 10,000 records, with `ActiveDataProvider` 35 items at a time will be loaded, while through `ArrayDataProvider` they will be loaded all from scratch (with big performance issues).

The last one, `SqlDataProvider`, uses a SQL query as a data source. If we create pagination with this provider, we will need to also pass the `totalCount` attribute to the constructor to inform DataProvider how many records the SQL query should return:

```
// return total items count for this sql query
$itemsCount = \Yii::$app->db->createCommand('SELECT COUNT(*) FROM
room')->queryScalar();

// build a SqlDataProvider with a pagination with 10 items for
page

$dataProvider = new \yii\data\SqlDataProvider([
    'sql' => 'SELECT * FROM room',
```

```
        'totalCount' => $itemsCount,
        'pagination' => [
                'pageSize' => 10,
        ],
    ]);

    // get the user records in the current page
    $models = $dataProvider->getModels();
```

Using a grid

Now that we know how to get a data input source to pass to GridView, let's look at how to implement it. Minimal implementation of GridView requires two attributes for an array passed to a constructor: dataProvider and columns. The first parameter, dataProvider, is the one we want to use in order to manipulate the data.

The second parameter, columns, represents the columns of the table to be displayed, for example:

```
<?= \yii\grid\GridView::widget([
    'dataProvider' => $dataProvider,
    'columns' => [
      'id',
      'floor',
      'room_number',
       'available_from:datetime',
       'price_per_day:currency',
    ],
]) ?>
```

This code will display a table with data from $dataProvider and five columns: id, floor, room_number, available_from, and price_per_day; the last two columns are formatted firstly using datetime and secondly using currency. Colons are used to specify the formatter to be applied to the column data.

> The aspect of the table can be customized with many attributes and by default, the table layout is rendered using Bootstrap.

Columns in the grid table can be identified using strings, but in general they are configured in terms of yii\grid\Column classes.

Custom columns in a grid

As mentioned in the previous paragraph, the `columns` property of the GridView widget is mainly filled with strings.

When we need to apply a specific format, such as currency or date/time, we can append this specification to the column name with a colon and the type used for formatting, as `currency` or `datetime`.

But the most general form of a GridView column is an object of the `yii\grid\ Column` class, derived by the `yii\grid\DataColumn` class.

A GridView column extended by the `yii\grid\Column` class is rendered using an array with the following keys:

```
    [
  // can be omitted, as it is the default
  'class' => 'yii\grid\DataColumn',

        'attribute',     // name of model attribute
        'format',         // format use to display data
        'header',        // header of column
        'footer',        // footer of column
        'visible',        // flag to set visibility
        'content'         // callback to print data
        ],
```

There are also other parameters but these ones are the most used.

Example – displaying a reservations list by clicking on a customer grid row

We are now ready to create a customer grid that contains a reference to the linked reservation list in every row. First of all, make sure that the structure and the data for the customer and reservation tables is the following:

```
--
-- Structure of Table `customer`
--

CREATE TABLE IF NOT EXISTS `customer` (
  `id` int(11) NOT NULL PRIMARY KEY AUTO_INCREMENT,
  `name` varchar(50) NOT NULL,
```

```
  `surname` varchar(50) NOT NULL,
  `phone_number` varchar(50) DEFAULT NULL,
  PRIMARY KEY (`id`)
);


--
-- Data Dump of Table `customer`
--

INSERT INTO `customer` (`id`, `name`, `surname`, `phone_number`)
VALUES
(1, 'James', 'Foo', '+39-12345678'),
(2, 'Bar', 'Johnson', '+47-98438923');


--
-- Structure of Table `reservation`
--

CREATE TABLE IF NOT EXISTS `reservation` (
  `id` int(11) NOT NULL PRIMARY KEY AUTO_INCREMENT,
  `room_id` int(11) NOT NULL,
  `customer_id` int(11) NOT NULL,
  `price_per_day` decimal(20,2) NOT NULL,
  `date_from` date NOT NULL,
  `date_to` date NOT NULL,
  `reservation_date` timestamp NOT NULL DEFAULT CURRENT_TIMESTAMP,
  PRIMARY KEY (`id`),
  KEY `room_id` (`room_id`),
  KEY `customer_id` (`customer_id`)
);


--
-- Data Dump of table `reservation`
--

INSERT INTO `reservation` (`id`, `room_id`, `customer_id`,
`price_per_day`, `date_from`, `date_to`, `reservation_date`)
VALUES
(1, 2, 1, 90.00, '2015-04-01', '2015-05-06', '2015-05-24
22:45:37'),
(2, 2, 1, 48.00, '2019-08-27', '2019-08-31', '2015-05-24
22:45:37'),
(3, 1, 2, 105.00, '2015-09-24', '2015-10-06', '2015-06-03
00:21:14');
```

Create a new controller named `CustomersController` in `basic/controllers/`
`CustomersController.php` with the `actionGrid` action to display a list in the
grid view:

```php
<?php

namespace app\controllers;

use Yii;
use yii\web\Controller;
use app\models\Customer;
use yii\data\ActiveDataProvider;

class CustomersController extends Controller
{
    public function actionGrid()
    {
        $query = Customer::find();

        $dataProvider = new ActiveDataProvider([
            'query' => $query,
            'pagination' => [
                'pageSize' => 10,
            ],
        ]);

        return $this->render('grid', [ 'dataProvider' =>
        $dataProvider ]);

    }
}
```

This action `actionGrid` simply creates a data provider with all the data from the
customer (unfiltered) and with a pagination that displays ten items on a page.
Finally, render the grid view.

This is the content of the grid view in `basic/views/customers/grid.php`:

```php
<?php
use yii\grid\GridView;
use yii\helpers\Html;
?>

<h2>Customers</h2>

<?= GridView::widget([
```

```
        'dataProvider' => $dataProvider,
        'columns' => [
            'id',
            'name',
            'surname',
            'phone_number',

            [
                'header' => 'Reservations',
                'content' => function ($model, $key, $index, $column) {
                    return Html::a('Reservations',
                    ['reservations/grid', 'Reservation[customer_id]'
                    => $model->id]);
                }
            ],

            [
                'class' => 'yii\grid\ActionColumn',
                'template' => '{delete}',
                'header' => 'Actions',
            ],
        ],
    ]) ?>
```

The last two columns require particular explanation.

The penultimate one, Reservation, displays a link to give you access to the list of all customer reservations. We have put Reservations as the header and filled the content property with dynamic data passed from the callback function, which returns an HTML link to the reservations/index route with a parameter indicating customer_id selected.

The last column headed Actions displays the ActionColumn with the single action delete to remove the selected record.

Point your browser to http://hostname/basic/customers/grid and you should have the following output:

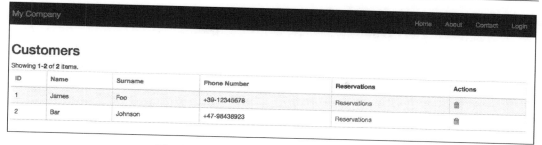

The Customers grid using the GridView widget

 The language used in GridView is configured in `basic/config/web.php` with the `language` property. This property has a global effect on every core widget.

We can complete this example by just putting a counter near the `Reservations` link to indicate the number of reservations for each customer.

For this purpose, we need to add a new relation named `getReservationsCount` to the Customer model in `basic/models/Customer.php`, which returns the number of reservations linked to the customer:

```
public function getReservationsCount()
{
  return $this->hasMany(\app\models\Reservation::className(),
  ['customer_id' => 'id'])->count();
}
```

Now we can modify the penultimate column with:

```
[
    'header' => 'Reservations',
    'content' => function ($model, $key, $index, $column) {
        $title = sprintf('Reservations (%d)', $model-
        >reservationsCount);
        return Html::a($title, ['reservations/grid',
        'Reservation[customer_id]' => $model->id]);
    }
],
```

If we refresh our browser now, we will see near the `Reservations` anchor link, the correct number of reservations for that customer appears.

This example represents the complete reservations list displayed when a user clicks on the link `Reservations`.

Create `ReservationsController` as a new file in `basic/controllers/ReservationsController.php` with an action `grid` and the following content:

```php
<?php

namespace app\controllers;

use Yii;
use yii\web\Controller;
use app\models\Reservation;
use yii\data\ActiveDataProvider;

class ReservationsController extends Controller
{
    public function actionGrid()
    {
        $query = Reservation::find();

        if(isset($_GET['Reservation']))
        {
            $query->andFilterWhere([
                'customer_id' =>
                isset($_GET['Reservation']['customer_id'])?
                $_GET['Reservation']['customer_id']:null,
            ]);
        }

        $dataProvider = new ActiveDataProvider([
            'query' => $query,
            'pagination' => [
                'pageSize' => 10,
            ],
        ]);

        return $this->render('grid', [ 'dataProvider' =>
        $dataProvider ]);

    }
}
```

In this controller, we applied an `andFilterWhere` condition to query whether `$_GET['Reservation']` is set. The `andFilterWhere()` method will apply a filter passed as a parameter only if the condition is not empty. So if `$_GET['Reservation']['customer_id']` is not set, the `andFilterWhere()` condition parameter will have a null value and will not be appended to any other query condition.

Filters in GridView

GridView has a core feature of being able to simplify filter rows just by putting an additional row below the header row.

Filters are mainly text input but in general they can be any type of control and we can customize them as much as we want.

Filters can be activated by filling out the GridView widget property `filterModel` with an instance of the model class and automatically a new row will be created below the header, containing working text inputs.

Filter text inputs have a name attribute filled with the model class name, which includes the field name. In this way, we will pass data to a controller, including everything in a single array; a variable that can easily be used to populate a search model massively.

 Automatic text input filters are created only for attributes that belong to at least one rule in the `rules()` method of `ActiveDataProvider`; otherwise it is enough that attributes belong to the `safe` validator.

Let's create an example with the reservations grid.

We will fill out the `filterModel` property to apply filters to GridView, for example:

```
<?= \yii\grid\GridView::widget([
    ...
    'filterModel' => $searchModel,
    ...
?>
```

Here, `$searchModel` is an instance of the `Reservation` model class that we will pass to the view from the grid action of `ReservationsController`.

Now let's create `actionGrid()` in `ReservationsController` in `basic/controllers/ReservationsController.php`:

```php
<?php

public function actionGrid()
    {
        $query = \app\models\Reservation::find();

        $searchModel = new \app\models\Reservation();
        if(isset($_GET['Reservation']))
        {
            $searchModel->load( \Yii::$app->request->get() );

            $query->andFilterWhere([
                'id' => $searchModel->id,
                'customer_id' => $searchModel->customer_id,
                'room_id' => $searchModel->room_id,
                'price_per_day' => $searchModel->price_per_day,
            ]);
        }

        $dataProvider = new \yii\data\ActiveDataProvider([
            'query' => $query,
            'pagination' => [
                'pageSize' => 10,
            ],
        ]);


        return $this->render('grid', [ 'dataProvider' =>
$dataProvider, 'searchModel' => $searchModel ]);

    }
```

The `$searchModel` instance is filled with the content of `$_GET['Reservation']`, in line:

```php
$searchModel->load( Yii::$app->request->get() );
```

Then, `$query` is updated with the content of non-null attributes.

Remember that the ActiveRecord's `load()` method will get values from the array enclosed in the model class name, applied as the key to the array passed as the first function parameter.

Browse to `http://hostname/basic/reservations/grid` and type 2 in the **Room ID** column filter (the second column). This should be the output:

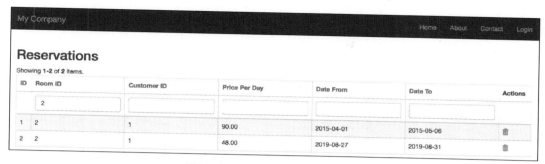

Reservations

Showing 1-2 of 2 items.

ID	Room ID	Customer ID	Price Per Day	Date From	Date To	Actions
	2					
1	2	1	90.00	2015-04-01	2015-05-06	🗑
2	2	1	48.00	2019-08-27	2019-08-31	🗑

Using filters in the GridView widget

We can also choose to customize the way we render a filter. Imagine using the **Room ID** column filter as a drop-down list instead of an input textbox.

We only need to fill out the `filter` property of **Room ID** with `dropDownList`. It is advisable to use the `Html` helper class to render `dropDownList` using the `activeDropDownList()` method. The `active` prefix stands for ActiveRecord. This method `dropDownList()` requires three parameters: the model class, the attribute of the model class, and finally an array key-value where `key` is the value attribute of the `<option>` tag and `value` is the text of the `<option>` tag.

We will use `yii\helpers\ArrayHelper` to create the array key-value, where the key is the `id` attribute of the model and the value is the return value of a callback function.

This is how the file in `basic/views/reservations/grid.php` changes:

```php
<?php
$roomsFilterData = yii\helpers\ArrayHelper::map( app\models\
Room::find()->all(), 'id', function($model, $defaultValue) {
    return sprintf('Floor: %d - Number: %d', $model->floor, $model-
>room_number);
});
?>

<?= \yii\grid\GridView::widget([
    'dataProvider' => $dataProvider,
    'filterModel' => $searchModel,
    'columns' => [
        'id',

        [
```

```
                'header' => 'Room',
                'filter' => \Html::activeDropDownList($searchModel,
                'room_id', $roomsFilterData, ['prompt' => '--- all']),
                'content' => function($model) {
                    return $model->room->floor;
                }
            ],
        ],
```

This is the expected output:

GridView with the dropdown list filter

Displaying and filtering ActiveRecord relational data in a grid's column

Let's now focus on relational data in GridView, a common topic that is easily solved by itself.

Think about the reservations grid, which has two relational fields: room_id and customer_id, referring respectively to room and customer tables. What if we want to immediately display the customer's surname, or room number?

At this point, our goal is to display relational data, for example, the customer's surname instead of customer_id in GridView. Fields that refer to related data are expressed with the relation attribute.

In the reservation grid view, customer is the relation to get a related customer and surname is the field to keep.

Therefore, to display the customer's surname, it is enough to insert this column (as a string) in the reservations grid view:

```
'customer.surname'
```

This is equivalent to:

```
[
    'attribute' => 'customer.surname'
]
```

A column named `surname` will be displayed. If we want to change column name to `Customer`, we use this:

```
[
    'header' => 'Customer',
    'attribute' => 'customer.surname'
]
```

We could use custom properties to get data, for example, `getnameAndSurname` to get the personal details of a specific customer.

Insert a new property in the `Customer` model:

```
public function getNameAndSurname() {
    return $this->name.' '.$this->surname;
}
```

Then this will be the column in the GridView:

```
[
    'header' => 'Customer',
    'attribute' => 'customer.nameAndSurname'
]
```

We now want to filter the `Customer` column. Since the `customer.surname` attribute is not in the `rules()` method of the `Reservation` model, we need to extend this class to handle extra attributes.

So, create a new class named `ReservationSearch` in `basic/models/ReservationSearch.php` with the following content:

```
<?php

class ReservationSearch extends app\models\Reservation
{
    public function attributes()
    {
        // add related fields to searchable attributes
```

```
        return array_merge(parent::attributes(),
        ['customer.surname']);
}

public function rules()
{
    // add related rules to searchable attributes
    return array_merge(parent::rules(),[ ['customer.surname',
    'safe'] ]);
}

}
```

This extension simply adds a new attribute and a new rule attached to this attribute. The name of the attribute is customer.surname.

We now have to change the actionGrid() action in ReservationsController to make a connection to the customer table that permits us to filter based on the customer's surname.

This is the content of actionGrid() of ReservationsController in basic/controllers/ReservationsController.php:

```
public function actionGrid()
{
    $query = \app\models\Reservation::find();

    $searchModel = new \app\models\ReservationSearch();
    if(isset($_GET['ReservationSearch']))
    {
        $searchModel->load( \Yii::$app->request->get() );

        $query->joinWith(['customer']);
        $query->andFilterWhere(
            ['LIKE', 'customer.surname', $searchModel-
            >getAttribute('customer.surname')]
        );

        $query->andFilterWhere([
            'id' => $searchModel->id,
            'customer_id' => $searchModel->customer_id,
            'room_id' => $searchModel->room_id,
            'price_per_day' => $searchModel->price_per_day,

        ]);
```

```
        }

        $dataProvider = new \yii\data\ActiveDataProvider([
            'query' => $query,
            'pagination' => [
                'pageSize' => 10,
            ],
        ]);


        return $this->render('grid', [ 'dataProvider' =>
        $dataProvider, 'searchModel' => $searchModel ]);

    }
```

 Be careful to ensure that $searchModel is instanced from the ReservationSearch class, as much as $_GET, parameter used to get data is instanced from ReservationSearch instead of Reservation (because it has changed class).

Filtering an action on the customer's surname in actionGrid() is made using these lines of code:

```
        $query->joinWith(['customer']);
        $query->andFilterWhere(
            ['LIKE', 'customer.surname', $searchModel-
            >getAttribute('customer.surname')]
        );
```

We make a join and if the customer.surname attribute is not null, then there will be a new filter. Browse to http://hostname/basic/reservations/grid and type Fo in the **Customer** column filter. You should see this:

Filtering using relational data

A summarized footer row in a grid

One feature of GridView is that it shows summarized or statistical data, usually as a footer row or first row, to get the data immediately (instead of scrolling down the page to the bottom of the grid).

A column of the GridView widget has an attribute named `footer` to identify the last row of the current pagination. A value filled in this attribute will be placed in the last row of the grid.

By default, showing the footer is disabled; to enable the footer, it is enough to set the attribute `showFooter` of GridView to `true`. Then, we need to insert data in the 'footer' attribute of the column that we want to show.

For example, we want to display the average price per day of rooms.

Add this code at the top of the grid view in `basic/views/reservations/grid.php` to calculate the average of price per day:

```php
<?php
use yii\grid\GridView;
use yii\helpers\Html;
?>

<h2>Reservations</h2>

<?php
$sumOfPricesPerDay = 0;
$averagePricePerDay = 0;

if(count($dataProvider->getModels()) > 0)
{
    foreach($dataProvider->getModels() as $m) $sumOfPricesPerDay
    += $m->price_per_day;
    $averagePricePerDay = $sumOfPricesPerDay /
    sizeof($dataProvider->getModels());
}
?>

<?php
$roomsFilterData = yii\helpers\ArrayHelper::map(
app\models\Room::find()->all(), 'id', function($model,
$defaultValue) {
    return sprintf('Floor: %d - Number: %d', $model->floor,
    $model->room_number);
```

```
    });
    ?>


    <?= app\components\GridViewReservation::widget([
        'dataProvider' => $dataProvider,
        'filterModel' => $searchModel,
        'showFooter' => true,
        'columns' => [
            'id',

            [
                'header' => 'Room',
                'filter' => Html::activeDropDownList($searchModel,
                'room_id', $roomsFilterData, ['prompt' => '--- all']),
                'content' => function($model) {
                    return $model->room->floor;
                }
            ],

            [
                'header' => 'Customer',
                'attribute' => 'customer.surname',
            ],

            [
                'attribute' => 'price_per_day',
                'footer' => Yii::$app->formatter-
                >asCurrency($resultQueryAveragePricePerDay, 'EUR')
            ],

            'date_from',
            'date_to',

            [
                'class' => 'yii\grid\ActionColumn',
                'template' => '{delete}',
                'header' => 'Actions',
            ],
        ],
    ]) ?>
```

Be careful! In this example, count is made using the models of the current pagination. If the grid is composed of more pages, it will only show the average value for the current page!

This count can consider all records (also filtered ones), making the calculation based not only on the models of the current pagination but also on the result of a query. Add the average count in `actionGrid()` of `ReservationsController`:

```php
public function actionGrid()
{
    $query = \app\models\Reservation::find();

    $searchModel = new \app\models\ReservationSearch();
    if(isset($_GET['ReservationSearch']))
    {
        $searchModel->load( \Yii::$app->request->get() );

        $query->joinWith(['customer']);
        $query->andFilterWhere(
            ['LIKE', 'customer.surname', $searchModel-
            >getAttribute('customer.surname')]
        );

        $query->andFilterWhere([
            'id' => $searchModel->id,
            'customer_id' => $searchModel->customer_id,
            'room_id' => $searchModel->room_id,
            'price_per_day' => $searchModel->price_per_day,

        ]);

    }
    $resultQueryAveragePricePerDay = $query-
    >average('price_per_day');

    $dataProvider = new \yii\data\ActiveDataProvider([
        'query' => $query,
        'pagination' => [
            'pageSize' => 10,
        ],
    ]);

    return $this->render('grid', [ 'dataProvider' =>
    $dataProvider, 'searchModel' => $searchModel,
    'resultQueryAveragePricePerDay' =>
    $resultQueryAveragePricePerDay ]);

}
```

The average is calculated from the `average()` method of the `$query` object (so the filter will be considered, if it is filled out) and passed to the view, so the code at the top of the view to execute calculation is no longer needed because we have correctly moved it to the Controller action.

Then change the `footer` content of the `price_per_day` column:

```
[
    'attribute' => 'price_per_day',
    'footer' => sprintf('Average: %0.2f',
    $resultQueryAveragePricePerDay)
],
```

Now the average count will be independent of pagination.

Example – extending GridView to customize the footer row in a grid

In a highly customized GridView, it is required to show data in positions not handled by default by GridView, or it is required to apply specific changes (such as merging a column).

In either of these cases and when it is impossible to create the desired output with attributes of GridView, it will be necessary to subclass the GridView widget.

The GridView widget has specific methods to render different parts of it: `renderTableBody()`, `renderTableFooter()`, `renderTableHeader()`, `renderTableRow()`, and so on.

Think about the previous example. Now, we also want to gather the first three columns in the footer to display the `Average` label, the unique value in the `price_per_day` column, and the last four columns with an empty space.

Create a new component that extends the `yii\grid\GridView` widget in `basic/components/GridViewReservation.php` with this content:

```php
<?php

namespace app\components;

use Yii;
use yii\web\Controller;
use yii\grid\GridView;

class GridViewReservation extends GridView
```

```
{
    public function renderTableFooter()
    {
        // Search column for 'price_per_day'
        $columnPricePerDay = null;
        foreach($this->columns as $column)
        {
            if(get_class($column) == 'yii\grid\DataColumn')
            {
                if($column->attribute == 'price_per_day')
                    $columnPricePerDay = $column;
            }
        }

        $html = '<tfoot><tr>';
        $html .= '<td colspan="3"><b>Average:</b></td>';
        $html .= $columnPricePerDay->renderFooterCell();
        $html .= '<td colspan="4"><i>this space is intentionally
        empty</i></td>';
        $html .= '</tr></tfoot>';


        return $html;
    }
}
```

This component just extends yii\grid\GridView and overrides the renderTableFooter() method to make the required customization (mainly merging cells). The only logic in this code is to find the price_per_day column, cycling the array of columns given by $this->columns, where $this refers to the GridView object.

Multiple grids on one page

Every Yii2 widget has so much encapsulated in it that using multiple GridView widgets is a simple activity that involves making few changes.

The only parameters indeed that are not customizable with the DataProvider model class are pageParam and sortParam, which define the current page index and the parameters used to order a grid.

Suppose, for example, that we have two GridViews filled with two different data providers, $firstDataProvider and $secondDataProvider.

In the controller, we will set the `pageParam` and `sortParam` parameters of each DataProvider:

```
$firstDataProvider->pagination->pageParam = 'first-dp-page';
$firstDataProvider->sort->sortParam = 'first-dp-sort';

$secondDataProvider->pagination->pageParam = 'second-dp-page';
$secondDataProvider->sort->sortParam = 'second-dp-sort';
```

If we miss these definitions when changing a page or sorting a column, this action will also affect the other GridView in the same page because we have not distinguished the two grid view parameters.

Example: managing the reservations and rooms grids in the same view

The purpose of this example is to display both the reservations and rooms grids in the same page completely independent from each other.

In ReservationsController in `basic/controllers/ReservationsController.php`, create a new action named `actionMultipleGrid()` with the following content:

```
public function actionMultipleGrid()
{
    /**
     * Reservations
     */
    $reservationsQuery = \app\models\Reservation::find();
    $reservationsSearchModel = new
    \app\models\ReservationSearch();

    if(isset($_GET['ReservationSearch']))
    {
        $reservationsSearchModel->load( \Yii::$app->request-
        >get() );

        $reservationsQuery->joinWith(['customer']);
        $reservationsQuery->andFilterWhere(
            ['LIKE', 'customer.surname',
            $reservationsSearchModel-
            >getAttribute('customer.surname')]
        );

        $reservationsQuery->andFilterWhere([
            'id' => $reservationsSearchModel->id,
```

```
                    'customer_id' => $reservationsSearchModel-
                    >customer_id,
                    'room_id' => $reservationsSearchModel->room_id,
                    'price_per_day' => $reservationsSearchModel-
                    >price_per_day,


        ]);
}

$reservationsDataProvider = new
\yii\data\ActiveDataProvider([
    'query' => $reservationsQuery,
    'sort' => [
        'sortParam' => 'reservations-sort-param',
    ],
    'pagination' => [
        'pageSize' => 10,
        'pageParam' => 'reservations-page-param'
    ],
]);


/**
 * Rooms
 */
$roomsQuery = \app\models\Room::find();
$roomsSearchModel = new \app\models\Room();

if(isset($_GET['Room']))
{
    $roomsSearchModel->load( \Yii::$app->request->get() );

    $roomsQuery->andFilterWhere([
        'id' => $roomsSearchModel->id,
        'floor' => $roomsSearchModel->floor,
        'room_number' => $roomsSearchModel->room_number,
        'has_conditioner' => $roomsSearchModel-
        >has_conditioner,
        'has_phone' => $roomsSearchModel->has_conditioner,
        'has_tv' => $roomsSearchModel->has_conditioner,
        'available_from' => $roomsSearchModel-
        >has_conditioner,

    ]);
```

```
    }

    $roomsDataProvider = new \yii\data\ActiveDataProvider([
        'query' => $roomsQuery,
        'sort' => [
            'sortParam' => 'rooms-sort-param',
        ],
        'pagination' => [
            'pageSize' => 10,
            'pageParam' => 'rooms-page-param'
        ],
    ]);

    return $this->render('multipleGrid', [
        'reservationsDataProvider' =>
        $reservationsDataProvider, 'reservationsSearchModel'
        => $reservationsSearchModel,
        'roomsDataProvider' => $roomsDataProvider,
        'roomsSearchModel' => $roomsSearchModel,
    ]);

}
```

We have detached the reservations declaration from the rooms declaration in order to clearly distinguish each from the other. Be careful to ensure that you defined sortparam and pageparam for either of the DataProvider.

Now we create a new view in basic/views/reservations/multipleGrid.php:

```php
<?php
use yii\grid\GridView;
use yii\helpers\Html;
?>

<h2>Reservations</h2>
<?= GridView::widget([
    'dataProvider' => $reservationsDataProvider,
    'filterModel' => $reservationsSearchModel,
    'columns' => [
        'id',
        'room_id',
        'attribute' => 'customer.surname',
        'price_per_day',
        'date_from',
```

```
                'date_to'
        ],
    ]) ?>


    <h2>Rooms</h2>
    <?= GridView::widget([
        'dataProvider' => $roomsDataProvider,
        'filterModel' => $roomsSearchModel,
        'columns' => [
            'id',
            'floor',
            'room_number',
            'has_conditioner:boolean',
            'has_phone:boolean',
            'has_tv:boolean',
            'available_from',
        ],
    ]) ?>
```

The two grids are completely independent and we can now order or change a page without interfering with other grids.

Summary

In this chapter, we presented the GridView widget to display data, directly or relational. A fundamental topic when discussing GridView is DataProvider, which is a way to provide data to GridView. You learned how to get DataProvider from ActiveRecord, an array, or SQL, based on the available source.

After the first simple implementation of GridView, you comprehended the customization in a column and displayed the relational data coming from other tables, using an extension of the model class to add extra features as new attributes. Next, we illustrated how to filter data in GridView to select only specific rows.

Just before the end of the chapter, you saw how to show, summarize, and customize a footer and more in the GridView by subclassing the core widget yii\grid\ GridView. Finally, the last topic concerned the use of more than one grid in the same page, with a special focus on the few changes that need to occur in order to avoid them interfering with each other.

In the next chapter, you will learn to customize the user interface with CSS, JavaScript, widgets, and tools such as Gii that are directly provided from the framework.

7
Working on the User Interface

In this chapter, you will discover how powerful Gii is as a tool. It provides support for CRUD actions, as well as creating a controller and its respective views.

We will cover the following topics related to the user interface in this chapter:

- Using Gii to generate create, read, update, and delete (CRUD) actions:
  - For example – using CRUD to manage rooms, reservations, and customers using Gii

- Customizing JavaScript and CSS:
  - For example – using JavaScript and CSS to display advertising columns that disappear if there is not enough space available

- Using AJAX:
  - For example: reservation details loaded from customers' drop-down lists

- Using the Bootstrap widget:
  - For example – using datepicker

- Viewing multiple models in the same view:
  - For example – saving multiple customers at the same time

- Saving linked models in the same view:
  - For example – creating a customer and reservation in the same view

It is now time for you to learn what Yii2 supports in order to customize the JavaScript and CSS parts of web pages. A recurrent use of JavaScript is to handle AJAX calls, that is, to manage widgets and compound controls (such as a dependent drop-down list) from jQuery and Bootstrap.

Finally, we will employ jQuery to dynamically create more models from the same class in the form, which will be passed to the controller in order to be validated and saved.

Using Gii to generate CRUD

We introduced Gii in *Chapter 5, Developing a Reservation System*, to generate models. Now we want to use Gii to create CRUD actions with a controller and views.

Type `http://hostname/basic/web/gii` in your browser to return to the Gii welcome page. Click on the **Start** button of the **CRUD** section. We have to fill out four fields:

- **Model Class**: This is the ActiveRecord class associated with the table where CRUD will be built; this class should be provided using the fully qualified namespaced path, for example: `app\models\ModelClass`.

- **Search Model Class**: This is the name of the search model class to be generated and extended from the model class; this class will provide useful methods and extensions to be used when searching the record. This should be provided using the fully qualified namespaced path, for example: `app\models\ModelClassSearch`.

- **Controller Class**: This is the name of the controller class to be generated; this class should be provided using the fully qualified namespaced path and the CamelCase format for the name, starting with an uppercase letter, for example: `app\controller\MyCustomController`.

- **View Path**: This is the directory where the view created from the controller actions will be stored. We can use path, alias `@app/views`, to indicate the base path for the views file, for example: `@app/views/myCustom` to indicate the base path of the `MyCustomController` views, that will be filled by default to `@app/views/controller-id`.

Then, we can customize `BaseControllerClass`, the widget used in the index page, to enable the state of I18N and the code template, but it is okay to leave them with the default values.

If we check **Enable I18N**, we must then look after the translations in app messages for each attribute label. This will be covered in a later chapter.

Example – using CRUD to manage rooms, reservations, and customers using Gii

In this example, we will create complete CRUD actions to manage rooms, reservations, and customers.

In the earlier chapter, we dealt with Gii CRUD actions to create a form. We must now repeat these instructions for all three models: the room, reservation, and customer model class. To distinguish files created with Gii from files created manually in the previous chapters, we will append the Gii suffix to the controller's class name.

Browse to the Gii welcome page at `http://hostname/basic/web/gii`, click on the **Start** button in the **CRUD** section, and fill out the fields with the following values to create CRUD actions for the `Room` model class:

- **Model Class**: `app\models\Room`
- **Search Model Class**: `app\models\RoomSearch`
- **Controller Class**: `app\controllers\RoomsWithGiiController`
- **View Path**: `@app/views/rooms-with-gii`

Then, repeat this operation for the `Reservation` model class:

- **Model Class**: `app\models\Reservation`
- **Search Model Class**: `app\models\ReservationSearch`
- **Controller Class**: `app\controllers\ReservationsWithGiiController`
- **View Path**: `@app/views/reservations-with-gii`

Finally, repeat them for the `Customer` model class:

- **Model Class**: `app\models\Customer`
- **Search Model Class**: `app\models\CustomerSearch`
- **Controller Class**: `app\controllers\CustomersWithGiiController`
- **View Path**: `@app/views/customers-with-gii`

Make sure that the View Path has a slash (/) in the path and not a backslash (\) as the namespaced path in the model class, search model class, and controller class.

The following screenshot shows the fields filled out to generate CRUD actions for the Room model class:

CRUD Generator from Gii

While navigating in the folder structure, you will see that Gii has created three new files in basic/controllers, named RoomsWithGiiController.php, ReservationsWithGiiController.php, and CustomersWithGiiController.php.

Each of these files contains five actions:

- `actionCreate()`: This action is used to create a new model object
- `actionView()`: This action is used to view the details of a model object
- `actionUpdate()`: This action is used to update an existing model object
- `actionDelete()`: This action is used to delete an existing model object
- `actionIndex()`: This action is used to display, using the grid layout, a list of model objects

Open the `basic/models` folder and you will find three new files: `RoomSearch.php`, `ReservationSearch.php` (which should already exist), and `CustomerSearch.php`.

Each of these files basically contains a `search()` method, which returns the ActiveDataProvider to be used to display data in GridView, passing some filter conditions.

Finally, open the `basic/views` folder and you will find three new folders: `roomsWithGii`, `reservationsWithGii`, and `customersWithGii`; each one containing six files:

- `_form.php`
- `_search.php`
- `create.php`
- `index.php`
- `update.php`
- `view.php`

View files that start with an underscore are considered by default in Yii2 as subviews, or rather views that are called by other views.

The first two files start with an underscore; effectively if we open `create.php` and `update.php`, we will notice that, at the end of these files, the `render()` method is called using the `_form.php` view. Both the create and update view will use the same `_form` view to display the form to edit fields.

The last four files, `create.php`, `index.php`, `update.php`, and `view.php` are views that refer to the same actions in the controller. By default, they all have a breadcrumb and a title for each page.

Make some tests that browse, for example, to `http://hostname/basic/web/rooms-with-gii/index` or `http://hostname/basic/web/rooms-with-gii/index`, to see some excellent works made by Gii.

This is the index action result of `RoomsWithGiiController`:

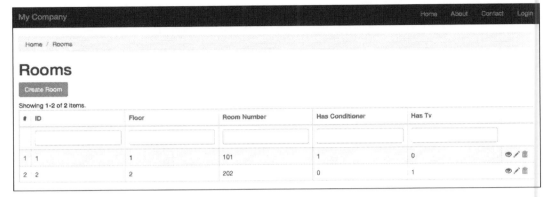

The output of the RoomsWithGiiController index action

Customize JavaScript and CSS

As mentioned before, in this chapter, you will discover how to use frontend interaction. Using JavaScript and CSS is fundamental to customize frontend output.

Differently from Yii1, where calling JavaScript and CSS scripts and files was done using the `Yii::app()` singleton, in the new framework version, Yii2, this task is part of the `yii\web\View` class.

There are two ways to call JavaScript or CSS: either directly passing the code to be executed or passing the path file.

 When passing the code directly to be executed, we will use the Heredoc syntax provided by PHP to avoid handling strings escaping.

The `registerJs()` function allows us to execute the JavaScript code with three parameters:

- The first parameter is the JavaScript code block to be registered
- The second parameter is the position where the JavaScript tag should be inserted (the header, the beginning of the body section, the end of the body section, enclosed within the jQuery `load()` method, or enclosed within the jQuery `document.ready()` method, which is the default)

- The third and last parameter is a key that identifies the JavaScript code block (if it is not provided, the content of the first parameter will be used as the key)

On the other hand, the `registerJsFile()` function allows us to execute a JavaScript file with three parameters:

- The first parameter is the path file of the JavaScript file
- The second parameter is the HTML attribute for the script tag, with particular attention given to the depends and position values, which are not treated as tag attributes
- The third parameter is a key that identifies the JavaScript code block (if it's not provided, the content of the first parameter will be used as the key)

CSS, similar to JavaScript, can be executed using the code or by passing the path file.

The `registerCss()` function allows us to execute CSS code with three parameters:

- The first one is the CSS code block to be registered
- The second one is the HTML attributes for the `style` tag
- The third and last parameter is a key that identifies the JavaScript code block (if it is not provided, the content of the first parameter will be used as the key)

The `registerCssFile()` function allows us instead to execute a CSS file with three parameters:

- The first one is the path file of the CSS file
- The second parameter is the HTML attribute for the link tag, with particular attention given to the depends value, which is not treated as a tag attribute
- The third parameter is a key that identifies the JavaScript code block (if it's not provided, the content of the first parameter will be used as the key)

Generally, JavaScript or CSS files are published in the `basic/web` folder, which is accessible without restrictions.

So, when we have to use custom JavaScript or CSS files, it is recommended to put them in a subfolder of the `basic/web` folder, which can be named as `css` or `js`.

 By default, the folder for CSS files `basic/web/css` should already exist. But we still need to create `basic/web/js` for JavaScript files.

In some circumstances, we might be required to add a new CSS or JavaScript file for all web application pages. The most appropriate place to put these entries is `AppAsset.php`, a file located in `basic/assets/AppAsset.php`. In it we can add CSS and JavaScript entries required in web applications, even using dependencies if we need to.

Example – using JavaScript and CSS to display advertising columns that disappear if not enough space is available

This sample is suitable if you need to use JavaScript and CSS customizations together.

Think about the layout built as three vertical columns, typical of a blog system. One column of 200 pixels on the left (usually for advertising), one central column of 1000 pixels (usually for content) and one of 200 pixels on the right (usually again for advertising).

If the browser size is at least 1,400 pixels wide, we want all three columns to be shown (the content and two columns for advertising).

If there is not enough space for all the columns and the browser's width size is between 1,200 and 1,400 pixels, only the left and central columns will be shown (only a column for advertising and one for the content. Finally, if the browser's width size is under 1,200 pixels, only the central column with content will be shown).

Also, our goal is to ensure that these columns are always centered in the browser.

Create a new controller class in `basic/controllers/ThreeColumnsController.php`, to handle the action to render the view file:

```php
<?php
namespace app\controllers;

use Yii;
use yii\web\Controller;

class ThreeColumnsController extends Controller
{
    public function actionIndex()
    {
        return $this->render('index.php');
    }
}
```

Furthermore, create a new `view` folder in `basic/views/three-columns` and insert `index.php` file in it to store view content.

Basically, this is the content necessary to build a three column layout:

```
<div id="layout">
    <div id="colSx" class="column">
            Content of SX Column
    </div>
    <div id="colCenter" class="column">
            Content of Central Column
    </div>
    <div id="colDx" class="column">
            Content of DX Column
    </div>
</div>
```

The CSS class column will only be used to enhance cells' visibility with a black border around them.

At this point, we will center the layout and fix the columns' width using the `registerCss()` method at the top of the view file:

```php
<?php

$this->registerCss( <<< EOT_CSS

    .column
    {
            border:1px solid black;
    }

    #layout
    {
        position:relative;
        margin:0pt auto;
        width:1400px;
    }

    #colSx
    {
        width:200px;
        float:left;
    }
```

```
    #colCenter
    {
        width:1000px;
        float:left;
    }

    #colDx
    {
        width:200px;
        float:left;
    }

EOT_CSS
);


?>
```

Point your browser to `http://hostname/basic/web/three-columns/index` and you will get the following content:

Content width split into three columns

We must handle the resize browser event through JavaScript to manage the columns visualization using the dimension rules defined at the start of this chapter.

We will use the `registerJs()` method, passing only the code to be executed:

```
<?php
$this->registerJs( <<< EOT_JS

    function resizeLayout()
    {
        var windowWidth = $(window).width();

        if(windowWidth > 1400)
        {
            $('#colSx').css('display', 'block');
            $('#colCenter').css('display', 'block');
```

```
        $('#colDx').css('display', 'block');
        $('#layout').css('width', 1400);
    }
    else if((windowWidth>1200)&&(windowWidth<=1400))
    {
        $('#colSx').css('display', 'block');
        $('#colCenter').css('display', 'block');
        $('#colDx').css('display', 'none');
        $('#layout').css('width', 1200);
    }
    else if(windowWidth<1200)
    {
        $('#colSx').css('display', 'none');
        $('#colCenter').css('display', 'block');
        $('#colDx').css('display', 'none');
        $('#layout').css('width', 1000);
    }

}

$(window).resize(function() {
        resizeLayout();
});

$(function() {
        resizeLayout();
});

EOT_JS
);
?>
```

Refresh your browser to `http://hostname/basic/web/three-columns/index` and resize it to the desired width, and the columns visualization should change depending on the available space in the specific width.

Using AJAX

Yii2 provides appropriate attributes for some widgets to make AJAX calls; sometimes, however, writing a JavaScript code in these attributes will make code hard to read, especially if we are dealing with complex codes.

Consequently, to make an AJAX call, we will use external JavaScript code executed by `registerJs()`.

This is a template of the AJAX class using the GET or POST method:

```php
<?php
$this->registerJs( <<< EOT_JS

    // using GET method
$.get({
  url: url,
  data: data,
  success: success,
  dataType: dataType
});

    // using POST method
$.post({
  url: url,
  data: data,
  success: success,
  dataType: dataType
});

EOT_JS
);
?>
```

An AJAX call is usually the effect of a user interface event (such as a click on a button, a link, and so on). So, most of the time an AJAX call is directly connected to the `.on()` event of jQuery on the HTML elements (anchors, buttons, and so on). For this reason, it is important to remember how Yii2 renders the name and id attributes of input fields.

When we call `Html::activeTextInput($model, $attribute)` or in the same way use `<?= $form->field($model, $attribute)->textInput() ?>`.

The name and id attributes of the input text field will be rendered as follows:

- id : The model class name separated with a dash by the attribute name in lowercase; for example, if the model class name is Room and the attribute is floor, the id attribute will be room-floor

- name: The model class name that encloses the attribute name, for example, if the model class name is Reservation and the attribute is price_per_day, the name attribute will be Reservation[price_per_day]; so every field owned by the Reservation model will be enclosed all in a single array

Example – reservation details loaded from the customers' drop-down lists

In this example, there are two drop-down lists and a detail box. The two drop-down lists refer to customers and reservations; when user clicks on a customer list item, the second drop-down list of reservations will be filled out according to their choice.

Finally, when a user clicks on a reservation list item, a details box will be filled out with data about the selected reservation.

Create a new action in `basic/controllers/ReservationsController.php` named `actionDetailDependentDropdown()`:

```php
public function actionDetailDependentDropdown()
{
    $showDetail = false;

    $model = new Reservation();

    if(isset($_POST['Reservation']))
    {
        $model->load( Yii::$app->request->post() );

        if(isset($_POST['Reservation']['id'])&&
        ($_POST['Reservation']['id']!=null))
        {
            $model =
            Reservation::findOne($_POST['Reservation']['id']);
            $showDetail = true;
        }
    }


    return $this->render('detailDependentDropdown', [ 'model'
    => $model, 'showDetail' => $showDetail ]);
}
```

In this action, we will get the `customer_id` and `id` parameters from a form based on the `Reservation` model data and if it are filled out, the data will be used to search for the correct reservation model to be passed to the view.

There is a flag called `$showDetail` that displays the reservation details content if the `id` attribute of the model is received.

In `ReservationsController`, there is also an action that will be called using AJAX when the user changes the customer selection in the drop-down list:

```php
public function actionAjaxDropDownListByCustomerId($customer_id)
{
    $output = '';

    $items = Reservation::findAll(['customer_id' =>
    $customer_id]);
    foreach($items as $item)
    {
        $content = sprintf('reservation #%s at %s', $item->id,
        date('Y-m-d H:i:s', strtotime($item-
        >reservation_date)));
        $output .= \yii\helpers\Html::tag('option', $content,
        ['value' => $item->id]);
    }

    return $output;
}
```

This action will return the `<option>` HTML tags filled out with reservations data filtered by the customer ID passed as a parameter.

Now let's look at the view in `basic/views/reservations/detailDependentDropdown.php`:

```php
<?php
use yii\helpers\Html;
use yii\widgets\ActiveForm;
use yii\helpers\ArrayHelper;
use yii\helpers\Url;
use app\models\Customer;
use app\models\Reservation;

$urlReservationsByCustomer = Url::to(['reservations/ajax-drop-down-
list-by-customer-id']);
$this->registerJs( <<< EOT_JS

    $(document).on('change', '#reservation-customer_id',
      function(ev) {

        $('#detail').hide();

        var customerId = $(this).val();
```

```
        $.get(
            '{$urlReservationsByCustomer}',
            { 'customer_id' : customerId },
            function(data) {
                data = '<option value="">---
                choose</option>'+data;
                $('#reservation-id').html(data);
            }
        )
        ev.preventDefault();
    });

    $(document).on('change', '#reservation-id', function(ev) {
        $(this).parents('form').submit();
        ev.preventDefault();
    });

EOT_JS
);


?>


<div class="customer-form">
    <?php $form = ActiveForm::begin(['enableAjaxValidation' =>
    false, 'enableClientValidation' => false, 'options' => ['data-
    pjax' => '']]); ?>

    <?php $customers = Customer::find()->all(); ?>
    <?= $form->field($model, 'customer_id')-
    >dropDownList(ArrayHelper::map( $customers, 'id',
    'nameAndSurname'), [ 'prompt' => '--- choose' ]) ?>

    <?php $reservations = Reservation::findAll(['customer_id' =>
    $model->customer_id]); ?>
    <?= $form->field($model, 'id')->label('Reservation ID')-
    >dropDownList(ArrayHelper::map( $reservations, 'id',
    function($temp, $defaultValue) {
      $content = sprintf('reservation #%s at %s', $temp->id,
      date('Y-m-d H:i:s', strtotime($temp->reservation_date)));
        return $content;
    }), [ 'prompt' => '--- choose' ]); ?>

    <div id="detail">
    <?php if($showDetail) { ?>
        <hr />
```

```
            <h2>Reservation Detail:</h2>
            <table>
                <tr>
                    <td>Price per day</td>
                    <td><?php echo $model->price_per_day ?></td>
                </tr>
            </table>
        <?php } ?>
        </div>

        <?php ActiveForm::end(); ?>

    </div>
```

At the top of the view, there are handlers for changes in the customers and reservations drop-down list.

If the customer drop-down list is changed, the detail div will be hidden, an AJAX call will get all the reservations filtered by customer_id, and the result will be passed as content to the reservations drop-down list. If the reservations drop-down list is changed, a form will be submitted.

Next in the form declaration, we can find first of all the customer drop-down list and then the reservations list, which uses a closure to get the value from the ArrayHelper::map() methods. We could add a new property in the Reservation model by creating a function starting with the prefix get, such as getDescription(), and put in it the content of the closure, or rather:

```
public function getDescription()
{
$content = sprintf('reservation #%s at %s', $this>id, date('Y-m-d
H:i:s', strtotime($this>reservation_date)));
            return $content;
}
```

Or we could use a short syntax to get data from ArrayHelper::map() in this way:

```
<?= $form->field($model, 'id')->dropDownList(ArrayHelper::map(
$reservations, 'id', 'description'), [ 'prompt' => '---
choose' ]); ?>
```

Finally, if $showDetail is flagged, a simple details box with only the price per day of the reservation will be displayed.

Point your browser to `http://hostname/basic/web/reservations/detail-dependent-dropdown`:

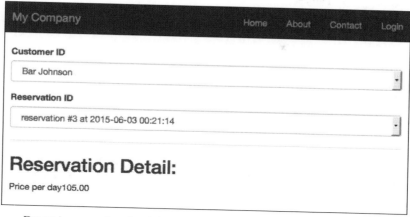

Dynamic reservation details being loaded from the customer drop-down list

Using the Bootstrap widget

Yii2 supports Bootstrap as a core feature. Bootstrap framework CSS and JavaScript files are injected by default in all pages and we could even use this feature to only apply CSS classes or call our own JavaScript function provided by Bootstrap.

However, Yii2 embeds Bootstrap as a widget, and we can access this framework's capabilities like any other widget.

The most used are:

Class name	Description
`yii\bootstrap\Alert`	This class renders an alert Bootstrap component
`yii\bootstrap\Button`	This class renders a Bootstrap button
`yii\bootstrap\Dropdown`	This class renders a Bootstrap drop-down menu component
`yii\bootstrap\Nav`	This class renders a nav HTML component
`yii\bootstrap\NavBar`	This class renders a navbar HTML component

For example, `yii\bootstrap\Nav` and `yii\bootstrap\NavBar` are used in the default main template.

This is an extract from the main layout view (in `basic/views/layouts/main.php`):

```php
<?php
NavBar::begin([
    'brandLabel' => 'My Company',
    'brandUrl' => Yii::$app->homeUrl,
    'options' => [
        'class' => 'navbar-inverse navbar-fixed-top',
    ],
]);
echo Nav::widget([
    'options' => ['class' => 'navbar-nav navbar-right'],
    'items' => [
        ['label' => 'Home', 'url' => ['/site/index']],
        ['label' => 'About', 'url' =>
        ['/site/about']],
        ['label' => 'Contact', 'url' =>
        ['/site/contact']],
        Yii::$app->user->isGuest ?
            ['label' => 'Login', 'url' =>
            ['/site/login']] :
            ['label' => 'Logout (' . Yii::$app->user->identity->username . ')',
            'url' => ['/site/logout'],
            'linkOptions' => ['data-method' =>
            'post']],
    ],
]);
NavBar::end();
?>
```

Example: using datepicker

Yii2 also supports, by itself, many jQuery UI widgets through the JUI extension for Yii2, `yii2-jui`.

If we do not have the `yii2-jui` extension in the `vendor` folder, we can get it from Composer using this command:

```
php composer.phar require --prefer-dist yiisoft/yii2-jui
```

In this example, we will discuss the two most used widgets: `datepicker` and `autocomplete`. First let's have a look at the `datepicker` widget. This widget can be initialized using a model attribute or by filling out a value property. The following is an example made using a model instance and one of its attributes:

```
echo DatePicker::widget([
    'model' => $model,
    'attribute' => 'from_date',
    //'language' => 'it',
    //'dateFormat' => 'yyyy-MM-dd',
]);
```

And here is a sample of the value property's use:

```
echo DatePicker::widget([
    'name'  => 'from_date',
    'value' => $value,
    //'language' => 'it',
    //'dateFormat' => 'yyyy-MM-dd',
]);
```

Now create a new controller named `JuiWidgetsController` in `basic/controllers/JuiWidgetsController.php`:

```php
<?php

namespace app\controllers;

use Yii;
use yii\web\Controller;
use app\models\Reservation;

class JuiWidgetsController extends Controller
{
    public function actionDatePicker()
    {
        $reservationUpdated = false;

        $reservation = Reservation::findOne(1);

        if(isset($_POST['Reservation']))
        {
            $reservation->load( Yii::$app->request->post() );
```

```
            $reservation->date_from = Yii::$app->formatter-
            >asDate(  date_create_from_format('d/m/Y',
            $reservation->date_from), 'php:Y-m-d' );
            $reservation->date_to = Yii::$app->formatter->asDate(
            date_create_from_format('d/m/Y', $reservation-
            >date_to), 'php:Y-m-d' );

            $reservationUpdated = $reservation->save();
        }

        return $this->render('datePicker', ['reservation' =>
        $reservation, 'reservationUpdated' =>
        $reservationUpdated]);
    }
}
```

In this action, we define the $reservation model, picking from the reservations database table with id 1.

When data is sent via POST, the date_from and date_to fields will be converted from the d/m/y to the y-m-d format to make it possible for the database to save data. Then the model object is updated through the save() method. Using the Bootstrap widget, an alert box will be displayed in the view after updating the model.

Create the datePicker view in basic/views/jui-widgets/datePicker.php:

```php
<?php

use yii\helpers\Html;
use yii\widgets\ActiveForm;
use yii\jui\DatePicker;

?>

<div class="row">
    <div class="col-lg-6">
        <h3>Date Picker from Value<br />(using MM/dd/yyyy format
        and English language)</h3>
        <?php
            $value = date('Y-m-d');

        echo DatePicker::widget([
            'name'  => 'from_date',
            'value' => $value,
            'language' => 'en',
```

```
                    'dateFormat' => 'MM/dd/yyyy',
        ]);
        ?>
</div>
<div class="col-lg-6">

        <?php if($reservationUpdated) { ?>
            <?php
            echo yii\bootstrap\Alert::widget([
                'options' => [
                    'class' => 'alert-success',
                ],
                'body' => 'Reservation successfully updated',
            ]);
            ?>
        <?php } ?>

        <?php $form = ActiveForm::begin(); ?>

        <h3>Date Picker from Model<br />(using dd/MM/yyyy format
        and italian language)</h3>

        <br />

        <label>Date from</label>
        <?php
        // First implementation of DatePicker Widget
        echo DatePicker::widget([
            'model'  => $reservation,
            'attribute' => 'date_from',
            'language' => 'it',
            'dateFormat' => 'dd/MM/yyyy',
        ]);
        ?>

        <br />
        <br />

        <?php
        // Second implementation of DatePicker Widget
        echo $form->field($reservation, 'date_to')-
        >widget(\yii\jui\DatePicker::classname(), [
                'language' => 'it',
                'dateFormat' => 'dd/MM/yyyy',
```

```
        ]) ?>

        <?php
            echo Html::submitButton('Send', ['class' => 'btn btn-
            primary'])
        ?>

        <?php $form = ActiveForm::end(); ?>

    </div>
</div>
```

The view is split into two columns, left and right. The left column simply displays a DataPicker example from the value (fixed to the current date). The right column displays an alert box if the $reservation model has been updated and the next two kinds of widget declaration too; the first one without using $form and the second one using $form, both outputting the same HTML code.

In either case, the DatePicker date output format is set to dd/MM/yyyy through the dateFormat property and the language is set to Italian through the language property.

Point your browser to http://hostname/basic/web/jui-widgets/date-picker to see the following output:

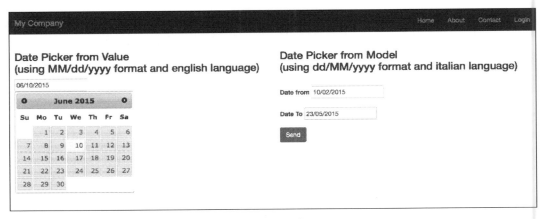

Using datepicker

Multiple models in the same view

Often, we can find many models of same or different class in a single view. First of all, remember that Yii2 encapsulates all the views' form attributes in the same container, named the same as the model class name. Therefore, when the controller receives the data, these will all be organized in a key of the `$_POST` array named the same as the model class name.

If the model class name is `Customer`, every form input name attribute will be `Customer[attributeA_of_model]` This is built with: `$form->field($model, 'attributeA_of_model')->textInput()`.

In the case of multiple models of the same class, the container will again be named as the model class name but every attribute of each model will be inserted in an array, such as:

```
Customer[0][attributeA_of_model_0]
Customer[0][attributeB_of_model_0]
...
...
...
Customer[n][attributeA_of_model_n]
Customer[n][attributeB_of_model_n]
```

These are built with:

```
$form->field($model, '[0]attributeA_of_model')->textInput();
$form->field($model, '[0]attributeB_of_model')->textInput();
...
...
...
$form->field($model, '[n]attributeA_of_model')->textInput();
$form->field($model, '[n]attributeB_of_model')->textInput();
```

 Notice that the array key information is inserted in the attribute name!

So, when data is passed to the controller, `$_POST['Customer']` will be an array composed by the `Customer` models and every key of this array, for example, `$_POST['Customer'][0]` is a model of the `Customer` class.

Example – saving multiple customers at the same time

Now let's see how to save three customers at once. We will create three containers, one for each model class that will contain some fields of the Customer model.

Create a view in basic/views/customers/createMultipleModels.php that contains a block of input fields repeated for every model passed from the controller:

```php
<?php

use yii\helpers\Html;
use yii\widgets\ActiveForm;

/* @var $this yii\web\View */
/* @var $model app\models\Room */
/* @var $form yii\widgets\ActiveForm */
?>

<div class="room-form">

    <?php $form = ActiveForm::begin(); ?>

    <div class="model">

      <?php for($k=0;$k<sizeof($models);$k++) { ?>
          <?php $model = $models[$k]; ?>
          <hr />
          <label>Model #<?php echo $k+1 ?></label>
          <?= $form->field($model, "[$k]name")->textInput() ?>
          <?= $form->field($model, "[$k]surname")->textInput() ?>
          <?= $form->field($model, "[$k]phone_number")-
          >textInput() ?>
      <?php } ?>

    </div>

<hr />

    <div class="form-group">
      <?= Html::submitButton('Save', ['class' => 'btn btn-
      primary']) ?>
    </div>
</div>
```

```php
<?php ActiveForm::end(); ?>

</div>
```

For each model all the fields will have the same validator rules of the Customer class, and every single model object will be validated separately.

Next create a new action in the customers controller in `basic/controllers/CustomersController.php`, named `actionCreateMultipleModels`. If the `$_POST['Customer']` content is set, and if they are all validated and finally redirected to the grid action, it will save them all together; otherwise it will create three models of the Customer class:

```php
public function actionCreateMultipleModels()
{
    $models = [];

    if(isset($_POST['Customer']))
    {
        $validateOK = true;

        foreach($_POST['Customer'] as $postObj)
        {
            $model = new Customer();
            $model->attributes = $postObj;
            $models[] = $model;

            $validateOK = ($validateOK && ($model-
            >validate()));
        }

        // All models are validated and will be saved
        if($validateOK)
        {
            foreach($models as $model)
            {
                $model->save();
            }

            // Redirect to grid after save
            return $this->redirect(['grid']);
        }
    }
}
```

```
        else
        {
            for($k=0;$k<3;$k++)
            {
                $models[] = new Customer();
            }
        }

        return $this->render('createMultipleModels', ['models' =>
        $models]);
    }
```

It can be useful to create models in the controller because a large number of them and other validation checks are configured here.

Browse to `http://hostname/basic/web/customers/create-multiple-models` to see the complete page:

Multiple models in the same view

Saving linked models in the same view

It could be convenient to save different kind of models in the same view. This approach allows us to save time and to navigate from every single detail until a final item that merges all data is created. Handling different kind of models linked to each other it is not so different from what we have seen so far. The only point to take care of is the link (foreign keys) between models, which we must ensure is valid.

Therefore, the controller action will receive the `$_POST` data encapsulated in the model's class name container; if we are thinking, for example, of the customer and reservation models, we will have two arrays in the `$_POST` variable, `$_POST['Customer']` and `$_POST['Reservation']`, containing all the fields about the customer and reservation models.

Then all data must be saved together. It is advisable to use a database transaction while saving data because the action can be considered as ended only when all the data has been saved.

Using database transactions in Yii2 is incredibly simple! A database transaction starts with calling `beginTransaction()` on the database connection object and finishes with calling the `commit()` or `rollback()` method on the database transaction object created by `beginTransaction()`.

To start a transaction:

```
$dbTransaction = Yii::$app->db->beginTransaction();
```

Commit a transaction, to save all the database activities:

```
$dbTransaction->commit();
```

Rollback a transaction, to clear all the database activities:

```
$dbTransaction->rollback();
```

So, if a customer was saved and the reservation was not (for any possible reason), our data would be partial and incomplete. Using a database transaction, we will avoid this danger.

Example – creating a customer and reservation in the same view

We now want to create both the customer and reservation models in the same view in a single step. In this way, we will have a box containing the customer model fields and a box with the reservation model fields in the view.

Create a view in `basic/views/reservations/createCustomerAndReservation.php`, with the fields from the customer and reservation models:

```php
<?php

use yii\helpers\Html;
use yii\widgets\ActiveForm;
use yii\helpers\ArrayHelper;
use \app\models\Room;
?>

<div class="room-form">

    <?php $form = ActiveForm::begin(); ?>

    <div class="model">

        <?php echo $form->errorSummary([$customer, $reservation]); ?>

        <h2>Customer</h2>
        <?= $form->field($customer, "name")->textInput() ?>
        <?= $form->field($customer, "surname")->textInput() ?>
        <?= $form->field($customer, "phone_number")->textInput() ?>

        <h2>Reservation</h2>
        <?= $form->field($reservation, "room_id")-
        >dropDownList(ArrayHelper::map(Room::find()->all(), 'id',
        function($room, $defaultValue) {
            return sprintf('Room n.%d at floor %d', $room-
            >room_number, $room->floor);
        })); ?>
        <?= $form->field($reservation, "price_per_day")->textInput()
        ?>
        <?= $form->field($reservation, "date_from")->textInput() ?>
        <?= $form->field($reservation, "date_to")->textInput() ?>

    </div>

    <div class="form-group">
        <?= Html::submitButton('Save customer and room', ['class'
        => 'btn btn-primary']) ?>
```

```
        </div>

        <?php ActiveForm::end(); ?>

    </div>
```

We have created two blocks in the form to fill out the fields for the customer and the reservation.

Now, create a new action named `actionCreateCustomerAndReservation` in `ReservationsController` in `basic/controllers/ReservationsController.php`:

```php
public function actionCreateCustomerAndReservation()
{
    $customer = new \app\models\Customer();
    $reservation = new \app\models\Reservation();

    // It is useful to set fake customer_id to reservation
    model to avoid validation error (because customer_id is
    mandatory)
    $reservation->customer_id = 0;

    if(
        $customer->load(Yii::$app->request->post())
        &&
        $reservation->load(Yii::$app->request->post())
        &&
        $customer->validate()
        &&
        $reservation->validate()
    )
    {

        $dbTrans = Yii::$app->db->beginTransaction();

        $customerSaved = $customer->save();

        if($customerSaved)
        {
            $reservation->customer_id = $customer->id;
            $reservationSaved = $reservation->save();

            if($reservationSaved)
            {
                $dbTrans->commit();
            }
            else {
                $dbTrans->rollback();
            }
```

```
            }
            else {
                $dbTrans->rollback();
            }
        }


        return $this->render('createCustomerAndReservation', [
    'customer' => $customer, 'reservation' => $reservation ]);
        }
```

Ensure you pay attention to these two matters:

- `$reservation->customer_id = 0`: With this code, we avoid the validation error relating to the `customer_id` requirement that appears when `$reservation` is validated

- The database transaction will be committed only if the customer model and reservation model's save action are completed

Browse to `http://hostname/basic/web/reservations/create-customer-and-reservation` to see the complete page:

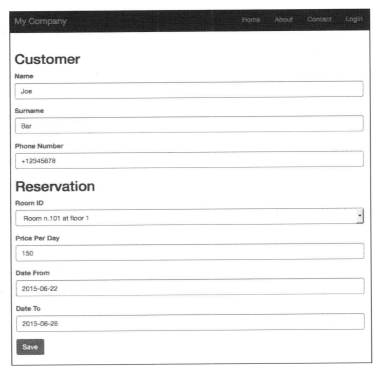

A customer and reservation created together

Summary

In this chapter, we discussed about the user interface and how Yii helps us with its core functionalities. The first important tool that Yii provides is Gii, which facilitates CRUD actions and views' creation, which we used in Gii to manage rooms, reservations, and customers, for example.

Next we saw how to embed JavaScript and CSS in a layout and views, with file content or an inline block. This was applied to an example that showed you how to change the number of columns displayed based on the browser's available width; this is typically a task for websites or web apps that display advertising columns.

Again on the subject of JavaScript, you learned how to implement direct AJAX calls, taking an example where the reservation detail was dynamically loaded from the customers drop-down list.

Next we looked at Yii's core user interface library, which is built on Bootstrap and we illustrated how to use the main Bootstrap widgets natively, together with DatePicker (probably the most commonly used jQuery UI widget).

Finally, the last topics covered were multiple models of the same and different classes. We looked at two examples on these topics: the first one to save multiple customers at the same time and the second to create a customer and reservation in the same view.

In the next chapter, we will explain how to set up login authentication and authorization, and will reach these goals from scratch.

8

Log in to the App

This chapter will explain how to set up login authentication and authorization. Logging in is a fundamental step to protect our application and you will learn how to reach these goals from scratch, using the web management free extension that is broadly available on the Internet.

We will cover the following topics in this chapter:

- Creating a user login:
  - ° For example: creating login form to access
- Configure a user authorization
  - ° For example: creating an access control filter to authorize
- **Role Based Access Control (RBAC)**
  - ° For example: configuring RBAC to set permissions for users
- Mixing **Access Control Filter (ACF)** and RBAC
  - ° For example: managing users' roles to access rooms, reservations, and customers

The first step will be creating an authenticated access to our app using a database table to manage users and associate it to the Yii user component, through a user model that extends `IdentityInterface`. We will provide an example of how to use it: building a login form to authenticate the user.

The next step will be to control what actions a user can perform, using ACF and RBAC. We will follow some examples using ACF and RBAC, and in the latter case we will build a complete authorization manager from scratch.

Creating a user login

The application's security starts with two well distinguished phases of the same user login: authentication and authorization.

The first one, authentication, is the process of verifying a user's identity, usually using a username and password, or email and password, process. Authentication is completed when the user has been recognized and their state has been preserved for further requests.

The second one, authorization, is the process of verifying that the user has the permission to execute a specific action.

> Since http requests are stateless, we need to preserve the login status, which means that there is no data context sharing among them. This limit is solved by sessions, mainly files where the web server stores the data. A filename is used as a session identifier and passed to the browser through a cookie or URL parameter of links contained in the HTML response.
> In this way, the browser keeps the session active by sending the session identifier to the web server through a cookie or a parameter in the request URL, and the web server knows which file contains the session data.
> A database table can be used instead of files with the same functionalities.

Yii2 implements authentication through the `yii\web\User` component, which manages the user authentication status and also contains a reference to the `identityClass` that represents the concrete object that we are referring to.

An `identityClass` class should implement five methods:

- `findIdentity()`: This method looks for an instance of an identity class using the ID provided as parameter. It is commonly used when we need to keep the login status via a session.

- `findIdentityByAccessToken()`: This one looks for an instance of the identity class using the access token provided by the parameter. It is commonly used when we need to authenticate using a single secret token.

- `getId()`: This one returns the ID of the identity instance.

- `getAuthKey()`: This method returns the key used to verify the cookie-based login when the login has been completed using a cookie sent by the browser (when **Remember me** is checked during the login).

- `validateAuthKey()`: This method verifies that the provided `authKey` passed as a parameter is correct (in the cookie-based login).

Often the `identityClass` class corresponds to a record of the `User` database table. For this reason, usually the `identityClass` class implements `IdentityInterface` and extends `ActiveRecord`.

It is now time to implement authentication. The first thing to do is to configure `yii\web\User` components and its `identityClass`. Open the `basic/config/web.php` file and add the `user` property to `components` if it does not already exist:

```
'components' => [
    ...
    ...
    'user' => [
        'identityClass' => 'app\models\User',
    ],
],
```

Next, we have to create a database table where we store the users' records:

```
CREATE TABLE `user` (
 `id` int(11) NOT NULL AUTO_INCREMENT,
 `username` varchar(255) NOT NULL,
 `auth_key` varchar(32) NOT NULL,
 `password_hash` varchar(255) NOT NULL,
 `access_token` varchar(100) DEFAULT NULL,
 PRIMARY KEY (`id`)
) ENGINE=InnoDB DEFAULT CHARSET=utf8
```

> Notice that we do not have a password field, but we have a `password_hash` field. This because passwords are stored using the hashing method. In models, we will have a setter `setPassword()` method that gets plain text passwords to fill in the `password_hash` field.

Finally, let's update the `basic/models/User` class that handles the login status by implementing `IdentityInterface` and connect it to the `user` table of database. This is a common implementation for `basic/models/User`:

```php
<?php
namespace app\models;

use Yii;
use yii\base\NotSupportedException;
use yii\db\ActiveRecord;
use yii\web\IdentityInterface;
```

```
class User extends ActiveRecord implements IdentityInterface
{
    public static function tableName()
    {
        return 'user';
    }

    public static function findIdentity($id)
    {
        return static::findOne(['id' => $id]);
    }

    public static function findIdentityByAccessToken($token, $type
    = null)
    {
        return static::findOne(['access_token' => $token]);
    }

    public static function findByUsername($username)
    {
        return static::findOne(['username' => $username]);
    }

    public function getId()
    {
        return $this->getPrimaryKey();
    }

    public function getAuthKey()
    {
        return $this->auth_key;
    }

    public function validateAuthKey($authKey)
    {
        return $this->getAuthKey() === $authKey;
    }

    public function validatePassword($password)
    {
        return Yii::$app->security->validatePassword($password,
        $this->password_hash);
    }
```

```
public function setPassword($password)
{
    $this->password_hash = Yii::$app->security-
    >generatePasswordHash($password);
}

public function generateAuthKey()
{
    $this->auth_key = Yii::$app->security-
    >generateRandomString();
}
}
```

If our application also uses a cookie-based authentication, we need to fill in the auth_key field too, as this will be passed to the client in the http response. It is convenient to populate the auth_key field automatically when a new user is inserted by overriding the beforeSave() method in the \app\models\User model:

```
public function beforeSave($insert)
{
    if (parent::beforeSave($insert)) {
        if ($this->isNewRecord) {
            $this->auth_key = \Yii::$app->security-
            >generateRandomString();
        }
        return true;
    }
    return false;
}
```

User components provide methods to log in, log out, and access the identityClass, and they verify the effectiveness of the user authentication.

To verify whether the user is well authenticated, use the following:

```
// whether the current user is a guest (not authenticated)
$isGuest = Yii::$app->user->isGuest;
```

When a user is authenticated and we have an instance of the \app\models\User model, we could complete the authentication by calling:

```
// find a user identity with the specified username.
// note that you may want to check the password if needed
```

```
$userModel = User::findOne(['username' => $username]);

// logs in the user
Yii::$app->user->login($userModel);
```

Then, when we need to access the identity class:

```
// access to identity class that it is equivalent to $userModel
$identity = Yii::$app->user->identity;
```

Finally, to log the user out:

```
Yii::$app->user->logout();
```

Example – a login form to access

In this example, we will create a login form and complete the user authentication. To proceed it is necessary to create a user database table from a SQL query, as described in the previous paragraph.

To add a user, just insert a new record in the user table, with foo as the username and foopassword as the password:

```
INSERT INTO `user` (
`username` ,
`password_hash` ,
)
VALUES (
'foo',
'$2a$12$hL0rmIMjxhLqI.xr7jD1FugNWEgZNh62HuJj5.y34XBUfBWB4cppW'
);
```

A password is hashed using the bcrypt method and cost with value 12, available on the Internet through a quick Google search.

Then, create a new controller named MyAuthentication in basic/controllers/ MyAuthenticationController.php and ensure it contains two actions: actionLogin and actionLogout.

The actionLogin method gets the username and password data from $_POST and uses an $error variable to pass an error description to the view. If the username and password data is filled in, the user will be found in the database table and the inserted password will be validated, and after that the user will be logged in.

Finally, `actionLogout` simply logs the user out from the session and redirects the browser to the login page:

```php
<?php

namespace app\controllers;

use Yii;
use yii\web\Controller;

use app\models\User;


class MyAuthenticationController extends Controller
{
    public function actionLogin()
    {
        $error = null;

        $username = Yii::$app->request->post('username', null);
        $password = Yii::$app->request->post('password', null);

        $user = User::findOne(['username' => $username]);

        if(($username!=null)&&($password!=null))
        {
            if($user != null)
            {
                if($user->validatePassword($password))
                {
                    Yii::$app->user->login($user);
                }
                else {
                    $error = 'Password validation failed!';
                }
            }
            else
            {
                $error = 'User not found';
            }
        }

        return $this->render('login', ['error' => $error]);
    }
```

```
        public function actionLogout()
        {
            Yii::$app->user->logout();
            return $this->redirect(['login']);
        }

    }
```

Now, create the view with this content in `basic/views/my-authentication/login.php`. Before a user can log in, a form with the username and password to be filled in will be displayed. When the username and password match an entry in the user database table, a confirmation message and a logout button will be displayed:

```
<?php
use \yii\bootstrap\ActiveForm;
use \yii\helpers\Html;
use \yii\bootstrap\Alert;
?>


<?php
if($error != null) {
    echo Alert::widget([ 'options' => [ 'class' => 'alert-danger'
    ], 'body' => $error ]);
}
?>


<?php if(Yii::$app->user->isGuest) { ?>

    <?php ActiveForm::begin(); ?>

    <div class="form-group">
    <?php echo Html::label('Username', 'username'); ?>
    <?php echo Html::textInput('username', '', ['class' => 'form-
    control']); ?>
    </div>

    <div class="form-group">
    <?php echo Html::label('Password', 'password'); ?>
    <?php echo Html::passwordInput('password', '', ['class' =>
    'form-control']); ?>
    </div>

    <?php echo Html::submitButton('Login', ['class' => 'btn btn-
    primary']); ?>
```

```
    <?php ActiveForm::end(); ?>

<?php } else { ?>

    <h2>You are authenticated!</h2>
    <br /><br />
    <?php echo Html::a('Logout',  ['my-authentication/logout'],
    ['class' => 'btn btn-warning']); ?>

<?php } ?>
```

Test it by pointing the browser to `http://hostname/basic/web/my-authentication/login` and after filling out the form with `foo` as the username and `foopassword` as the password, this should be displayed:

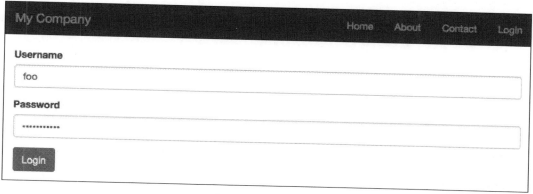

Login form to access

After clicking on the **Login** button, you should see:

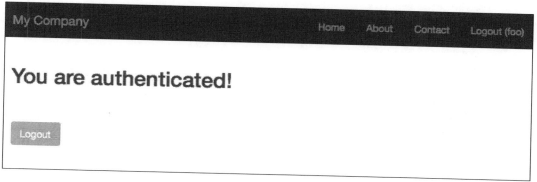

Successful authentication

This method does not provide error handling for the fields, because we are not using a model to create form fields. If we had created a form model with username and password fields, we could have added rules validation to this model and seen input error handling (such as missing field value, wrong field length, and so on). Fortunately, Yii2 has a login form model ready to use in `basic/models/LoginForm.php`.

If we had wanted to use this model, we would have created a new action named `actionLoginWithForm` in `MyAuthenticationController` that handles login fields through the model instead of parameters from `$_POST`:

```php
public function actionLoginWithModel()
{
    $error = null;

    $model = new \app\models\LoginForm();
    if ($model->load(Yii::$app->request->post())) {
        if(($model->validate())&&($model->user != null))
        {
            Yii::$app->user->login($model->user);
        }
        else
        {
            $error = 'Username/Password error';
        }
    }

    return $this->render('login-with-model', ['model' =>
    $model, 'error' => $error]);
}
```

This is the content of `basic/views/my-authentication/login-with-model.php`:

```php
<?php
use \yii\bootstrap\ActiveForm;
use \yii\helpers\Html;
use \yii\bootstrap\Alert;
?>

<?php
if($error != null) {
    echo Alert::widget([ 'options' => [ 'class' => 'alert-danger'
    ], 'body' => $error ]);
}
?>
<?php if(Yii::$app->user->isGuest) { ?>
```

```php
<?php $form = ActiveForm::begin([
    'id' => 'login-form',
]); ?>

    <?= $form->field($model, 'username') ?>

    <?= $form->field($model, 'password')->passwordInput() ?>

    <div class="form-group">
        <?= Html::submitButton('Login', ['class' => 'btn btn-
        primary', 'name' => 'login-button']) ?>
    </div>

    <?php ActiveForm::end(); ?>
<?php } else { ?>
    <h2>You are authenticated!</h2>
    <br /><br />
    <?php echo Html::a('Logout',  ['my-authentication/logout'],
    ['class' => 'btn btn-warning']); ?>
<?php } ?>
```

We can look at the output by pointing our browser to `http://hostname/basic/web/my-authentication/login-with-model`.

If we try to submit the form without filling out all the fields, we will immediately get errors because they are activated by the form client-side validation:

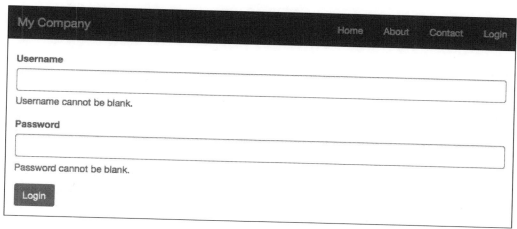

Login error using the model

We can customize the `LoginForm` model class as we want if standard behavior is not enough for our purposes.

Configuring user authorization

Yii has two methods to authorize users: ACF and RBAC.

The first one, ACF, is used in applications that require a minimal and simple access control. Basically, its behavior is based on five parameters:

- `allow`: This parameter specifies whether this is an allow or deny rule; possible values are `allow` or `deny`

- `actions`: This parameter specifies which actions this rule matches, and they are declared using an array of string

- `roles`: This parameter specifies which user roles this rule matches; possible values are ?' and @, which mean respectively guest user and authenticated user

- `ips`: This parameter specifies which client IP address this rule matches; the IP address that can contain * as a wildcard

- `verbs`: This parameter specifies which verb (request method) this rules matches

By default, if no rule matches, access will be denied.

ACF is enabled by overwriting the `behaviors()` method of `Controller` and populating its `access` property with the content of some (or every one) of the preceding parameters.

```php
public function behaviors()
{
    return [
        'access' => [
            'class' => AccessControl::className(),
            'only' => ['login', 'logout', 'signup', 'index'],
            'rules' => [
                [
                    'allow' => true,
                    'actions' => ['login', 'signup', 'index'],
                    'roles' => ['?'],
                ],
                [
                    'allow' => true,
                    'actions' => ['logout'],
                    'roles' => ['@'],
                ],
            ],
        ],
    ];
}
```

In this example, the `login`, `logout`, `signup`, and `index` actions are enabled for guest users (all users) and the logout action is enabled only for authenticated ones.

ACF has many other parameters that can be defined, such as `controllers`, to define which controllers this rule matches (if it is empty, this means all controllers); `matchCallback` whose value is a PHP callable function called to verify whether this rule can be applied or not; and finally `denyCallback`, whose value is a PHP callable function used when this rule will deny access.

When a rule is denied, there are two different behaviors according to the role of the user. If a guest is denied, a denied rule will call the `yii\web\User::loginRequired()` method to redirect the user's browser to the login page; if the user is authenticated, it will throw a `yii\web\ForbiddenHttpException` exception.

This behavior can be customized using the `denyCallback` property mentioned earlier, and by defining the correct callable PHP function.

Obviously, any detail about the logged in user is not considered by this type of authorization. During configuration in the `behaviors()` method, in fact, no detail about the user ever appears (for example, `role`). So we cannot define more precisely which conditions a user can execute or not a controller action.

ACF suggests only if we have to limit access to an authenticated user, without needing some other details to allow the controller action to be executed.

But in all those cases in which it is enough to limit access based on the condition that the user is logged in or not, it is the best approach. In the REST API with limited access (where only the authenticated users are able to make calls), ACF is probably the best solution.

Example – creating an ACF to authorize the users

Now let's look at how to create an ACF to authorize the user to display or not display the page content.

We have two actions: `actionPrivatePage` and `actionPublicPage`. The first one is accessible only from an authenticated user and the second one is publically accessible.

In `MyAuthenticationController.php`, let's add the `behaviors()` method with the following content:

```
public function behaviors()
{
    return [
```

```php
'access' => [
    'class' => AccessControl::className(),
    'only' => ['public-page', 'private-page'],
    'rules' => [
        [
            'allow' => true,
            'actions' => ['public-page'],
            'roles' => ['?'],
        ],
        [
            'allow' => true,
            'actions' => ['private-page'],
            'roles' => ['@'],

        ],
    ],

    // Callable function when user is denied
    'denyCallback' => function($rule, $data) {
            $this->redirect(['login']);
    }
    ],
    ];
}
```

This method applies an ACF to only two actions, `actionPublicPage` and `actionPrivatePage` (based only on the property value) and restricts access for private pages that specify the roles as @.

Then, we added the `denyCallback` property to indicate how the behavior should appear when access is denied to the user. In this case, we set it so that the user should be redirected to the `login` action of `MyAuthenticationController`.

RBAC

RBAC is the right choice when we need more granularity of authorization controls.

RBAC involves two parts:

- The first one is to build up the RBAC authorization data
- The second one is to use the authorization data to perform further access controls

We'll start now by building up the RBAC authorization data. RBAC can be initialized in two ways: through PhpManager, instancing the `yii\rbac\PhpManager` component that will store RBAC data in the `@app/rbac` folder, and through DbManager, instancing the `yii\rbac\DbManager` component, which will use four database tables to store its data.

We need to configure the `authManager` application component in the main configuration file using one of the authorization managers, `yii\rbac\PhpManager` or `yii\rbac\DbManager`.

The following code shows how to configure `authManager` in `basic/config/web.php` using the `yii\rbac\PhpManager` class:

```
return [
    // ...
    'components' => [
        'authManager' => [
            'class' => 'yii\rbac\PhpManager',
        ],
        // ...
    ],
];
```

The following code shows how to configure `authManager` in `basic/config/web.php` using the `yii\rbac\DbManager` class:

```
return [
    // ...
    'components' => [
        'authManager' => [
            'class' => 'yii\rbac\DbManager,
        ],
        // ...
    ],
];
```

Both these methods are based on three objects: `permissions`, `roles`, and `rules`. The `permissions` method represents actions that can be controlled; `roles` are a set of permissions to which the target can be enabled or less; and `rules` are extra validations that will be executed when a permission is checked. Finally, `permissions` or `roles` can be assigned to users and identified by the `IdentityInterface::getId()` value of the `Yii::$app->user` component.

When access permissions do not change, we could create a console command to launch in case, or once, permissions are changed. However, we will not discuss that now as you will see the console command in-depth in the next chapters.

Instead, we will write permissions using a fake action to only execute permissions, roles, and assignments settings.

In `basic/controllers/MyAuthenticationController.php`, add this action named `actionInitializeAuthorizations`:

```
public function actionInitializeAuthorizations()
{
    $auth = Yii::$app->authManager;

    // Reset all
    $auth->removeAll();

    // add "createReservation" permission
    $permCreateReservation = $auth-
    >createPermission('createReservation');
    $permCreateReservation->description = 'Create a
    reservation';
    $auth->add($permCreateReservation);

    // add "updatePost" permission
    $permUpdateReservation = $auth-
    >createPermission('updateReservation');
    $permUpdateReservation->description = 'Update
    reservation';
    $auth->add($permUpdateReservation);

    // add "operator" role and give this role the
    "createReservation" permission
    $roleOperator = $auth->createRole('operator');
    $auth->add($roleOperator);
    $auth->addChild($roleOperator, $permCreateReservation);

    // add "admin" role and give this role the
    "updateReservation" permission
    // as well as the permissions of the "operator" role
    $roleAdmin = $auth->createRole('admin');
    $auth->add($roleAdmin);
    $auth->addChild($roleAdmin, $permUpdateReservation);
    $auth->addChild($roleAdmin, $roleOperator);

    // Assign roles to users. 1 and 2 are IDs returned by
    IdentityInterface::getId()
    // usually implemented in your User model.
    $auth->assign($roleOperator, 2);
    $auth->assign($roleAdmin, 1);
}
```

Before calling this action from your browser, make sure that the folder in `basic/rbac` already exists and that it is writable.

In order to start this action from the beginning, two permissions and two roles are created, then the `createReservation` permission is added as a child to the operator role and the `updateReservation` permission is added as a child to the admin role, together to the operator role.

If we check the `createReservation` permission for the user with the `roleOperator` role, it will be successfully confirmed. The same happens if we check the user with `adminOperator`. But when we check the `updateReservation` permission on the user with the `roleOperator` role, it will be denied since that permission is not assigned to that specific role.

 Permissions and role names can be chosen without restrictions, because they are used as parameters when checking permissions.

Now let's point our browser to `http://hostname/basic/my-authentication/initialize-authorizations` in order to launch the permissions creation.

The content of files created through this action in the `basic/rbac` folder are simply arrays. This is the content of the `items.php` file:

```php
<?php
return [
    'createReservation' => [
        'type' => 2,
        'description' => 'Create a reservation',
    ],
    'updateReservation' => [
        'type' => 2,
        'description' => 'Update reservation',
    ],
    'operator' => [
        'type' => 1,
        'children' => [
            'createReservation',
        ],
    ],
    'admin' => [
        'type' => 1,
        'children' => [
```

```
                'updateReservation',
                'operator',
            ],
        ],
    ];
```

This is the content of `assignments.php`:

```php
<?php
return [
    2 => [
        'operator',
    ],
    1 => [
        'admin',
    ],
];
```

Finally, to check the user authorization, it is enough to call the `yii\web\User::can()` method:

```php
if (\Yii::$app->user->can()) {
    // create reservation permission is enabled to current user
}
```

Example – configuring RBAC to set permissions for users

In this example, we will create a user permissions management system from scratch, based on RBAC. We will create a new controller named `AuthorizationManagerController` in `basic/controllers/AuthorizationManagerController.php` that will display all the users and all the available permissions and roles from the database. This example is based on the user database table already used in the previous paragraphs.

Let's take a look at its structure again:

```sql
CREATE TABLE `user` (
 `id` int(11) NOT NULL AUTO_INCREMENT,
 `username` varchar(255) COLLATE utf8_unicode_ci NOT NULL,
 `auth_key` varchar(32) COLLATE utf8_unicode_ci NOT NULL,
 `password_hash` varchar(255) COLLATE utf8_unicode_ci NOT NULL,
 `access_token` varchar(100) COLLATE utf8_unicode_ci DEFAULT NULL,
 PRIMARY KEY (`id`)
)
```

We will truncate the database table and insert these records, five items, to be used in the next examples:

```
TRUNCATE user;

INSERT INTO `user` (`id`, `username`, `auth_key`, `password_hash`,
`access_token`) VALUES
(1, 'foo', '', '$2a$12$hL0rmIMjxhLqI.xr7jD1FugNWEgZNh62HuJj5.
y34XBUfBWB4cppW',
NULL),
(2, 'userA', '',
'$2a$12$hL0rmIMjxhLqI.xr7jD1FugNWEgZNh62HuJj5.y34XBUfBWB4cppW',
NULL),
(3, 'userB', '',
'$2a$12$hL0rmIMjxhLqI.xr7jD1FugNWEgZNh62HuJj5.y34XBUfBWB4cppW',
NULL),
(4, 'userC', '',
'$2a$12$hL0rmIMjxhLqI.xr7jD1FugNWEgZNh62HuJj5.y34XBUfBWB4cppW',
NULL),
(5, 'admin', '',
'$2a$12$hL0rmIMjxhLqI.xr7jD1FugNWEgZNh62HuJj5.y34XBUfBWB4cppW',
NULL);
```

Now that we have data to work with, we can pass to write code.

The first method to create in this controller is `initializeAuthorizations()`, which has to initialize all the available authorizations in the system:

```php
<?php

namespace app\controllers;

use Yii;
use yii\web\Controller;
use yii\filters\AccessControl;
use app\models\User;
use app\models\LoginForm;

class MyAuthenticationController extends Controller
{

public function initializeAuthorizations()
    {
        $auth = Yii::$app->authManager;

        $permissions = [
```

```php
        'createReservation' => array('desc' => 'Create a
        reservation'),
        'updateReservation' => array('desc' => 'Update
        reservation'),
        'deleteReservation' => array('desc' => 'Delete
        reservation'),

        'createRoom' => array('desc' => 'Create a room'),
        'updateRoom' => array('desc' => 'Update room'),
        'deleteRoom' => array('desc' => 'Delete room'),

        'createCustomer' => array('desc' => 'Create a
        customer'),
        'updateCustomer' => array('desc' => 'Update
        customer'),
        'deleteCustomer' => array('desc' => 'Delete
        customer'),
    ];

    $roles = [
        'operator' => array('createReservation', 'createRoom',
        'createCustomer'),
    ];

    // Add all permissions
    foreach($permissions as $keyP=>$valueP)
    {
        $p = $auth->createPermission($keyP);
        $p->description = $valueP['desc'];
        $auth->add($p);

        // add "operator" role and give this role the
        "createReservation" permission
        $r = $auth->createRole('role_'.$keyP);
        $r->description = $valueP['desc'];
        $auth->add($r);
        if( false == $auth->hasChild($r, $p)) $auth-
        >addChild($r, $p);
    }

    // Add all roles
    foreach($roles as $keyR=>$valueR)
    {
        $r = $auth->createRole($keyR);
        $r->description = $keyR;
```

```
$auth->add($r);

foreach($valueR as $permissionName)
{
  if( false == $auth->hasChild($r, $auth-
  >getPermission($permissionName))) $auth-
  >addChild($r, $auth->getPermission($permissionName));
}

}

// Add all permissions to admin role
$r = $auth->createRole('admin');
$r->description = 'admin';
$auth->add($r);
foreach($permissions as $keyP=>$valueP)
{
    if( false == $auth->hasChild($r, $auth-
    >getPermission($permissionName))) $auth->addChild($r,
    $auth->getPermission($keyP));
}
}
}
```

At the top of this method, we created a permissions and roles list, then we assigned them to the Yii authorization component. Take care to ensure that, after calling this method for the first time, you check whether any children already exist by calling the hasChild method on every addChild() insert attempt.

 We have created a role for each permission, because assign() and revoke() take a role and not a permission as a first parameter, so we are required to replicate a role for every permission.

Next, we can create actionIndex(), which launches the previous initialize authorizations, getting all the users and populating an array with all the permissions assigned to every user. This is the content of the actionIndex() method:

```
public function actionIndex()
{
    $auth = Yii::$app->authManager;

    // Initialize authorizations
    $this->initializeAuthorizations();
```

```php
    // Get all users
    $users = User::find()->all();

    // Initialize data
    $rolesAvailable = $auth->getRoles();
    $rolesNamesByUser = [];

    // For each user, fill $rolesNames with name of roles
    assigned to user
    foreach($users as $user)
    {
        $rolesNames = [];

        $roles = $auth->getRolesByUser($user->id);
        foreach($roles as $r)
        {
            $rolesNames[] = $r->name;
        }

        $rolesNamesByUser[$user->id] = $rolesNames;
    }

    return $this->render('index', ['users' => $users,
    'rolesAvailable' => $rolesAvailable, 'rolesNamesByUser' =>
    $rolesNamesByUser]);
}
```

Follow the content of the index action view in basic/views/authorization-manager/index.php:

```php
<?php
use yii\helpers\Html;
?>

<table class="table">
    <tr>
        <td>User</td>
        <?php foreach($rolesAvailable as $r) { ?>
            <td><?php echo $r->description ?></td>
        <?php } ?>
    </tr>

    <?php foreach($users as $u) { ?>
        <tr>
```

```php
        <td><?php echo $u->username ?></td>

        <?php foreach($rolesAvailable as $r) { ?>
            <td align="center">
            <?php if(in_array($r->name, $rolesNamesByUser[$u-
            >id])) { ?>
                <?php echo Html::a('Yes', ['remove-role',
                'userId' => $u->id, 'roleName' => $r->name]); ?>
            <?php } else { ?>
                <?php echo Html::a('No', ['add-role', 'userId'
                => $u->id, 'roleName' => $r->name]); ?>
            <?php } ?>
            </td>
        <?php } ?>
    </tr>
    <?php } ?>

</table>
```

This loops for each user's content of the `$rolesAvailable` array. To see this output, point your browser to `http://hostname/basic/web/authorization-manager/index`:

User	Create a reservation	Update reservation	Delete reservation	Create a room	Update room	Delete room	Create a customer	Update customer	Delete customer	operator	admin
foo	No	No	No	No	No	No	No	No	No	No	No
userA	Yes	Yes	No	No	No	Yes	No	No	No	No	Yes
userB	No	No	No	No	No	No	Yes	No	No	No	No
userC	No	Yes	No	No	No	No	No	No	No	No	No
admin	No	Yes	No	Yes	No	No	No	No	No	No	No

Users/Permissions table

Every permission status is a link to the actions of adding a role or removing a role (depending on the current status).

Now we must create the last two actions: add a role and revoke a role to the user:

```php
    public function actionAddRole($userId, $roleName)
    {
        $auth = Yii::$app->authManager;

        $auth->assign($auth->getRole($roleName), $userId);
```

```
        return $this->redirect(['index']);
    }

    public function actionRemoveRole($userId, $roleName)
    {
        $auth = Yii::$app->authManager;

        $auth->revoke($auth->getRole($roleName), $userId);

        return $this->redirect(['index']);
    }
```

Mixing ACF and RBAC

ACF contains a property named `role` that is usually filled with `?` to indicate that access is available for all users, and `@` to indicate that access is restricted to authenticated ones. But there is a third option that refers its content to the role name of the RBAC system.

For each controller, therefore, it is enough to overwrite `behaviors()` by specifying the roles that can access the actions inside the controller and then to associate users to the role, in order to allow or deny access.

Example – managing users' roles to access rooms, reservations, and customers

In this example, we will show you how to manage the access to the controller actions using ACF and RBAC.

We will use the `foo` user to simulate an authenticated user for `RoomsController`. The first thing to do is to extend the `behaviors()` method of `RoomsController` in `basic/controller/RoomsController.php` with this content:

```
Use yii\filters\AccessControl;

    public function behaviors()
    {
        return [
            'access' => [
                'class' => AccessControl::className(),
                'rules' => [
```

```
                    [
                        'allow' => true,
                        'actions' => ['create'],
                        'roles' => ['operator'],
                    ],
                    [
                        'allow' => true,
                        'actions' => ['index'],
                    ],
                ],
            ],
        ];
    }
```

With this code, we will guarantee access to the `create` action only to users with the `operator` role, while the `index` action access is given to all users and all other actions are denied to everyone.

So, if we try to browse to `http://hostname/basic/web/rooms/create`, we should see an error page with a forbidden error. This is because we are trying to access a page with insufficient permissions.

Now, we can execute the authentication simply by going to `http://hostname/basic/web/my-authentication/login` and typing `foo` as the username and `foopassword` as the password, since we already created a user with these credentials in the database in the previous chapter. We should see a successfully logged in page.

The last thing to do is to assign the `operator` role to the `foo` user. We can use the authorization manager just created in `http://hostname/basic/web/authorization-manager/index`. Now, click on the cell referring to the `foo` user and the `operator` role. In this way, we have assigned the `operator` role to the `foo` user.

Finally, we can refresh the rooms creation page at `http://hostname/basic/web/rooms/create`. We can see now the create action page of the rooms controller.

Summary

In this chapter, you learned how to apply user authentication and authorization to an app. The first step was to create an authenticated access to the application. For this purpose, we created a database table to manage users and associated it to the Yii user component through a user model that extends `IdentityInterface`.

The first example in this chapter was building a login form to authenticate the user. The next step was to control which actions a user can perform or not, and this was the case for the authorization phase too. As you saw, Yii provides two solutions for this matter: ACF and RBAC. We configured a controller to use ACF and then you saw how RBAC is a more powerful tool to manage user authorization with more granularity. Finally, we built an authorization manager all by ourselves.

In the next chapter, we will cover topics such as installing and using an advanced template and having multiple apps in the same context.

Frontend to Display Rooms to Everyone

9

This chapter will cover topics about using templates to have multiple apps in the same context.

Yii, indeed, allows you to have an advanced installation able to contain multiple instances of an Yii application. Therefore, every folder in the project is actually a new Yii application.

We will see how to install and configure the project, share data between them, and finally customize the URL to make them pretty for the search engine.

We will cover the following topics in this chapter:

- Using an advanced template to split frontend and backend
- Configuring an application using init
    - Example – creating frontend for public access
- Sharing ActiveRecord models among applications
    - Example – displaying available rooms in frontend site
- Customizing a URL in an advanced template
    - Example – using advanced templates in the same domain
- How to use advanced templates in shared hosting

Using an advanced template to split frontend and backend

Until now, we have seen simple applications with only one single entry point to access. However, a single entry point isn't enough for more general applications. In advanced web applications, in fact, we have not just a single entry point but often three: frontend, backend, and a common area used as shared zone for every entry point.

The frontend entry point is a public access that is available to all users without restrictions.

On the other hand, the backend entry point is a restricted access available only for authenticated users that have administration roles for managing content in the web application.

Finally, the common entry point is used to share data between entry points.

Think about a reservation system, where frontend is the website displaying room availability and prices, while backend is the administration area, where operators can manage rooms.

In the same way, another example of frontend and backend could be a newspaper website that comprises a frontend area with news publically visible to all users, and a backend area where journalists can insert news.

Now that we know the differences between frontend and backend and their aim, we will create an advanced Yii application.

The steps to install an advanced template of the Yii application are similar to the ones to install basic templates.

 It is highly recommended, at this point, to have a console access the host, where we can put files.

Locate the web hosting document root folder in the web hosting. Starting from it, we will launch commands to create the advanced application in a new subfolder named yiiadv, which stands for Yii installation with the advanced template.

We will install the Yii advanced template using Composer as it is the most recommended way. If we have not installed Composer as the global application yet, we can install it now in the yiiadv folder.

The following are the instructions to install Yii advanced template starting from document root folder:

```
$ curl -sS https://getcomposer.org/installer | php
$ php composer.phar global require "fxp/composer-asset-plugin:~1.0.0"
$ php composer.phar create-project --prefer-dist yiisoft/yii2-app-advanced yiiadv
```

By opening the `yiiadv` subfolder, we can see some new folders beside the basic template, which are as follows:

- `backend`: This folder is the entry point for the backend application of the project

- `common`: This folder is the entry point for the application containing common data for the other applications in the project

- `console`: This folder is the entry point for the console application of the project

- `frontend`: This folder is the entry point for the frontend application of the project

This structure is the result of the experience on developing the web application. Backend and frontend entry points have been formerly discussed; the common entry point is an area where to put data (common models, components, and so on) shared among all the other applications in the project.

> Every application in the project (backend, frontend, common, and console) is considered as a single namespace in the web application. So, when we refer to `RoomsController` in the frontend, the complete class namespace will be `frontend/controllers/RoomsController`.

This installation is still raw and requires an initialization using the `init` command. However, if we try to open any of these applications, we can recognize the same basic template structure with `assets`, `config`, `controllers`, `models`, `runtime`, `views`, and `web` subfolders. So, a basic template application can be considered the only unique application in an advanced template one.

Finally, in the advanced template properties, every application starting point is always in `web/index.php`. For example, for the frontend application, the starting point is `frontend/web/index.php`.

Configuring an application using init

Apart from having multiple kinds of configuration, we can have multiple entry points in advanced applications.

In advanced web applications, in fact, we also have a different approach in the development stage. We usually have two environments: development and production. In the first one, we make tests using fake users, data, and so on, while in the second one we must take care to guarantee the proper functioning of the project.

Therefore, we will have different sets of configuration files and parameters based on environments where we will work in.

We could wish, in fact, to test the application using the development database instead of the production database, or specific parameters available only in a specific environment.

Indeed, the `init` command offers this capability to switch different configuration and parameters for different environments. Basically, there are two environments: development and production.

 A first initialization is needed to make sure that the project could work.

The `init` command can be launched both in interactive mode as well as in noninteractive (silent) one.

In the interactive mode, starting from the `yiiadv` folder:

```
$ php init
```

And in a noninteractive (silent) mode:

```
$ php init --env=Development --overwrite=All
```

In both modalities, we need to specify only the target environment if we want to overwrite all the current configuration files.

This command will simply copy the content of the chosen environment (according to the type of selected environment) in the respective application folder, with the same name starting from root.

For example, open the folder in `environments/dev/backend`. We will see two folders: `config` and `web`, containing the first two configuration files and the other files `index.php` and `index-test.php`. These files will overwrite the corresponding files in the `backend` folder starting from the root folder of the project.

So, if we launch the preceding command with parameters of init, the content of the folders in environments/dev (the backend, common, console, and frontend folders) will be copied in the backend, common, console, and frontend folders starting from the root folder of the project.

Also, with this command, other operations such as making some folders writable or applying specific values to configuration properties, are accomplished. However, the init command is mainly used to switch different configurations and index.php files.

Starting from any application of the project (backend, frontend, common, and console), configuration values and parameters taken from the top of any application's index. php file (backend, frontend, common, or console) are read in the following sequence:

- common/config/main.php
- common/config/main-local.php
- config/main.php
- config/main-local.php

This means that the config parameters are initially read firstly from common/config/main.php then from common/config/main-local.php, then again from application config/main.php, and finally from application config/main-local.php. The properties with same name will be overwritten during the reading of other configuration files.

Therefore, if the same configuration property is declared in all four configuration files, its value will be the same as config/main-local.php, which is the last configuration file to be read.

Since, we locally have a last chance to apply differences towards a specific property of configuration with the -local version of files, the content of environment subfolders will be only about the -local version of a specific file. For example, if we open environments/dev/backend/config path, we will see only main-local.php and params-local.php, practically the last two filenames that index.php will read in sequence.

So if we change the database connection parameters in environments/dev/backend/config/main-local.php and then apply init with the dev target environment, this file will overwrite backend/config/main-local.php. This is the last configuration file that backend/web/index.php will read during its bootstrap (if we browse /backend/web/index.php).

Now that we have executed the `init` command in the `dev` environment, we can point the browser to `http://hostname/yiiadv/frontend/web` and we should see the same congratulations page of the basic template.

In the same way, the backend entry point is also available pointing to `http://hostname/yiiadv/backend/web`, where a login form is displayed by default (this is because it is a restricted area).

 If we want to add a new application in the project, it is enough to copy the content of frontend or backend folder to another new folder in the project.

Example – creating frontend for public access

As we have seen, the frontend application is a reachable pointing browser to `http://hostname/yiiadv/frontend/web`.

However, the first thing to set in the frontend access is URL-friendly customization; this is because it is important that our public website is well positioned in the search engine.

As we have done in the basic template, we can render pretty URLs in the advanced template too, following these two steps:

1. Create the `.htaccess` file in `yiiadv/frontend/web`.
2. Add the `urlManager` component in `yiiadv/frontend/config/main.php`.

In step 1, it is enough to create a file in `yiiadv/frontend/web/.htaccess` with the following content:

```
RewriteEngine on

# If a directory or a file exists, use it directly
RewriteCond %{REQUEST_FILENAME} !-f
RewriteCond %{REQUEST_FILENAME} !-d
# Otherwise forward it to index.php
RewriteRule . index.php
```

This code will make the web server URL rewrite work, rewriting all requests to the `index.php` file in `yiiadv/frontend/web`.

While, in step 2, we must add the `urlManager` property in `yiiadv/frontend/config/main.php`:

```
'urlManager' => [
    'enablePrettyUrl' => true,
    'showScriptName' => false,
],
```

Now we can refresh the web browser to `http://hostname/yiiadv/frontend/web` and navigation to the URL link on the top, and we can see, for instance, that URL is in pretty form.

We can consider the `frontend` folder as a Yii standalone application and we can create controllers, views, models, and so on.

Sharing ActiveRecord models among applications

Although every folder in the main Yii project could be considered a Yii standalone application, with its own controllers, models, views, and so on, it is conventionally accepted that all shared data are located in the `common` folder.

So every shared model (such as `User`, `Room`, `Reservation`, and `Customer`) that could be used in other Yii applications, should be inserted in `common/models`, under the `common\models` namespace.

From my point of view, when an application needs to use an ActiveRecord from `common/models`, I rather prefer to point to an extended version in its namespace, so as to have a chance again to add custom methods or properties to model for that application.

For example, consider we have the `Room` model in `common/models`:

```php
<?php
namespace common\models;
class Room extends ActiveRecord
{
....
....
}
```

In the backend application, we will create an empty extension to the Room class from common namespace:

```php
<?php
namespace backend\models;
class Room extends \common\models\Room
{
}
```

In this way, we have the possibility to add custom methods or properties to that specific application (namespace), if needed.

Therefore, every controller, view, or model in backend namespace will point to \backend\models\Room, when it needs to refer to the Room ActiveRecord.

Example – displaying available rooms in the frontend site

This example will emphasize the few differences between basic and advanced applications occurring in the developing phase.

The first thing to do is to check whether the database configuration is right, since we have just initialized an advanced application.

 The database configuration on the production server can be found in common/config/main.php, whereas the database configuration on the developing server is located in common/config/main-local.php, which overwrites the configuration in common/config/main.php.

Open common/config/main.php and add the db property to the configuration array:

```php
'db' => [
    'class' => 'yii\db\Connection',
    'dsn' => 'mysql:host=localhost;dbname=yii_db',
    'username' => 'my_username',
    'password' => 'my_password',
    'charset' => 'utf8',
],
```

Change the database properties (host, username, and password) according to our configuration parameters.

Remember to comment out the database configuration in `common/config/main-local.php` to avoid overwriting configurations.

In this way, we will have complete access to the database and tables previously created, and to rooms' data, indeed.

Now, we are ready to create:

1. The Room model.
2. The Rooms controller.
3. View of index action of the Rooms controller.

The first step requires the use of Gii. By default, Gii is enabled with basic configuration in the frontend application (only from localhost).

We will overwrite this configuration so as to use Gii from everywhere. Therefore, in the frontend local configuration (`frontend/config/main-local.php`), which has the following lines:

```
$config['bootstrap'][] = 'gii';
$config['modules']['gii'] = 'yii\gii\Module';
```

Replace them with these ones:

```
$config['bootstrap'][] = 'gii';
$config['modules']['gii'] = [
        'class' => 'yii\gii\Module',
        'allowedIPs' => ['*']
];
```

Now, we can finally access Gii from everywhere. Using the browser, go to `http://hostname/yiiadv/frontend/web/gii`; a welcome page should be displayed.

Go to **Model Generator** and fill the first field, Table Name, with room, the name of model we are creating, just as we have done in the previous chapters.

Since, we are working with the advanced template, model files (like other objects created by Gii) will be created in the frontend namespace, or rather in `frontend/models`.

Therefore, it is necessary to change the first field of **Model Generator**, **Namespace**, so as to switch from `app/models` to `common/models`, the shared area of common data:

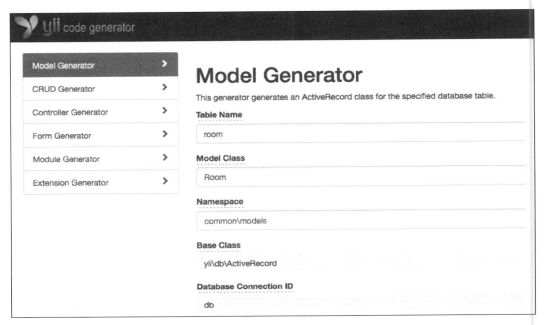

Gii model generator in advanced template

In `common/models`, there should be a `Room.php` file containing the model of the `Room` table.

The second step it is to create the controller and the action of the controller to display the rooms list.

Let's create the controller under `frontend/controllers/RoomsController.php` with the following content:

```php
<?php
namespace frontend\controllers;

use Yii;
use yii\web\Controller;
use yii\data\ActiveDataProvider;
use common\models\Room;
```

```
class RoomsController extends Controller
{
    public function actionIndex()
    {
        $dataProvider = new ActiveDataProvider([
            'query' => Room::find(),
            'pagination' => [
                'pageSize' => 20,
            ],
        ]);

        return $this->render('index', [
            'dataProvider' => $dataProvider,
        ]);
    }
}
```

Make sure that the namespace declaration on top is `frontend\controllers`, since every application in the web project has its own namespace (in this case, `frontend`).

 We should never directly subclass `yii\web\Controller`, instead we should create a custom controller for each application, for example, `frontend\controllers\BaseController`, and then subclass it from every controller that we will create in `frontend\controllers`.

Finally, the third step is to create view content of index action in `frontend/views/rooms/index.php`:

```
<div class="row">
<?php foreach ($dataProvider->getModels() as $model) { ?>
    <div class="col-md-3" style="border:1px solid gray; margin-
    right:10px; padding:20px;">
        <h2>Room #<?= $model->id ?></h2>
        Floor: <?= $model->floor ?>
        <br />
        Number: <?= $model->room_number; ?>
    </div>
<?php } ?>
</div>
```

This will produce the following output with the data available in the database:

Rooms availability in the frontend

Customizing a URL in the advanced template

When working with multiple applications in the same project, you might require access from an application to another, for example, from the backend to a frontend link. This is because we want to display public page rendering in the frontend after inserting data in the backend.

The `urlManager` property is customized with references about the application where it is defined. However, we can add specific properties to refer to the respective application.

Therefore, in `common/config/main.php`, we can add these two properties:

```
'urlManagerFrontend' => [
    'class' => 'yii\web\urlManager',
    'baseUrl' => '/yiiadv/frontend/web',
    'enablePrettyUrl' => true,
    'showScriptName' => false,
],

'urlManagerBackend' => [
    'class' => 'yii\web\urlManager',
    'baseUrl' => '/yiiadv/backend/web',
    'enablePrettyUrl' => true,
    'showScriptName' => false,
],
```

For example, we can get a URL to frontend from everywhere. It is enough to write this code `echo Yii::$app->urlManagerFrontend->createUrl(...)` to create a URL from frontend.

 It is necessary to put the `.htaccess` file in the web folder of each application that has the `enablePrettyUrl` property in the `urlManager` configuration.

Yii also provides convenient aliases to application paths, other than the default aliases of the basic template:

- `@common`: This is the common directory
- `@frontend`: This is the frontend web application directory
- `@backend`: This is the backend web application directory
- `@console`: This is the console directory

Example – using the advanced template in the same domain

We have seen that the advanced template creates more applications in the same web application than we can reach using `/frontend` or `/backend` or any other application name prefix in the URL. However, it is not advisable, especially for frontend, that all URLs contain a `/frontend` prefix.

We want to have this URL format for frontend: `http://hostname/yiiadv/`; and this one for backend: `http://hostname/yiiadv/admin` (we can choose the name we want).

All requests have to be managed on the `/yiiadv` folder level. So, we will add an `.htaccess` file in the `/yiiadv` folder that it will dispatch to the correct route.

Here is a list of the actions that must be performed:

1. Configure `.htaccess` in `/yiiadv` to handle all requests.
2. Configure the backend application to customize its `baseUrl`.
3. Configure the frontend application to customize its `baseUrl`.

It is obvious that steps 2 and 3 must be repeated for any other application, for which we want to manipulate the base URL.

For step 1, let's put the .htaccess file with the following content in the /yiiadv folder:

```
RewriteEngine on
# For Backend
RewriteCond %{REQUEST_FILENAME} !-f
RewriteCond %{REQUEST_FILENAME} !-d
RewriteCond %{REQUEST_URI} ^/yiiadv/admin
RewriteRule ^admin(/.+)?$ /yiiadv/backend/web/$1 [L,PT]
# For Frontend
RewriteCond %{REQUEST_URI} !index.php
RewriteCond %{REQUEST_FILENAME} !-f
RewriteRule ^(.*)$ /yiiadv/frontend/web/$1
```

Therefore, in the Backend block of .htaccess, we catch requests in /yiiadv/admin and redirect them to the yiiadv/backend/web/ base URL.

For step 2, the backend requests capture is completed when we also make these changes in backend configuration, adding the request property in backend/config/main.php:

```
'request' => [
    // !!! insert a secret key in the following (if it is
    empty) - this is required by cookie validation
    'cookieValidationKey' => '20ofX7Q9e-
    EQLSK5BEk70_07fUXkka8y',
    'baseUrl' => '/yiiadv/admin',
],
```

Now, point the browser to http://hostname/yiiadv/admin and if we did everything correctly we should finally be able to see the login page.

 Make sure there is a request attribute in the configuration array in backend/config/main-local.php; we need to comment this otherwise it will overwrite request in the backend/config/main.php file that we have just changed.

Finally, just like we have done with backend requests, in step 3, we need to change the request property for frontend requests under frontend/config/main.php in the configuration:

```
'request' => [
    // !!! insert a secret key in the following (if it is
    empty) - this is required by cookie validation
```

```
        'cookieValidationKey' =>
        'ear8GcRjBGXQgKVwfEpbApyj7Fb0UKXk',
        'baseUrl' => '/yiiadv',
    ],
```

Now, point the browser to `http://hostname/yiiadv` and if we did everything correctly, we should see the congratulation page of the frontend.

As the last part of this example, if we want to reach the frontend to the `http://hostname` URL and backend to the `http://hostname/admin` URL, we must put an `.htaccess` file in the document root folder with this content:

```
RewriteEngine on
# For Backend
RewriteCond %{REQUEST_FILENAME} !-f
RewriteCond %{REQUEST_FILENAME} !-d
RewriteCond %{REQUEST_URI} ^/admin
RewriteRule ^admin(/.+)?$ /yiiadv/backend/web/$1 [L,PT]
# For Frontend
RewriteCond %{REQUEST_URI} !index.php
RewriteCond %{REQUEST_FILENAME} !-f
RewriteRule ^(.*)$ /yiiadv/frontend/web/$1
```

Then, we must change the `request` property of the frontend configuration in `frontend/config/main.php` with:

```
'request' => [
    // !!! insert a secret key in the following (if it is
    empty) - this is required by cookie validation
    'cookieValidationKey' =>
    'ear8GcRjBGXQgKVwfEpbApyj7Fb0UKXk',
    'baseUrl' => '',
],
```

Finally, change the `request` property of the backend configuration in `backend/config/main.php` with:

```
'request' => [
    // !!! insert a secret key in the following (if it is
    empty) - this is required by cookie validation
    'cookieValidationKey' => '2OofX7Q9e-
    EQLSK5BEk70_07fUXkka8y',
    'baseUrl' => '/admin',
],
```

In this way, the frontend is now reachable pointing the browser to `http://hostname` and the backend to `http://hostname/admin`.

How to use the advanced template in the shared hosting

In my opinion, almost all applications should use the advanced template, since it provides the right project structure from the very start, so as to immediately handle frontend and backend occurring in every web project.

However, we have also seen that the advanced template requires a console access to execute installation and initialization commands. So, if we have a remote hosting without this capability, it could be difficult for us to install and use Yii with the advanced template.

If we cannot add the console capability to remote hosting, we have two possibilities:

- Create the project in the local environment where we can install what we want and need; it is enough to locally install a WAMP or a LAMP distribution (based on the operating system of the hosting machine) and then launch the composer command to install Yii
- Launch the `init` command to initialize the project (it could be initialized from start in production mode so that no other changes are needed)

Therefore, the project is ready to be uploaded to remote hosting. Remember that project environment is in production mode, but in this way, we do not have to change the configuration manually if we want to pass from development to production mode.

Summary

In this chapter, we saw how to use Yii to build a modern web project based on frontend and backend applications. We have found out differences between basic and advanced templates, installing our first advanced project based on advanced templates.

Then we have used the `init` command to customize development or production environment in which to make the application run. Then we have written an example to display in the frontend rooms list, similar to what we have done in the previous basic template.

Finally, we customized URLs to make them pretty also in the advanced template, to refer to frontend and backend without URL application prefix. We also learned how to use advanced templates in shared hosting that does not have access to the console.

In the next chapter, we will explain how to write a multilingual app, adapt, and render the app in different languages without changes to the source code.

10
Localize the App

This chapter explains how to write a multilingual app. Localization, also known as Internationalization (I18N), takes care that a software application can be adapted and rendered in different languages without changes in the source code. This is particularly important in a web application where users speak different languages.

Yii provides powerful tools to handle this task, choosing from the file or database approach (according to the application's complexity). We will cover the following topics:

- Setting the default language
- File-based translations
  - Example – using file-based translation for the entire website
- Placeholders formatting
- DB-based translations
  - Example – translating the room's description using DB

Setting the default language

A Yii application uses two kinds of languages: source language and target language.

Source language specifies the language employed to write the source code; the default setting is en-US, and it is advisable not to change this value since English is the most used and known language in software development. On the other hand, there is a target language used to display content to end users, and we are going to work specifically on this aspect.

This language can be set in the configuration file using the `language` property:

```
return [
    // set target language to be Italian
    'language' => 'it-IT',

        . . . .
        . . . .
  •  ];
```

Alternatively, you can use the following code:

```
// change target language to Italian
\Yii::$app->language = 'it-IT';
```

Now, let's see how to handle app localization in practice.

File-based translations

This is the most simple way to translate text messages from one language to another. Basically, there are one or more files for each language containing keywords with text representations; we will put these keywords in the source code where the framework will replace them with text.

The pairs of keyword-text translations are grouped by categories representing the filenames where they are stored. These pairs are array keys-values, where key indicates keywords, and value indicates text translations.

By default, the path folder containing translations for a specific language is in `@app/messages/<language>/<category>.php`. Therefore, if we are writing translations for the `app` category and the `en-US` language, for example, the complete path for the translation file will be in `@app/messages/en-US/app.php`.

Going to the source code, translations are activated using the `Yii::t()` static method that accepts four parameters, but only the first two are required; the first one is the category, and the second one is the message to translate.

Now, we want to make an example where we will write a classic `Hello World!` in two languages: English and Italian. However, it will be just as easy to translate it in any other language.

Working on the previous basic templated project, write a new controller named `FileTranslatorController` in `basic/controllers/FileTranslatorController.php` with the following content:

```php
<?php

namespace app\controllers;

use Yii;
use yii\web\Controller;

class FileTranslatorController extends Controller
{
    public function actionIndex()
    {
        \Yii::$app->language = 'en-US';
        $englishText = \Yii::t('app', 'Hello World!');

        \Yii::$app->language = 'it-IT';
        $italianText = \Yii::t('app', 'Hello World!');

        return $this->render('index', ['englishText' =>
        $englishText, 'italianText' => $italianText]);
    }
}
```

The first two source code rows in `actionIndex()` will set the app language to `en-US`, and then they will store the content of `Hello World!` key of the `basic/messages/en-US/app.php` file in the `$englishText` variable.

In the same way, the last two source code rows in `actionIndex()` will set the app language to `it-IT`, and then they will store the content of `Hello World!` key of the `basic/messages/it-IT/app.php` file in the `$italianText` variable.

The view content in `basic/views/file-translator/index.php` is simply as follows:

```
<b>Display Hello World! in two language: English and Italian</b>

<br /><br />

In English:
```

```
<?= $englishText ?>

<br /><br />
In Italian:
<?= $italianText ?>
```

Now, we need to define file languages for English and Italian translations.

If the `messages` folder does not exist in `basic/messages`, we will just create it; then, create two new folders named `en-US` and `it-IT`. In each folder, add a new file named `app.php`.

For the file with the English translations in `basic/messages/en-US/app.php`, let's write:

```php
<?php

return [
    'Hello World!' => 'Hello world!',
];

?>
```

While for Italian translations in `basic/messages/it-IT/app.php`, let's write:

```php
<?php

return [
    'Hello World!' => 'Ciao Mondo!',
];

?>
```

You can browse to `http://hostname/basic/file-translator/index` to view the output.

Example – using file-based translation for the entire website

Applying translations to the entire website is tedious, and, above all, there is a high possibility that you will miss some translations. Yii provides a powerful tool to automatically produce the message's PHP files for all the languages we want.

This powerful tool is a console command named `message`; therefore, we require a console access.

This command requires two steps:

1. Creating a configuration file where we will indicate the `languages` property, or which languages we want to support in the project and the `messagePath` property, or rather, where to store translated messages.

2. Launching the `message` command.

For step 1, go to the console, in the project's root folder, where the `yii` file is located.

If we are working on a basic template, we will launch the following command:

```
$ ./yii message/config config/i18n.php
```

The first parameter, `message/config`, is the action `config` invoked on the controller `message`, and the second parameter is the file path where we want to save the configuration (in this case, `config/i18n.php`, but we can write anything).

If we are working on an advanced template, we will launch the following command:

```
./yii message/config common/config/i18n.php
```

The only difference is that, in the last command, we specified that the configuration file for message command translations is in `common/config` instead of the `config` folder.

Now, if we open `config/i18n.php`, we should see the default configuration file for the `message` command that should look like this:

```php
<?php

return [
    // string, required, root directory of all source files
    'sourcePath' => __DIR__ . DIRECTORY_SEPARATOR . '..',
    // array, required, list of language codes that the extracted
    messages
    // should be translated to. For example, ['zh-CN', 'de'].
    'languages' => ['de'],
    // string, the name of the function for translating messages.
    // Defaults to 'Yii::t'. This is used as a mark to find the
    messages to be
    // translated. You may use a string for single function name
    or an array for
```

```
// multiple function names.
'translator' => 'Yii::t',
// boolean, whether to sort messages by keys when merging new
messages
// with the existing ones. Defaults to false, which means the
new (untranslated)
// messages will be separated from the old (translated) ones.
'sort' => false,
// boolean, whether to remove messages that no longer appear
in the source code.
// Defaults to false, which means each of these messages will
be enclosed with a pair of '@@' marks.
'removeUnused' => false,
// array, list of patterns that specify which
files/directories should NOT be processed.
// If empty or not set, all files/directories will be
processed.
// A path matches a pattern if it contains the pattern string
at its end. For example,
// '/a/b' will match all files and directories ending with
'/a/b';
// the '*.svn' will match all files and directories whose name
ends with '.svn'.
// and the '.svn' will match all files and directories named
exactly '.svn'.
// Note, the '/' characters in a pattern matches both '/' and
'\'.
// See helpers/FileHelper::findFiles() description for more
details on pattern matching rules.
'only' => ['*.php'],
// array, list of patterns that specify which files (not
directories) should be processed.
// If empty or not set, all files will be processed.
// Please refer to "except" for details about the patterns.
// If a file/directory matches both a pattern in "only" and
"except", it will NOT be processed.
'except' => [
    '.svn',
    '.git',
    '.gitignore',
    '.gitkeep',
    '.hgignore',
    '.hgkeep',
    '/messages',
```

```
    ],

    // 'php' output format is for saving messages to php files.
    'format' => 'php',
    // Root directory containing message translations.
    'messagePath' => __DIR__,
    // boolean, whether the message file should be overwritten
    with the merged messages
    'overwrite' => true,


    /*
    // 'db' output format is for saving messages to database.
    'format' => 'db',
    // Connection component to use. Optional.
    'db' => 'db',
    // Custom source message table. Optional.
    // 'sourceMessageTable' => '{{%source_message}}',
    // Custom name for translation message table. Optional.
    // 'messageTable' => '{{%message}}',
    */


    /*
    // 'po' output format is for saving messages to gettext po
    files.
    'format' => 'po',
    // Root directory containing message translations.
    'messagePath' => __DIR__ . DIRECTORY_SEPARATOR . 'messages',
    // Name of the file that will be used for translations.
    'catalog' => 'messages',
    // boolean, whether the message file should be overwritten
    with the merged messages
    'overwrite' => true,
    */
];
```

The configuration is very clear to read, so we will only explain its main properties: languages, messagePath, and except.

The languages property defines which languages are supported in the web project. For example, we could write:

```
'languages' => ['en', 'it', 'fr'],
```

The preceding command supports and autogenerates messages for the English, Italian, and French languages.

The `messagePath` property defines where autogenerated messages should be saved. It is advisable to point to the `messages` folder (that must be created if it does not exist); in this way, we can write the following in the basic template:

```
'messagePath' => __DIR__ . DIRECTORY_SEPARATOR . '..' .
DIRECTORY_SEPARATOR . 'messages',
```

Here, `__DIR__` refers to the `config` file folder, while in the basic template, it is the `basic/config` folder.

Once we have launched the `message` command, it will look for all folders and subfolders containing `.php` files, as indicated in the `only` property (only `.php` files will be processed).

Therefore, in the project's root folder, there are some folders, such as `vendor`, not relevant for our purpose.

So, we will add the `/vendor` value to the `except` property, in order to indicate that the `message` command will not look inside this folder, in this way:

```
'except' => [
    '.svn',
    '.git',
    '.gitignore',
    '.gitkeep',
    '.hgignore',
    '.hgkeep',
    '/messages',
    '/vendor'
],
```

For step 2, we will now try to launch the command:

```
$ ./yii message config/i18n.php
```

It will find the `Yii::t` marker, defined in the `translator` property, in all the files in the folders and subfolders specified in the `sourcePath` property, considering the `except` property to exclude files and folders where we do not want to look.

The translated messages will be created (if they do not exist) in the `messagePath` folder, in our case, in the `messages` folder starting from the project's root folder.

If there are no `Yii::t` markers in all the searched files, the relative language's subfolder will be empty.

For example, open `SiteController` in `basic/controller/SiteController.php` and change the `actionIndex` content as follows:

```
public function actionIndex()
{
    $message = \Yii::t('app', 'this message must be translated!');

    return $this->render('index');
}
```

Now, relaunch the `message` command:

$ ./yii message config/i18n.php

Then, check the `basic/messages/en` folder. We will find an `app.php` file that contains the `this message must be translated` key to which we must fill the value to specify the translation.

Placeholders formatting

The `Yii:t` method is not only limited to replace strings with their translation in other languages, but it handles the specific formatting of source strings to support many kinds of generalization.

Firstly, `Yii:t()` supports placeholders in the following two formats:

- String in the {nameOfPlaceholder} format
- Integer in the {0} format, and this type of placeholder is zero-based

Value arrays to replace the placeholder are passed as the third parameter to the `Yii:t()` method.

For example, we want to display a page with only `Hello World, I'm ...` by appending the custom name to the text.

Create `basic/controllers/FileTranslatorController.php`:

```
public function actionHelloWorldWithName($name='')
{
    $text = \Yii::t('app', 'Hello World! I\'m {name}', ['name'
    => $name]);

    return $this->render('helloWorldWithName', ['text' =>
    $text]);
}
```

Now, create the view in `basic/views/file-translator/helloWorldWithName.php` simply with the following command:

```
<?= $text ?>
```

It will display the `$text` value passed from the controller.

Test it by pointing the browser to `http://hostname/basic/web/file-translator/hello-world-with-name`, also passing the `?name=` parameter, otherwise there will be no name at the end of the text.

Translations can be prepared using the `message` command that we have just seen:

```
$ ./yii message config/i18n.php
```

This will automatically create a new marker `Hello World! I\'m {name}` in the `basic/messages` subfolders.

The placeholders can be specialized with two other attributes: `ParameterType` and `ParameterStyle`, adding a comma after `PlaceholderName`. So, the full form to specify a placeholder will be as follows:

```
{PlaceholderName, ParameterType, ParameterStyle}
```

Here, `ParameterType` can be:

- `number` : The ParameterStyle can be an integer, currency, percent, or custom pattern (for example, 000)
- `date`: The ParameterStyle can be short, medium, long, full, or custom pattern (for example, dd/mm/yyyy)
- `time`: The ParameterStyle can be short, medium, long, full or custom pattern (for example, hh:mm)
- `spellout`: There is no ParameterStyle
- `ordinal`: There is no ParameterStyle
- `duration`: There is no ParameterStyle

The most used message formatting is probably `plural`, and that allows us to specify different key strings based on the number passed as a parameter.

Consider the following code as an example:

```
// if $n = 0, it shows "There are no books!"
// if $n = 1, it shows "There is one book!"
```

```
// if $n = 4, it shows "There are 4 books!"
```

```
echo \Yii::t('app', 'There {n, plural, =0{are no books} =1{is one
book} other{are # books}}!', ['n' => $n]);
```

Here, =0 stands for the message to be displayed when $n is 0, =1 stands for the message to be displayed when $n is 1, and other stands for the message to be displayed when $n is other than 0 and 1.

DB-based translations

Yii also supports database as a storage option for message translations.

It has to be explicitly configured in the config/web.php file if we are working in the basic template, or in common/config/main.php, if we are working in the advanced template.

Next, we need to add two more database tables to manage message sources and message translations.

Start by creating database tables, as suggested in Yii's official documentation at http://www.yiiframework.com/doc-2.0/yii-i18n-dbmessagesource.html:

```
CREATE TABLE source_message (
    id INTEGER PRIMARY KEY AUTO_INCREMENT,
    category VARCHAR(32),
    message TEXT
);
```

```
CREATE TABLE message (
    id INTEGER,
    language VARCHAR(16),
    translation TEXT,
    PRIMARY KEY (id, language),
    CONSTRAINT fk_message_source_message FOREIGN KEY (id)
        REFERENCES source_message (id) ON DELETE CASCADE ON UPDATE
RESTRICT
);
```

 Table names can be customized in the configuration file.

Table `source_message` will store all messages written with the source language; table `message` will store all translations; both tables are joined together by the `id` field.

In the next example, let's insert one record for each table:

```
INSERT INTO `source_message` (`id`, `category`, `message`) VALUES
(1, 'app', 'Hello World from Database!');

INSERT INTO `message` (`id`, `language`, `translation`) VALUES
(1, 'it', 'Ciao Mondo dal Database!');
```

Now, it is time to apply some changes to the configuration. We need to insert the `i18n` property in the `components` section of the configuration in `config/web.php` (based on the basic template):

```
'components' => [
    // ...
    'i18n' => [
        'translations' => [
            'app' => [
                'class' => 'yii\i18n\DbMessageSource',
                //'messageTable' => 'message,
                //'sourceMessageTable' => 'source_message,

            ],
        ],
    ],
],
```

This component, i18n, uses `yii\i18n\PhpMessageSource` as a class by default, and has employed itself for file-based translation.

Now, we want to display the message in Italian. Create a new action in `basic/controllers/FileTranslatorController.php` named `actionHelloWorldFromDatabase()`, with the following content:

```
public function actionHelloWorldFromDatabase()
{
    \Yii::$app->language = 'it';
    $text = \Yii::t('app', 'Hello World from Database!');

    return $this->render('helloWorldFromDatabase', ['text' =>
$text]);
}
```

The view in `basic/views/file-translator/helloWorldFromDatabase` will show the `$text` content:

```
<?= $text ?>
```

Test it by pointing the browser to `http://hostname/basic/web/file-translator/hello-world-from-database`. If all is correct, we should see `Ciao Mondo dal Database!`, which is the Italian version of `Hello World from Database!`.

Example – translating room descriptions using DB

This example will show you how to translate the room's description using the database as the storage option. We will create models for `message` and `source_message` database tables, since we are going to use ActiveRecord to manage records in all the tables that control translations.

Firstly, we are going to create models for `message` and `source_message` database tables using Gii. In the basic template, point the browser to `http://hostname/basic/web/gii`, and then go to the model generator. Gii will create `Message` and `SourceMessage` models in the `basic/models` folder.

Next, we want to create a form that contains descriptions both in the original language and in all other translations.

For this purpose, we will create a view in `basic/views/rooms/indexWithTranslatedDescriptions.php`, as follows:

```php
<?php
use yii\helpers\Url;
use yii\widgets\ActiveForm;
?>

<div class="row">
    <div class="col-md-4">
        <legend>Rooms with translated descriptions</legend>

        <?php $form = ActiveForm::begin([]); ?>
        <table class="table">
            <tr>
                <th>#</th>
                <th>Floor</th>
                <th>Room number</th>
                <th>Description - English</th>
```

```
            <th>Description - Italian</th>
            <th>Description - French</th>
    </tr>
    <?php for($k=0;$k<count($rooms);$k++) : ?>
        <?php $room = $rooms[$k]; ?>
        <input type="hidden" name="Room[<?= $k ?>][id]"
        value="<?= $room->id ?>" />
        <tr>
            <td><?php echo $k+1 ?></td>
            <td><?php echo $room->floor ?></td>
            <td><?php echo $room->room_number ?></td>
            <td><input type="text" name="Room[<?= $k
            ?>][description][en]" value="<?= $room-
            >description ?>" /></td>
            <td><input type="text" name="Room[<?= $k
            ?>][description][it]" value="<?= Yii::$app-
            >i18n->translate('app', $room->description,
            [], 'it') ?>" /></td>
            <td><input type="text" name="Room[<?= $k
            ?>][description][fr]" value="<?= Yii::$app-
            >i18n->translate('app', $room->description,
            [], 'fr') ?>" /></td>
        </tr>
    <?php endfor; ?>
    </table>
    <br />
    <input type="submit" class="btn btn-primary" value="Submit
    descriptions" />
    <?php ActiveForm::end(); ?>
    </div>
</div>
```

We will check for other language translations using the `Yii::$app->i18n->translate` method that accepts:

- Category
- Message to be translated
- Parameters of messages
- Language

It is now time to add `actionIndexWithTranslatedDescriptions()` in `basic/controllers/RoomsController.php`:

```php
public function actionIndexWithTranslatedDescriptions()
{
    if(isset($_POST['Room']))
    {
        $roomsInput = $_POST['Room'];
        foreach($roomsInput as $item)
        {
            $sourceMessage =
            \app\models\SourceMessage::findOne(['message' =>
            $item['description']]);

            // If null, I need to create source message
            if($sourceMessage == null)
            {
                $sourceMessage = new
                \app\models\SourceMessage();
            }
            $sourceMessage->category = 'app';
            $sourceMessage->message =
            $item['description']['en'];
            $sourceMessage->save();

            $otherLanguages = ['it', 'fr'];

            foreach($otherLanguages as $otherLang)
            {
                $message = \app\models\Message::findOne(['id'
                => $sourceMessage->id, 'language' =>
                $otherLang]);
                if($message == null)
                {
                    $message = new \app\models\Message();
                }
                $message->id = $sourceMessage->id;
                $message->language = $otherLang;
                $message->translation =
                $item['description'][$otherLang];
                $message->save();
            }
```

```
                       // Room to update
                       $roomToUpdate =
                       \app\models\Room::findOne($item['id']);
                       $roomToUpdate->description =
                       $item['description']['en'];
                       $roomToUpdate->save();
                   }
               }

           $rooms = Room::find()
           ->all();

           return $this->render('indexWithTranslatedDescriptions',
           ['rooms' => $rooms]);
       }
```

> If we have trouble accessing the URL, check the `access` property
> returned by the `behaviors()` method of this controller to ensure that
> this action is allowed.

On top of this code, we will check whether the `$_POST` array is filled; in this case, we will get the `$sourceMessage` object from descriptions passed from the view. Next, we can create or update the message model for whatever language we want. In the end, we will also save the room object, eventually with its description field changed.

With this solution, anytime we want to change a description, a new record will be created since the text has been changed.

Summary

In this chapter, we have seen how to configure multiple languages in our app. We have found out that there are two storage options to handle internationalization: file and database. File is suggested for small projects and database for bigger ones.

We have discovered how to grab placeholders from the entire website through the 'message' command from the console and how to create placeholders that contain formatting information.

Finally, we have configured the database as a storage target for translations, and we have created a complete example to handle room description in different languages.

In the next chapter, we will learn how to create RESTful web services using the new integrated management of Yii 2.

11
Creating an API for Use in a Mobile App

In this chapter, you will learn how to create RESTful Web Services with the new integrated management of Yii 2.

You will learn how to create a new application to manage the `api` environment and how to create a controller using the default base classes provided by the framework.

Then, we will cover authentication methods and you'll learn how to customize the response output format. We'll also discuss:

- Configuring the REST app in the advanced template
- Creating a controller:
    - For example: creating a controller to manage rooms
- Authentication:
    - For example: using authentication to get a customers list
- New controller actions:
    - For example: getting a rooms list for a reservation
- Customizing authentication and the response
    - For example: status response node in received data
- Other forms of export – RSS:
    - For example: creating RSS with a list of available rooms

Configuring a REST app in the advanced template

Before using the advanced template, it is advisable to configure RESTful Web Services, since, as you saw in previous chapters, this configuration allows you to easily add a new application in the same project.

Yii provides many built-in features to create RESTful Web Services and it reduces the code needed to implement it that is always structured with models, controllers, and actions.

These are its main features:

- Default actions (`index`, `view`, `create`, `update`, `delete`, and `options`) in `yii\rest\ActiveController`, which is the base controller suggested to override
- A response format selectable from input
- Customized authentication and authorization
- Caching and rate limiting

Yii applies well-established knowledge about RESTful Web Services creation, such as how to present metadata in the response output. So, it is advisable that we follow the framework guidelines as far as possible; in this way, we will write commonly manageable REST APIs.

The first thing to do with an advanced template is to create a new application in the same project, for example renaming it `api`. Yii has not got a built-in functionality to create a new application, but it only takes a few steps to complete this task.

Starting from the root of our project, we will create, as well as for other applications (`common`, `backend`, `frontend`, and `console`), a new folder named `api` with the following command:

```
$ mkdir api
```

Now, enter in `api` and let's create these five subfolders:

```
$ mkdir config
$ mkdir web
$ mkdir controllers
$ mkdir runtime
```

We must only create files for the first two folders, and the others will be left temporarily empty.

Another possible solution would be to copy complete content from other applications, such as frontend or backend, to the new application destination folder and then to clear content that is not useful.

In the `config` folder, we must create two files: `main.php` and `params.php`. The second file, `params.php`, will be temporarily empty as we have not got any parameters to store in it, such as:

```php
<?php
return [
];
```

The content of `api/config/main.php` will, instead, be:

```php
<?php
$params = array_merge(
    require(__DIR__ . '/../../common/config/params.php'),
    require(__DIR__ . '/../../common/config/params-local.php'),
    require(__DIR__ . '/params.php')
);

return [
    'id' => 'app-api',
    'basePath' => dirname(__DIR__),
    'controllerNamespace' => 'api\controllers',
    'bootstrap' => ['log'],
    'modules' => [],

    'components' => [

        'urlManager' => [
            'enablePrettyUrl' => true,
            'showScriptName' => false,
        ],

        'user' => [
            'identityClass' => '\common\models\User',
            'enableSession' => false,
            'loginUrl' => null
        ],

        'log' => [
```

```
                    'traceLevel' => YII_DEBUG ? 3 : 0,
                    'targets' => [
                        [
                            'class' => 'yii\log\FileTarget',
                            'levels' => ['error', 'warning'],
                        ],
                    ],
                ],
            ],
        'params' => $params,
    ];
```

Then, we will create an index.php file in the web folder with the following content:

```php
<?php
defined('YII_DEBUG') or define('YII_DEBUG', true);
defined('YII_ENV') or define('YII_ENV', 'dev');

require(__DIR__ . '/../../vendor/autoload.php');
require(__DIR__ . '/../../vendor/yiisoft/yii2/Yii.php');
require(__DIR__ . '/../../common/config/bootstrap.php');

$config = yii\helpers\ArrayHelper::merge(
    require(__DIR__ . '/../../common/config/main.php'),
    require(__DIR__ . '/../../common/config/main-local.php'),
    require(__DIR__ . '/../config/main.php')
);

$application = new yii\web\Application($config);
$application->run();
```

Still in the web folder, we will create the .htaccess file to handle a pretty URL:

```
RewriteEngine on

# If a directory or a file exists, use it directly
RewriteCond %{REQUEST_FILENAME} !-f
RewriteCond %{REQUEST_FILENAME} !-d
# Otherwise forward it to index.php
RewriteRule . index.php
```

Finally, we have to add a new alias in `common/config/bootstrap` regarding the
`api` application:

```
Yii::setAlias('api', dirname(dirname(__DIR__)) . '/api');
```

Our job is complete, as we finally have a brand new application from scratch.

 Be sure to make the `runtime` folder writable, since the framework
will write in it runtime data such as log files.

Creating a controller

Yii provides two base classes: `\yii\rest\Controller` and `\yii\rest\`
`ActiveController` that we can extend when we are creating a new controller
for RESTful web services.

Both of these classes contain the following useful common features, in execution order:

1. The response output as required from the request (content negotiator).
2. The HTTP method validation.
3. Authentication.
4. Rate limiting.

The second class `\yii\rest\ActiveController` adds more functionalities through
ActiveRecord, such as handling user authorization and a set of already existing
actions: `index`, `view`, `create`, `update`, `delete`, and `options`.

We will see that Yii provides all the necessary information to get the response
status and content through the body and HTTP header.

Let's create a controller to extend `\yii\rest\Controller` or rather
without ActiveRecord. Create a new controller in `api/controllers/`
`TestRestController.php`:

```php
<?php
namespace api\controllers;

use yii\rest\Controller;

class TestRestController extends Controller
```

```
{
    private function dataList()
    {
        return [
            [ 'id' => 1, 'name' => 'Albert', 'surname' =>
            'Einstein' ],
            [ 'id' => 2, 'name' => 'Enzo', 'surname' => 'Ferrari'
            ],
            [ 'id' => 4, 'name' => 'Mario', 'surname' => 'Bros' ]
        ];
    }


    public function actionIndex()
    {
            return $this->dataList();
    }
}
```

In the preceding code, we have a method `dataList`, which returns an array of objects, and an `actionIndex` method that provides the `index` action for `TestRestController` and returns that list.

 Many examples can be executed using a web browser (requested by employing the GET verb). Generally, however, we need a specific tool to test RESTful web services, such as `Postman` for example, an excellent extension for the Chrome browser or the `curl` command for advanced users.

The first feature of `\yii\rest\Controller` is to arrange the response output format, dynamically based on the request, which is also called **content negotiation**.

Indeed, we can try to launch this request through `http://hostname/yiiadv/api/web/test-rest/index` in our browser, or through specific tools using the GET verb and the `Accept` HTTP header set to `application/xml`, or by using `curl`, as follows:

```
$ curl -H "Accept: application/xml"
http://hostname/yiiadv/api/web/test-rest/index

<?xml version="1.0" encoding="UTF-8"?>

<response><item><id>1</id><name>Albert</name><surname>Einstein</
surname></item><item><id>2</id><name>Enzo</name><surname>Ferrari</
surname></item><item><id>4</id><name>Mario</name><surname>Bros</
surname></item></response>
```

In these cases, we will get a response based on the XML data:

```
1   <?xml version="1.0" encoding="UTF-8"?>
2 ▾ <response>
3 ▾     <item>
4           <id>1</id>
5           <name>Albert</name>
6           <surname>Einstein</surname>
7       </item>
8 ▾     <item>
9           <id>2</id>
10          <name>Enzo</name>
11          <surname>Ferrari</surname>
12      </item>
13  </response>
```

The XML data response to test-rest/index

However, if we change the `Accept` header to `application/json`, we will get a response based on the JSON data:

```
$ curl -H "Accept: application/json" http://hostname/yiiadv/api/web/test-rest/index
```

[{"id":1,"name":"Albert","surname":"Einstein"},{"id":2,"name":"Enzo","surname":"Ferrari"},{"id":4,"name":"Mario","surname":"Bros"}]

In these cases, we will get a response based on the JSON data:

```
1 ▾ [
2 ▾     {
3           "id": 1,
4           "name": "Albert",
5           "surname": "Einstein"
6       },
7 ▾     {
8           "id": 2,
9           "name": "Enzo",
10          "surname": "Ferrari"
11      },
12 ▾    {
13          "id": 4,
14          "name": "Mario",
15          "surname": "Bros"
16      }
17  ]
```

The JSON data response to test-rest/index

The same data will be rendered in different ways according to the `Accept` header sent from the client.

The second feature, HTTP method validation, allows you to specify which verbs are available for a resource. Verbs are defined in the `behaviors()` method, which must be extended to modify this setting:

```
public function behaviors()
{
    $behaviors = parent::behaviors();
    $behaviors['verbs'] = [
            'class' => \yii\filters\VerbFilter::className(),
            'actions' => [
                'index'  => ['get'],
            ],
    ];
    return $behaviors;
}
```

In this case, we only set the GET verb to the `index` action, because keys of the `actions` attribute of `behaviors['verbs']` are the actions and the value is an array containing supported HTTP methods.

If we launch `http://hostname/yiiadv/api/web/test-rest/index` using the GET verb (as a browser request), we will continue to display the result. However, if we change the HTTP method to the POST verb, for example, we will get an exception error:

```
1 ▼ {
2     "name": "Method Not Allowed",
3     "message": "Method Not Allowed. This url can only handle the following request methods: GET.",
4     "code": 0,
5     "status": 405,
6     "type": "yii\\\\web\\\\MethodNotAllowedHttpException"
7 }
```

An exception error using the wrong verb

This is because only the GET verb is supported by the `index` action.

In the next sections, we will explain the third and fourth features, authentication and rate limiting.

Example – creating a controller to manage rooms

With this example, we will apply the concepts dealt with in the previous chapter, in this case using `\yii\rest\ActiveController` as the base class instead of `\yii\rest\Controller`, since we are going to employ an ActiveRecord class to manipulate data.

Create a new controller in `api/controllers/RoomsController.php`:

```php
<?php
namespace api\controllers;

use yii\rest\ActiveController;

class RoomsController extends ActiveController
{
    public $modelClass = 'common\models\Room';
}
```

This controller implicitly contains these actions:

- `actionIndex` that returns a list of models, accessible only with GET and HEAD HTTP methods
- `actionView` that returns details about the mode, accessible only with the GET and HEAD HTTP methods by passing the `id` parameter
- `actionCreate` that creates a new model, accessible only with the POST HTTP methods
- `actionUpdate` that updates an existing model, accessible only with the PUT and PATCH HTTP methods
- `actionDelete` that deletes an existing model, accessible only with the DELETE HTTP method
- `actionOptions` that returns the allowed HTTP methods

Now, let's try to launch all these methods.

Launch `actionIndex` at `http://hostname/yiiadv/api/web/rooms` using the GET method:

```
[
{
    "id": 1,
    "floor": 1,
    "room_number": 101,
    "has_conditioner": 1,
    "has_tv": 0,
    "has_phone": 1,
    "available_from": "2015-05-20",
    "price_per_day": "120.00",
```

```
        "description": "description 1"

    },

    {
        "id": 2,
        "floor": 2,
        "room_number": 202,
        "has_conditioner": 0,
        "has_tv": 1,
        "has_phone": 1,
        "available_from": "2015-05-30",
        "price_per_day": "118.00",
        "description": "description 2"
    }
]
```

We will get all the records in the database as an array of the JSON object and HTTP header, along with the successful status code and pagination details:

```
X-Pagination-Current-Page: 1
X-Pagination-Page-Count: 1
X-Pagination-Per-Page: 20
X-Pagination-Total-Count: 2
```

If we launch the same URL using the HEAD HTTP method, we will only get the HTTP HEADER response without a body, so we will get only the pagination information.

Finally, if we launch the same URL with an unsupported HTTP method, for example the PUT method, we will get two important HTTP headers:

- The `status code` header set to `405 Method Not Allowed`
- The `Allow` header set to `GET, HEAD`

The `status code` header says that a method is not supported, and the `Allow` header returns a list of supported HTTP methods for that action.

Now, launch `actionView` on `http://hostname/yiiadv/api/web/rooms/view?id=1` using the GET method:

```
{
    "id": 1,
    "floor": 1,
```

```
    "room_number": 101,
    "has_conditioner": 1,
    "has_tv": 0,
    "has_phone": 1,
    "available_from": "2015-05-20",
    "price_per_day": "120.00",
    "description": "description 1"
}
```

If we try to launch a nonexistent ID, for example `http://hostname/yiiadv/api/web/rooms/view?id=100`, using the GET method, we will get this body response:

```
{
    "name": "Not Found",
    "message": "Object not found: 100",
    "code": 0,
    "status": 404,
    "type": "yii\\\\web\\\\NotFoundHttpException"
}
```

The HTTP `status code` header will be set to `404 Not Found` to specify that the requested item (`id=100`) does not exist. Using only the HEAD HTTP method, we will get information from the HTTP `status code` set to `404`. The `Create` and `Update` actions require that the client sends body content of the object to be created or updated.

By default, Yii recognizes only the `application/x-www-form-urlencoded` and `multipart/form-data` input formats. In order to enable the JSON input format, we need to configure the `parsers` property of the request's application component in the `api/config/main.php` file:

```
'request' => [
    'parsers' => [
        'application/json' => 'yii\web\JsonParser',
    ]
]
```

After configuring the JSON input parser, we can call `http://hostname/yiiadv/api/web/rooms/create` using the POST HTTP method to create a new room and pass, for example, this JSON:

```
{
    "floor": 99,
    "room_number": 999,
    "has_conditioner": 1,
```

```
        "has_tv": 1,
        "has_phone": 1,
        "available_from": "2015-12-30",
        "price_per_day": "48.00",
        "description": "description room 999"
}
```

If no error occurred, we will get:

`201 Created as HTTP Header Status Code`

`Object just created as body content`

If we are missing some required fields and there are validation errors, we will get:

`422 Data Validation Failed`

`An array of field-message to indicate which validation errors occurred`

The same thing needs to be done for an update action, in this case, however, we will call `http://hostname/yiiadv/api/web/rooms/update` and pass the id URL parameter using the PUT or PATCH HTTP method. In this case, only the HTTP header status code `200 OK` will be a successful response and the update object will be returned as body content.

Finally, `actionDelete` is used by calling `http://hostname/yiiadv/api/web/rooms/delete`, by passing the id URL parameter, and using the DELETE HTTP method. A successful execution will return `204 No Content` as the HTTP status code; otherwise, it will be `404 Not Found`.

Authentication

There are three kinds of authentication:

- **HTTP Basic Auth** (the `HttpBasicAuth` class): This method uses the WWW-Authenticate HTTP header to send the username and password for every request

- **Query parameter** (the `QueryParamAuth` class): This method uses an access token passed as query parameter in the API URL

- **OAuth 2** (the `HttpBearerAuth` class): This method uses an access token that is obtained by the consumer from an authorization server and sent to the API server via HTTP bearer tokens

Yii supports all the methods mentioned, but we can also easily create a new one.

To enable authentication, follow these steps:

1. Configure the user application component in the configuration, setting `enableSession` to `false` in order to make user authentication status not persistent using a session across requests. Next, set `loginUrl` to `null` to show the HTTP 403 error instead of redirecting it to the login page.

2. Specify which authentication method we want to use, configuring the `authenticator` behavior in API controller classes.

3. Implement `yii\web\IdentityInterface::findIdentityByAccessToken()` in the user identity class.

> The first step ensures that REST requests are really stateless, but if you need to persist or store session data, you can skip this step.

Step 1 can be configured in `api/config/main.php`:

```
'components' => [
    . . .
    'user' => [
        'identityClass' => 'common\models\User',
        'enableSession' => false,
        'loginUrl' => null
    ],
];
```

Step 2 requires that we extend the `behaviors()` controller method, specifying a single authenticator:

```
public function behaviors()
{
    $behaviors = parent::behaviors();
    $behaviors['authenticator'] = [
        'class' => yii\filters\auth\HttpBasicAuth::className(),
    ];
    return $behaviors;
}
```

Or we can do this by specifying multiple authenticators:

```
public function behaviors()
{
    $behaviors = parent::behaviors();
    $behaviors['authenticator'] = [
```

```
            'class' => yii\filters\auth\CompositeAuth::className(),
            'authMethods' => [
                yii\filters\auth\HttpBasicAuth::className(),
                yii\filters\auth\HttpBearerAuth::className(),
                yii\filters\auth\QueryParamAuth::className(),
            ],
        ];
        return $behaviors;
    }
```

Finally, step 3 requires the implementation of findIdentityByAccessToken() of the identityClass specified in the configuration file.

In a simple scenario, the access token can be stored in a column of the User table and then retrieved:

```
public static function findIdentityByAccessToken($token, $type
= null)
{
    return static::findOne(['access_token' => $token]);
}
```

At the end of the configuration, every request will try to authenticate the user in the beforeAction() method of the same controller.

Now, let's take a look at the first authentication method, HTTPBasicAuth. This method requires us to set the auth property to the callable PHP function; if it is not set, the username will be used as the access token passed to the \yii\web\ User::loginByAccessToken() method.

The basic implementation of the HttpBasicAuth authentication is:

```
public function behaviors()
{
    $behaviors = parent::behaviors();
    $behaviors['authenticator'] = [
            'class' =>
            yii\filters\auth\HttpBasicAuth::className(),
            'auth' => function($username, $password) {
            // return null or identity interface
    // For example search by username and password
    return \common\models\User::findOne(['username' => $username,
    'password' => $password);
        }

        /*
```

```
                    'auth' => [$this, 'httpBasicAuthHandler'],
                    */
        ];
        return $behaviors;
    }


    public function httpBasicAuthHandler($username, $password)
    {
        // For example search by username and password
        return \common\models\User::findOne(['username' => $username,
        'password' => $password]);
    }
```

The callable PHP function stored by the `auth` property can be represented as an inline function, or as an array, whose first value is the object and the second is the function name to be called, by passing `$username` and `$password` parameters.

Check how PHP is running through `phpinfo()`. If you display CGI/FCGI, then you need to add `SetEnvIf Authorization .+ HTTP_AUTHORIZATION=$0` in `.htaccess` to use HTTP Auth from PHP.

The second authentication method is query parameter, by using the `QueryParamAuth` class. With this method, a query parameter named `access-token` must be passed to the URL. Then, it will call the `\yii\web\user::loginByAccessToken()` method, passing `access-token` as the first parameter. This function will return an `IdentityInterface` or `null`.

The URL parameter name can be changed using `tokenParam` in the authentication declaration:

```
public function behaviors()
{
    $behaviors = parent::behaviors();
    $behaviors['authenticator'] = [
            'class' =>
            yii\filters\auth\QueryParamAuth::className(),
            'tokenParam' => 'myAccessToken'
    ];
    return $behaviors;
}
```

With this configuration, the URL must be `http://hostname/url?myAccessToken=...`

The last authentication method, OAuth 2, requires an authorization server from which we will get the bearer token to pass to the REST API server, which is similar to `QueryParamAuth`.

Example – using authentication to get a customers list

In this example, we are going to authenticate ourselves by using two methods at the same time: `HTTPBasicAuth` and `QueryParamAuth`. When using `QueryParamAuth` with an access token, we will first call a publically accessible action to get an access token that the user will pass to all the other actions as the query URL parameter.

We will start by creating a new model from the `Customer` database table and putting it into the `common/models` folder. Then, we will create a new user in the `User` database table using, for example, `foo` as the username and `$2a$12$xzGZB29iqBHva4sEYbJeT.pq9g1/VdjoD0S67ciDB30EWSCE18sW6` as the password (this is equivalent to the hashed `bar` text).

Create a new controller in `api/controllers/CustomersController.php` that only extends the `behaviors()` method to implement `HTTPBasicAuth` and `QueryParamAuth`:

```php
<?php
namespace api\controllers;

use yii\rest\ActiveController;
use yii\filters\auth\CompositeAuth;
use yii\filters\auth\HttpBasicAuth;
use yii\filters\auth\QueryParamAuth;

class CustomersController extends ActiveController
{
  public $modelClass = 'common\models\Customer';

  public function behaviors()
  {
    $behaviors = parent::behaviors();

    $behaviors['authenticator'] = [
      'class' => CompositeAuth::className(),
      'authMethods' => [
        [
          'class' => HttpBasicAuth::className(),
```

```
        'auth' => function($username, $password)
        {
          $out = null;
          $user =
          \common\models\User::findByUsername($username);
          if($user!=null)
          {
            if($user->validatePassword($password)) $out = $user;
          }
          return $out;
        }
      ],
      [
          'class' => QueryParamAuth::className(),
      ]
    ]
  ];

  return $behaviors;
}
}
```

In `HTTPBasicAuth`, we implement the `auth` property inside the configuration array by checking `$username` and then validating the password. If the username and password match each other, it will return the user found or will otherwise be null.

`QueryParamAuth`, instead, does not need any property other than the class, since we will use `access-token` as the query parameter name. Nevertheless, to complete this task, we need an action that will return the related user's access token after passing both the username and password.

For this purpose, we will add the `actionAccessTokenByUser()` method, which looks for the user with the `$username` and `$password` parameters passed. If the user already exists, its `access_token` property will be updated with a random string, so every time we call this action, `access_token` will change and the previous one will be cancelled:

```
public function actionAccessTokenByUser($username,
$passwordHash)
{
    $accessToken = null;

    $user = \common\models\User::findOne(['username' =>
    $username, 'password_hash' => $passwordHash]);
    if($user!=null)
```

```
        {
            $user->access_token = Yii::$app->security-
            >generateRandomString();
            $user->save();
            $accessToken = $user->access_token;
        }
        return [ 'access-token' => $accessToken ];
    }
```

Finally, to test `HTTPBasicAuth`, we need to pass the WWW-Authentication header by calling the `http://hostname/yiiadv/api/web/customers/index` URL.

If we want to use `QueryParamAuth`, we need to:

- Get `access-token` returned from `http://hostname/yiiadv/api/web/customers/access-token-by-user`, by passing the username and hashed password

- Call `http://hostname/yiiadv/api/web/customers/index?access-token`, by passing the access-token property value received from the previous request

`QueryParamAuth` calls the `findIdentityByAccessToken()` function of `IdentityInterfaces`(the user mode). So, check that the method is implemented, and if it's not, implement it as follows:

```
public static function findIdentityByAccessToken($token,
$type = null)
    {
    return User::findOne(['access_token' => $token]);
    }
```

Pay attention, as this way of using access tokens allows the use of the REST API with the same credentials for only one client at a time. This is because any time an `access-token-by-user` is called, a new `access-token` will be created. Therefore, it should be created a relation one-to-many between users and `access-token` in order to provide multiple clients with access using the same username/password credentials.

New controller action

It is very simple to add new actions to the REST API controller. We only need to remember three differences in the web controller:

- Verb setting for the new action

- Authenticate the setting for the new action

- Output for the new action

The first two steps are configured in the `behaviors()` method of the controller:

```
public function behaviors()
{
    $behaviors = parent::behaviors();
    $behaviors['verbs'] = [
            'class' => \yii\filters\VerbFilter::className(),
            'actions' => [
                'myCustomAction'  => ['get', 'head'],
            ],
    ];

    $behaviors['authenticator'] = [
    'except' => 'myCustomAction',
        'class' => HttpBasicAuth::className(),
    ];

    return $behaviors;
}

public function actionMyCustomAction()
{
    ...
    ...

}
```

In the first part of the `behaviors()` method, we will only set the `get` and `head` HTTP methods to call the `myCustomAction` action. If we try to call this action with other HTTP methods, we will get a not supported exception.

In the last part of the `behaviors()` method, we will set it so that `myCustomAction` has not got authentication, since it is in the `except` property.

The third difference, output for the new action, states that we have different ways to return data. We can use:

- A key-value pair array to create a single object from scratch
- An ActiveRecord instance to create a single object
- An ActiveRecord array to create a list of objects
- A data provider

In this last case, the framework will automatically output pagination information and links to other pages (if present).

Example – getting a rooms list for a reservation

In this example, we need to create a `Reservation` model in the `common/models` folder using Gii.

Then, we create a new controller in `api/controllers/ReservationsController.php`:

```php
<?php
namespace api\controllers;

use Yii;
use yii\rest\ActiveController;
use yii\filters\auth\CompositeAuth;
use yii\filters\auth\HttpBasicAuth;
use yii\filters\auth\QueryParamAuth;

class ReservationsController extends ActiveController
{
    public $modelClass = 'common\models\Reservation';

    public function actionIndexWithRooms()
    {
        $reservations = \common\models\Reservation::find()->all();

        $outData = [];
        foreach($reservations as $r)
        {
            $outData[] = array_merge($r->attributes, ['room' =>
            $r->room->attributes]);
        }
        return $outData;
    }

}
```

Now, let's call `http://hostname/yiiadv/api/web/reservations/index-with-rooms`, where we will display a list of reservations, in each of which the room property is expanded together with the content of room object related to the reservation.

Take care to ensure that the `room` relation already exists in the `Reservation` model. If not, we must add this relation to the `Reservation` model:

```
public function getRoom()
{
        return $this->hasOne(Room::className(),
['id' =>
        'room_id']);
}
```

However, this solution is inefficient since we always get all the rows and if there are too many of them, this can result in it being too expensive for us. To solve this problem, we could use a DataProvider created from a set of data found, or better yet, a more simple solution automatically provided by Yii.

Indeed, Yii provides some easy ways to display relations and filter returned fields. For example, there could be fields that we do not want to show, such as a password, private data, and so on.

Models have these methods:

- `fields()`: By default, classes that extend `yii\base\Model::fields()` return all the model attributes as fields, while classes that extend `yii\db\ActiveRecord::fields()` only return the attributes that have been populated from the DB

- `extraFields()`: By default, classes that extend `yii\base\Model::extraFields()` return nothing, while classes that extend `yii\db\ActiveRecord::extraFields()` return the names of the relations that have been populated from the DB

The first method, `fields()`, is a key-value array where the key is the name of the field returned. The value can be empty if the returned content is the attribute with the same name as the key, a string indicating which attribute to get the returned value from, or a callable PHP function to manipulate the returned value.

The second method, `extraFields()`, is a string array whose values are relations defined in the model class.

Finally, to dynamically filter the requested field, we append the `fields` parameter to the requested URL and the `expand` parameter to get a list of relations from the models.

So, if we call `http://hostname/yiiadv/api/web/reservations/index?expand=room`, we will get the same result but we will also have the pagination and loaded models that are only necessary for that page.

However, it would be more convenient for us to distribute an URL without special parameters, such as the expand and fields, for example, in order to avoid confusion among developers who will use these APIs.

We can use actionIndexWithRooms as a wrapper for actionIndex with an expanded parameter in this way:

```
public function actionIndexWithRooms()
{
        $_GET['expand'] = 'room';
        return $this->runAction('index');
}
```

With this solution, the http://hostname/yiiadv/api/web/reservations/index-with-rooms URL is simply a wrapper for http://hostname/yiiadv/api/web/reservations/index?expand=room but this prevents developers from having to remember which parameters to pass to the URL to obtain the necessary nodes in the response.

Customizing authentication and response

Yii allows us to quickly create a custom authentication method for our application. This is useful because in some cases, the previously mentioned authentications are not sufficient.

A custom authentication model can be made by extending the yii\filters\auth\AuthMethod class, which implements yii\filters\auth\AuthInterface that requires overriding the authenticate ($user, $request, and $response) method:

```
<?php

namespace api\components;

use yii\filters\auth\AuthMethod;
use Yii;

class CustomAuthMethod extends AuthMethod {

    public function authenticate($user, $request, $response) {
    ...
    ...
    ...
}
```

```
    ...

    ...

    ...

    }
```

Even though the REST API should be stateless, or rather should not save session data, it could be necessary to store some information or preferences during a session across requests.

So, if we need to support a session, we can start it through the `authenticate()` method called in the `beforeAction()` event. The idea is to use `QueryParamAuth` using `access-token` as the session ID to identify the current session.

For this purpose, we will create a new folder in `api\components` to store the custom `SessionAuth` method.

This is the content of the `api/components/SessionAuth.php` file where the query URL parameter is named `sid`:

```php
<?php

namespace api\components;

use yii\filters\auth\AuthMethod;
use Yii;

class SessionAuth extends AuthMethod {
   public $tokenParam = 'sid';

   public function authenticate($user, $request, $response) {
     $accessToken = $request->get($this->tokenParam);

     if (is_string($accessToken)) {

        Yii::$app->session->id = $accessToken;

        $identity = isset(Yii::$app-
        >session['loggedUser'])?Yii::$app-
         >session['loggedUser']:null;

          if ($identity !== null) {
             return $identity;
          }
     }
     if ($accessToken !== null) {
        $this -> handleFailure($response);
```

```
        }
        return null;
    }

}
```

It is also necessary to create an action to start the session; otherwise, the user will not be stored in the session.

So, create a new controller called `UsersController` in `api/controllers/UsersController.php` to handle the login:

```php
<?php
namespace api\controllers;

use Yii;
use yii\rest\ActiveController;
use yii\filters\auth\CompositeAuth;
use yii\filters\auth\HttpBasicAuth;
use yii\filters\auth\QueryParamAuth;
use api\components\SessionAuth;
use common\models\User;

class UsersController extends ActiveController
{
    public $modelClass = 'common\models\User';

    public function behaviors()
    {
        $behaviors = parent::behaviors();

        $behaviors['authenticator'] = [
                'except' => ['login'],
                'class' => SessionAuth::className(),
        ];

        return $behaviors;
    }

    public function actionLogin($username, $passwordHash)
    {
        $dataOut = null;

        $user = User::findOne(['username' => $username,
        'password_hash' => $passwordHash]);
```

```
        if($user != null)
        {
            $session = Yii::$app->session;
            $session->open();

            $session['loggedUser'] = $user;

            $sid = $session->id;

            $dataOut = ['sid' => $sid];
        }

        return $dataOut;
    }
}
```

As earlier defined, in the `behaviors()` method, the actions of this controller, except for `login`, will authenticate against the `SessionAuth` component that checks primarily whether a user has successfully executed the login action.

We now call `http://hostname/yiiadv/api/web/users/login?username=&passwordHash=` and fill out the `username` and `passwordHash` fields. It returns the session ID to access the session data. Also, the `loggedUser` property is filled out in the session with the user model data.

Now, we can store shared information among requests as a typical web application.

Now, let's see how to customize a response in RESTful Web Services. First of all, this operation could be needed when we have to add, for example, extra information, such as explicit error messages to display in the client or operation status code.

The custom response must extend `\yii\web\Response` and override the `send()` method, as follows:

```php
<?php
namespace api\components;

use yii\rest\ActiveController;
use Yii;
use yii\web\Response;

class ApiResponse extends \yii\web\Response
{

    public function send()
```

```
    {
        ..
..
..
    }
}
```

This `send()` method manipulates data stored in the object properties, mainly in the `$this->data` variable.

This customization, which we will see in detail in the next example, is incomplete, as the `send()` method should implement all the manipulations of data made from the `\yii\web\Response` version. We must remember that Yii returns data based on the `Accept` HTTP header passed from the client and many other convenient functionalities.

It is possible to maintain this behavior simply by calling `parent::send()` before returning from the `send()` function, as follows:

```
    public function send()
    {
        ..
..
        parent::send();
}
```

Because, as said before, `send()` uses the `$this->data` variable as a container for data to be sent.

Example – status response node in data received

Now, let's apply the concepts seen in the previous chapter to add extra data into a response. This practice is useful when we need to return to client information about the operation status and extra data such as detailed error messages.

The purpose of this example is to return a response with two attributes:

- The `status` attribute containing three properties: `response_code` with an integer value indicating the operation state, `response_message` with a string value representation of `response_code` and `response_extra` with a custom text string
- The `data` attribute containing the expected output data

We will use a class containing all the integer codes and their text representations as a response code, since the integer value will be used to fill in the `response_code` property and a string representation to fill in the `response_message` property.

Create a new class file in `api/components/ApiResponseCode.php` with this content:

```php
<?php
namespace api\components;

class ApiResponseCode
{
    const ERR_OK = 0;
    const ERR_LOGIN_REQUIRED = 1;
    const ERR_METHOD_NOT_FOUND = 2;
    const ERR_NOT_FOUND = 3;
    const ERR_NOT_SAVED = 4;
    const ERR_DUPLICATE = 5;
    const ERR_INPUT_DATA_FORMAT = 6;

    public static function responsesExtras()
    {
        return [
            ApiResponseCode::ERR_OK => '',
            ApiResponseCode::ERR_LOGIN_REQUIRED => 'Login required
            to use this interface',
            ApiResponseCode::ERR_METHOD_NOT_FOUND => 'Interface
            not found',
            ApiResponseCode::ERR_NOT_FOUND => 'Record not found',
            ApiResponseCode::ERR_NOT_SAVED => 'Error in saving',
            ApiResponseCode::ERR_DUPLICATE => 'Duplicated record',
            ApiResponseCode::ERR_INPUT_DATA_FORMAT => 'Input data
            format incompatible',
        ];
    }

    public static function responseExtraFromCode($rc)
    {
        $al = ApiResponseCode::responsesExtras();
        return (isset($al[$rc]))?$al[$rc]:null;
    }

    public static function responseMessages()
    {
        return [
            ApiResponseCode::ERR_OK => 'OK',
```

```
                ApiResponseCode::ERR_LOGIN_REQUIRED =>
                'ERR_LOGIN_REQUIRED',
                ApiResponseCode::ERR_METHOD_NOT_FOUND =>
                'ERR_METHOD_NOT_FOUND',
                ApiResponseCode::ERR_NOT_FOUND => 'ERR_NOT_FOUND',
                ApiResponseCode::ERR_NOT_SAVED => 'ERR_NOT_SAVED',
                ApiResponseCode::ERR_DUPLICATE => 'ERR_DUPLICATED',
                ApiResponseCode::ERR_INPUT_DATA_FORMAT =>
                'ERR_INPUT_DATA_FORMAT',
            ];
        }

        public static function responseMessageFromCode($rc)
        {
            $al = ApiResponseCode::responseMessages();
            return (isset($al[$rc]))?$al[$rc]:null;
        }
    }
```

In this component, we defined a list of constants that represent all response codes that can be sent to a client. For each response code, there will be a relative text representation returned by the responseMessage() static method. Then, there will also be an array of extra text messages returned by responseExtras() that will fill the response_extra property if no specific text extra is passed.

Finally, we must write the component that extends \yii\web\Response named ApiResponse in api/components/ApiResponse.php. In this component, we will define three custom properties: statusResponseCode, statusResponseMessage, and statusResponseExtra, which we are going to fill with content composing in the status property.

In this way, we will have a convenient method, fillStatusResponse(), based on the $code parameter, which will automatically fill in both the statusResponseExtra and statusResponseMessage properties.

The core of this component is the overridden send() method that will return status with ERR_OK as response message and 0 as response code by default if there are no client errors (as authentication, not found, and so on.). This is unless a developer changes the values of statusResponseCode, statusResponseExtra, and statusResponseMessage, or manually or automatically calls its properties with fillStatusResponse().

Otherwise, if there are some client errors, we will support Not Authenticated and Not Found errors.

This is the content of the `api/components/ApiResponse.php` file:

```php
<?php
namespace api\components;

use Yii;
use yii\web\Response;

class ApiResponse extends Response
{
    public $statusResponseCode;
    public $statusResponseMessage;
    public $statusResponseExtra;

    /**
     * Set response code and extra from code.
     *
     * Response extra will be filled based on $extraData value
     * If $extraData is null, response extra will be value from
     ApiResponseCode::responseExtraFromCode($code)
     * If $extraData is string, response extra will be filled with
     this value
     */
    public function fillStatusResponse($code, $extraData=null)
    {
        $responseExtra =
        ApiResponseCode::responseExtraFromCode($code);
        $responseMessage =
        ApiResponseCode::responseMessageFromCode($code);

        if($extraData == null)
        {
            $statusResponseExtra = $responseExtra;
        }
        else
        {
            $statusResponseExtra = $extraData;
        }

        $this->statusResponseCode = $code;
        $this->statusResponseMessage = $responseMessage;
        $this->statusResponseExtra = $statusResponseExtra;
    }

    /**
```

```
 * Override send() method.
 *
 * $this->data member contains data released to client.
 */
public function send()
{
    $responseMessage =
    ApiResponseCode::responseMessageFromCode($this-
    >statusResponseCode);

    if($this->isClientError)
    {
        $dataOut = $this->data;

        if($this->statusCode == 401) {    // Not authorized
          $dataOut = null;

          $this->fillStatusResponse(ApiResponseCode:
          :ERR_LOGIN_REQUIRED);
        }
        else if($this->statusCode == 404) {   // Non found
            $dataOut = null;

            $this-
    >fillStatusResponse(ApiResponseCode:
    :ERR_METHOD_NOT_FOUND);
        }

        $this->data = ['status' => ['response_code' => $this-
        >statusResponseCode, 'response_message' => $this-
        >statusResponseMessage, 'response_extra' => $this-
        >statusResponseExtra ], 'data' => $dataOut ];

    }
    else
    {
        $this->data = ['status' => ['response_code' => $this-
        >statusResponseCode, 'response_message' =>
        $responseMessage, 'response_extra' => $this-
        >statusResponseExtra ], 'data' => $this->data ];
    }

    parent::send();
}

public function init()
```

```
{
    parent::init();

    $this->statusResponseCode = ApiResponseCode::ERR_OK;
}

}
```

Finally, we have to change the configuration file `api/config/main.php` by adding the `response` property as a component to indicate to use a custom response class:

```
'response' => [

    'format' => yii\web\Response::FORMAT_JSON,
    'charset' => 'UTF-8',
    'class' => '\api\components\ApiResponse',

],
```

Let's make some attempts. Try to call the non-existent URL `http://hostname/yiiadv/api/web/reservations/index-inexistent`.

This will be the output, correctly returning data as null and the status with the error explained:

```
1 ▾ {
2 ▾     "status": {
3           "response_code": 2,
4           "response_message": "ERR_METHOD_NOT_FOUND",
5           "response_extra": "Interface not found"
6       },
7       "data": null
8   }
```

The response with an error after calling a non-existent URL

Then, try to call a URL that requires authentication: `http://hostname/yiiadv/api/web/customers/index`, which we already implemented in the previous paragraphs.

This will be the output, correctly returning data as null and the status with the error explained:

```
1 ▾ {
2 ▾     "status": {
3           "response_code": 1,
4           "response_message": "ERR_LOGIN_REQUIRED",
5           "response_extra": "Login required to use this interface"
6       },
7       "data": null
8   }
```

The response with an error when calling the URL with authentication

Finally, we try to call a URL that returns data: `http://hostname/yiiadv/api/web/rooms/index`, which is already implemented in the previous paragraphs.

This will be the output, correctly returning data as filled and successful as the status:

```
1  {
2      "status": {
3          "response_code": 0,
4          "response_message": "OK",
5          "response_extra": null
6      },
7      "data": [
8          {
9              "id": 1,
10             "floor": 1,
11             "room_number": 101,
12             "has_conditioner": 1,
13             "has_tv": 0,
14             "has_phone": 1,
15             "available_from": "2015-05-20",
16             "price_per_day": "120.00",
17             "description": "description 1"
18         },
19         {
20             "id": 2,
21             "floor": 2,
22             "room_number": 202,
23             "has_conditioner": 0,
24             "has_tv": 1,
25             "has_phone": 1,
26             "available_from": "2015-05-30",
27             "price_per_day": "118.00",
28             "description": "description 2"
29         }
30     ]
31 }
```

A response with a successful output

Other forms of export – RSS

Yii allows us to create a custom format response to output data. The response format can be changed based on the `Accept` HTTP header sent by the client or done programmatically. When Yii receives a request, it searches for an available response formatter based on the `Accept` HTTP header value and finally calls the `format ($response)` method of the response formatter found.

Therefore, there are three steps to create custom responses:

1. Implementing the `yii\web\ResponseFormatterInterface` interface.
2. Adding a new custom formatter response property in the configuration file.
3. Extending the `behaviors()` method of the controller to handle specific `Accept` HTTP header values.

The first step requires us to implement the `yii\web\ResponseFormatterInterface` interface and extend its method `format ($response)`. Data to be formatted is stored in the `$response->data` property, and the response to client must be filled out in the `$response->content` property:

```php
<?php
namespace api\components;

use yii\web\ResponseFormatterInterface;

class RssResponseFormatter implements ResponseFormatterInterface
{
    public function format($response)
    {
        $response->getHeaders()->set('Content-Type',
        'application/rss+xml; charset=UTF-8');
        if ($response->data !== null) {
            $response->content = "<rss></rss>";
        }
    }
}
```

The second step requires us to add a reference to the custom response formatter. For this purpose, we will use the `formatters` property of `response`, which is an array where keys are the format names, and the array values are the corresponding configurations to create formatter objects:

```php
'response' => [
    'formatters' => [

        'rss' => [
            'format' => 'raw',
            'charset' => 'UTF-8',
            'class' =>
            '\api\components\RssResponseFormatter',
        ],

    ]

],
```

The third step requires us to extend the `behaviors()` method of the controller in order to handle specific `Accept` HTTP header values and indicate to the framework which response formatter to use according to the `Accept` HTTP header value, for example:

```php
public function behaviors()
{
    $behaviors = parent::behaviors();
    $behaviors['contentNegotiator']['formats']
    ['application/rss+xml'] = 'rss';
    return $behaviors;
}
```

When a client sends a request with the `Accept` HTTP header set to `application/rss+xml`, this controller will use the `rss` formatter (read from the configuration file) to prepare the response. If we specify a formatter that does not exist in the configuration file, we will get `InvalidConfigException`.

Example – creating an RSS with a list of available rooms

Now, let's look at how to create an RSS response formatter for the available rooms.

First of all, we must create the complete response formatter component in `api/components/RssResponseFormatter.php`:

```php
<?php
namespace api\components;

use yii\web\ResponseFormatterInterface;

class RssResponseFormatter implements ResponseFormatterInterface
{
    public function format($response)
    {
        $response->getHeaders()->set('Content-Type',
        'application/rss+xml; charset=UTF-8');
        if ($response->data !== null) {
            $rssOut = '<?xml version="1.0" encoding="UTF-8"?>';
            $rssOut .= '<rss>';
            $rssOut .= '<channel>';
            foreach ($response->data as $d)
            {
                $rssOut .= '<item>';
```

```
                    $rssOut .= sprintf('<title>Room #%d at floor
                    %d</title>', $d['id'], $d['floor']);
                    $rssOut .= '</item>';
              }
         $rssOut .= '</channel>';
         $rssOut .= '</rss>';

         $response->content = $rssOut;;
       }
    }
}
```

The RSS response formatter must implement the `format ($response)` method to correctly implement `yii\web\ResponseFormatterInterface`. When the `format ($response)` method is invoked, it will set the `Content-Type` HTTP header to `application/rss+xml`, use data that is ready to be sent from the `$response->data` property, and fill in the `$response->content` property, which is the final content received by the client.

Then, we must change the `api/config/main.php` file to add the `response` property with the support of the new response formatter:

```
'response' => [
    'formatters' => [

        'rss' => [
            'format' => 'raw',
            'charset' => 'UTF-8',
            'class' =>
            '\api\components\RssResponseFormatter',
        ],

    ]
],
```

The `formatter` property is an array of the response formatter where the keys are the format names and the values are the corresponding configurations to create formatter objects.

In this case, we configured a new formatter called `rss` that represents the `\api\components\RssResponseFormatter` component.

Finally, we have to configure the `behaviors()` method in the controller to handle the `Accept` HTTP header with the `application/rss+xml` value.

Open the `RoomsController` file in `api/controllers/RoomsController.php` and add the extension to the `behaviors()` method:

```
public function behaviors()
{
    $behaviors = parent::behaviors();
    $behaviors['contentNegotiator']['formats']
    ['application/rss+xml'] = 'rss';
    return $behaviors;
}
```

Starting from the base configuration of `$behaviors` inherited from `parent::behaviors()`, the `contentNegotiator` attribute contains a reference to `formats` for the `Accept` HTTP header value. The array keys are the `Accept` HTTP header value that is supported, and the values are the corresponding response formatter.

If we try to make the following request:

```
GET /yiiadv/api/web/rooms/index HTTP/1.1
Host: hostname
Accept: application/rss+xml
```

We should display the following response:

```
 1  <rss>
 2      <channel>
 3          <item>
 4              <title>Room #1 at floor 1</title>
 5          </item>
 6          <item>
 7              <title>Room #2 at floor 2</title>
 8          </item>
 9      </channel>
10  </rss>
```

The RSS response output

We can also use the response formatter programmatically. It is enough to set the format of the `Yii::$app->response` application component to a configured response formatter in the configuration file.

For example, we can add a new action named `actionIndexRss` in `RoomsController` that will output data using `RssResponseFormatter` in this way:

```
public function actionIndexRss()
{
    \Yii::$app->response->format = 'rss';

    $provider = new \yii\data\ActiveDataProvider([
```

```
        'query' => \common\models\Room::find(),
        'pagination' => [
            'pageSize' => 20,
        ],
    ]);

    return $provider;
}
```

Summary

In this chapter, we created `api` for use in a mobile app through the use of the powerful tools provided by Yii. We adopted the approach of creating a new application in order to distribute RESTful web services, instead of mixing web and `api` controllers. For this purpose, at the beginning of the chapter, we configured a new REST application using the advanced template.

After configuring the RESTful web service environment, we discovered two kinds of `api` controllers that Yii provides by default, then we created controllers with custom data and data from ActiveRecord.

Next, we found out the default authentication methods for RESTful Web Services provided by framework and you learned how to use them.

Finally, we focused on how to customize the response output format, taking an example of how to create an RSS version of the available data.

In the next chapter, you will learn how to write a console application and will look at the differences between web and console apps.

12
Create a Console Application to Automate the Periodic Task

In this chapter, we will learn how to write a console application and will discover the main differences between web and console apps.

Then, we will create our first console controller, using a practical example to illustrate how to update a database table.

In the final paragraphs, we will see how to set output colors and text formats and how to implement a complete periodic task, such as sending an e-mail with daily reservations. We will cover the following topics in this chapter:

- Interacting with console applications
- Creating a console controller
  - ○ Example – setting an alarm flag for expired reservation
- Formatting the output from the console
- Implementing and executing cron jobs
  - ○ Example – sending an e-mail with new reservations of the day

Interacting with console applications

The console is the third application installed by default with the advanced template.

This app is configured to launch commands through a console access, and it has the same application structure of those already seen in the previous chapters. Therefore, in this section, we require a console access to the host.

Compared to the web and API applications used until now, there are some differences.

The `public` properties of a controller, in fact, are visible from the command line as `option`. It is required to extend the `option()` method of the controller to make those properties available. Also, based on specific action, action parameters are passed as arguments of the command line.

Finally, a console controller action can return an exit code, a number where 0 indicates that everything is OK, a best practice for console application development.

Here is a typical usage of the console application starting from a shell:

```
yii <route> [--option1=value1 --option2=value2 ... argument1
argument2 ...]
```

The elements of the preceding code are explained as follows:

- `route`: This indicates the `controller/action` path to be called
- `option`: This indicates the accessible `public` properties of the controller for that specific action; we can access only the public properties returned by the `options()` method of the controller
- `argument`: This indicates the arguments to be passed to the controller action

 There is an option always available, `appconfig`, to indicate which path of the configuration files you must use. If it is not set, the default configuration file will be adopted.

Yii provides a set of core console applications, which we can access by calling the `help` controller (being a web application, the default action will be `index`), so as to display everything concerning the list of available console controllers or details about a single controller or action controller.

Let's consider an example; open the command line (in this case, a Linux shell) and type the following from the project root:

```
$ ./yii help
```

This will display an output similar to the following (partially displayed):

```
This is Yii version 2.0.4.

The following commands are available:

- asset                       Allows you to combine and compress
your JavaScript and CSS files.
    asset/compress (default)  Combines and compresses the asset files
according to the given configuration.
    asset/template            Creates template of configuration file
for [[actionCompress]].


- cache                       Allows you to flush cache.
    cache/flush               Flushes given cache components.
    cache/flush-all           Flushes all caches registered in the
system.
    cache/flush-schema        Clears DB schema cache for a given
connection component.
    cache/index (default)     Lists the caches that can be flushed.
...

...
```

Here, the first grouping level represents the controller names (with relative descriptions on the right), and the second level includes the actions of the relative controller. We will require a more deep response when passing the name of controller to help it:

```
$ ./yii help message
```

To display the controller description and the list of the actions, we can also require help about the complete route (controller/action) typing:

```
$ ./yii help message/config
```

This returns an output containing the description of the action, its usage, and the options available:

```
DESCRIPTION

Creates a configuration file for the "extract" command.

The generated configuration file contains detailed instructions on
```

how to customize it to fit for your needs. After customization, you may use this configuration file with the "extract" command.

USAGE

yii message/config <filePath> [...options...]

- filePath (required): string
  output file name or alias.

OPTIONS

--appconfig: string
  custom application configuration file path.
  If not set, default application configuration is used.

--color: boolean, 0 or 1
  whether to enable ANSI color in the output.
  If not set, ANSI color will only be enabled for terminals that support it.

--interactive: boolean, 0 or 1 (defaults to 1)
  whether to run the command interactively.

Creating a console controller

A console controller is totally similar to the web controllers that we created earlier. It extends the \yii\console\Controller base class and can return an integer value indicating the status response of the action (0 stands for successful execution of the action), also named exit code.

The public properties of the controller can be made available as an option only if their names are returned by the options() method that accepts actionID as the parameter; so the response can be customized according to actionID.

The response of the options() method is an array of text string that represents the public property names of the controller.

Starting from the advanced template application that we previously installed in the yiiadv folder, let's create a new console controller named MyExampleController in console/controllers/MyExampleController.php with the following content:

```php
<?php

namespace console\controllers;

use \yii\console\Controller;

/**
 * This is an example controller
 */
class MyExampleController extends Controller
{
    public $option1;
    public $option2;

    public function options($action)
    {
        return ['option1'];
    }

    /**
     * Simply return a welcome text
     */
    public function actionTest($param1)
    {
        echo 'this is my first controller using console
        application';
        echo "\n";
        echo "You have passed param1 with value: ".$param1;
        echo "\n";
        echo "Value of option1 is: ".$this->option1;
        echo "\n";

        // equivalent to return 0;
        return Controller::EXIT_CODE_NORMAL;
    }

}

?>
```

This controller contains two public properties, but only `option1` will be usable from the console, since it is returned by the `options()` method. We will display the result of the following command:

```
$ ./yii help my-example
```

The preceding command will return the following output:

```
DESCRIPTION


This is an example controller


SUB-COMMANDS


- my-example/test  Simply return a welcome text


To see the detailed information about individual sub-commands, enter:

  yii help <sub-command>
```

If we need other details about the `test` action, we can launch the preceding command specifying the complete route:

```
$ ./yii help my-example/test
```

Now, try to launch the command with the route `my-example/test`, without any parameter:

```
$ ./yii my-example/test
```

We will receive an error about missing `param1`. The following is the correct syntax:

```
$ ./yii my-example/test "this is value for param1"
```

The preceding command will return the following output without any value for `option1`:

```
this is my first controller using console application
You have passed param1 with value: this is value for param1
Value of option1 is:.
```

We can also pass the value `option1` by appending `--option1` to the command, as follows:

```
$ ./yii my-example/test "this is value for param1" --option1="this is
value for option1"
```

The preceding command will return a complete output, as follows:

```
this is my first controller using console application
You have passed param1 with value: this is value for param1
Value of option1 is: this is value for option1
```

Example – setting an alarm flag for expired reservation

Now, let's consider an example to illustrate how to use console commands to execute maintenance operations.

In console controllers, we can access all the models, components, and extensions available in the project, as well as what we have done in the web application. Therefore, we will manipulate data in the same way as we should do for a web application.

Starting from the reservation database table used in the previous chapters, we will add a new Boolean field, named expired, to set which reservations are out of the end date.

This is the structure of the `reservation` table to store data in the MySQL Server:

```
CREATE TABLE `reservation` (
  `id` int(11) NOT NULL AUTO_INCREMENT,
  `room_id` int(11) NOT NULL,
  `customer_id` int(11) NOT NULL,
  `price_per_day` decimal(20,2) NOT NULL,
  `date_from` date NOT NULL,
  `date_to` date NOT NULL,
  `reservation_date` timestamp NOT NULL DEFAULT CURRENT_TIMESTAMP,
  `expired` int(1) NOT NULL DEFAULT '0',
  PRIMARY KEY (`id`)
)
```

Now, let's insert some records to make a simulation. We will update the expired field with value 1 if today is after date_to value; otherwise, it will be 0.

These are the records to insert in the `reservation` database table:

```
INSERT INTO `reservation` (`id`, `room_id`, `customer_id`,
`price_per_day`, `date_from`, `date_to`, `reservation_date`,
`expired`) VALUES
(1, 2, 1, 90.00, '2015-02-10', '2015-05-23', '2015-05-24
22:45:37', 0),
```

```
(2, 2, 1, 48.00, '2019-08-27', '2019-08-31', '2015-05-24
22:45:37', 0),
(3, 1, 2, 105.00, '2015-09-24', '2015-10-06', '2015-06-03
00:21:14', 0),
(4, 1, 2, 150.00, '2015-06-22', '2015-06-28', '2015-06-21
22:24:25', 0),
(5, 1, 2, 150.00, '2015-07-22', '2015-08-28', '2015-06-21
22:24:34', 0);
```

[Make sure that users exist in user database table]

Now, create a new console controller in `console/controllers/`
`ReservationsController.php` with the following content:

```php
<?php

namespace console\controllers;

use \yii\console\Controller;

/**
 * Manage reservations
 */
class ReservationsController extends Controller
{
    /**
     * Update 'expired' field of reservations
     */
    public function actionUpdateExpired()
    {
        $models = \common\models\Reservation::find()->all();

        foreach($models as $m)
        {
            echo sprintf('Check reservation #%d - date_to = %s -
            status : %s', $m->id, $m->date_to, (strtotime($m-
            >date_to)<=time())?'OK':'Expired');
            echo "\n";
            // Set expired field. I'll for every model because if
            we could have changed 'date_to' value.
            $m->expired = (strtotime($m->date_to)<=time())?0:1;
            $m->save();
        }
```

```
                // equivalent to return 0;
                return Controller::EXIT_CODE_NORMAL;
            }
    }
    ?>
```

In `actionUpdateExpired`, we display for each model some data to the console, such as `id`, `date_to`, and `status`. Then, we will set for each model the value of the `expired` field, based on the `date_to` value.

Finally, we will launch this command:

`$ ./yii reservations/update-expired`

This will return the following output:

```
Check reservation #1 - date_to = 2015-05-23 - status : OK
Check reservation #2 - date_to = 2019-08-31 - status : Expired
Check reservation #3 - date_to = 2015-10-06 - status : Expired
Check reservation #4 - date_to = 2015-06-28 - status : OK
Check reservation #5 - date_to = 2015-08-28 - status : OK
```

Formatting the output from the console

The base class console controller `yii\console\Controller` supports methods to display colored and formatted output.

There are two standard methods to display the output, which are as follows:

- `stdout`: This prints a string to STDOUT
- `strerr`: This prints a string to STDERR

Both these methods support more parameters: the first is the text string to be displayed, and the other includes the formatting options that can be passed to make a pretty output.

There are formatting options for colors and typing; these are defined by constants from `\yii\helpers\Console`; for example, `BG_CYAN` for cyan background color, `BG_RED` for red background color, and `UNDERLINE` for underlined text.

Let's see an example using the following code:

```
$this->stdout("Hello?\n", Console::BOLD);
```

This will display `Hello?` (with a carriage return) with bold font. Sometimes, it could be possible that no effect will be displayed, since our terminal does not support colors.

In this case, a method of the console controller will help us verify our terminal capabilities: `isColorEnabled()` returns a Boolean indicating whether the terminal supports ANSI colors.

Both the methods `strout` and `strerr` are applied to the whole text string and are passed as the first parameter. If we want to apply some features only to a single part of the text, we must use the `ansiFormat` method that returns an ANSI-formatted string.

Let's take an example. Create a controller to check whether the console supports ANSI or not, and try to print the colored text if this feature is supported.

Then, create a new controller named `ColorController` in `console/controllers/ColorController.php` with this content:

```php
<?php

namespace console\controllers;

use \yii\console\Controller;
use \yii\helpers\Console;

/**
 * Colors dedicated controller
 */
class ColorController extends Controller
{
    /**
     * Simply return a welcome text
     */
    public function actionIsClientEnabled()
    {
        if($this->isColorEnabled())
        {
            $this->stdout('OK, terminal supports colors!');
        }
        else
        {
            $this->stdout('NOT OK, terminal does not support
            colors!');
```

```
        }

        $this->stdOut("\n");

        // equivalent to return 0;
        return Controller::EXIT_CODE_NORMAL;
    }

    public function actionPrintColouredText()
    {
        $colouredText = $this->ansiFormat('This text is coloured',
        Console::FG_RED);
        $normalText ="This text is normal";

        $this->stdout(sprintf("%s - %s\n", $normalText,
        $colouredText));
    }


}

?>
```

We call launch to check if client supports ANSI colors or not:

```
$ ./yii color/is-client-enabled
```

And to display colored text (if the client supports it):

```
$ ./yii color/print-coloured-text
```

The Console class under \yii\helpers\ contains many other useful methods to format text and output, such as confirm() or prompt() to get input from the user, or progress to create a progress bar to display the execution state.

Implementing and executing cron jobs

The main usage of console applications consists in the execution of periodic tasks using cron job (on Linux or Unix machines).

We can use console applications to send massive e-mails to perform system maintenance or to check a specific status of the application.

In the next example, we will see how to send an e-mail with a summary of the reservations made in the current date.

Example – sending an e-mail with new reservations of the day

This example illustrates how to send an e-mail with a summary of new daily reservations.

First of all, let's configure the `mailer` component in `console/config/main.php`, if it is not already configured.

It is enough to pass a few parameters to the component:

```
'components' => [
..
..

    'mailer' => [
        'class' => 'yii\swiftmailer\Mailer',
        'viewPath' => '@common/mail',
        // send all mails to a file by default. You have to
        set
        // 'useFileTransport' to false and configure a
        transport
        // for the mailer to send real emails.
        'useFileTransport' => true,
    ],
..
..
    ],
];
```

The `class` parameter indicates the class that handles the component, `viewPath`, which indicates where views of the e-mail, or rather e-mail templates, are stored; the last parameter `useFileTransport` indicates the e-mail sending method.

Now, in `ReservationsController`, under `console/controllers/ReservationsController.php`, add the method, `actionReservationsOfTheDay`, which sends the content of daily reservations:

```
public function actionReservationsOfTheDay($currentDate=null)
{
    if($currentDate == null) $currentDate = date('Y-m-d');
    $models = \common\models\Reservation::find()-
>where('DATE(reservation_date) = "'.$currentDate.'"')-
>all();
```

```
\Yii::$app->mailer->compose(['html' =>
'reservationsOfTheDay-html', 'text' =>
'reservationsOfTheDay-text'], ['models' => $models,
'currentDate' => $currentDate])
    ->setFrom('myemail@example.com')
    ->setTo('administrator@example.com')
    ->setSubject('Reservations of the day: '.$currentDate)
    ->send();

}
```

 It is advisable to put the from e-mail parameter, for example, in a params.php file, which contains all the global parameters available in the whole application.

This method simply gets the currentDate parameter from the input so that we can change the evaluation date as we need; the action body finds reservations for the input date and passes them to the e-mail view reservationsOfTheDay in the html and text format.

Now, we must create the content of the e-mail format, creating two files in common/mail: reservationsOfTheDay-html.php and reservationsOfTheDay-text.php.

This is the content of the HTML version:

```
There are <?= count($models) ?> reservations for the date <?=
$currentDate ?>

<br /><br />

<?php if(count($models)>0) { ?>
    <b>This is a summary:</b>

    <br />

    <table>
        <tr>
            <td>Reservation #</td>
            <td>Room</td>
            <td>Customer</td>
            <td>Price per day</td>
            <td>Date from</td>
```

```
            <td>Date to</td>
        </tr>

        <?php foreach($models as $m) { ?>
        <tr>
            <td><?= $m->id ?></td>
            <td><?= $m->room->floor.' '.$m->room->number ?></td>
            <td><?= $m->customer->surname.' '.$m->customer->name
            ?></td>
            <td><?= $m->price_per_day ?></td>
            <td><?= $m->date_from ?></td>
            <td><?= $m->date_to ?></td>
        </tr>
        <?php } ?>


    </table>
<?php } else { ?>
    <i>There is no summary for current date</i>
<?php } ?>
```

This is the corresponding content in text format (not required for the HTML e-mail client):

```
There are <?= count($models) ?> reservations for the date <?=
$currentDate ?>

<?php if(count($models)>0) { ?>
    This is a summary


    <?php foreach($models as $m) { ?>
        Reservation #: <?= $m->id ?> - Room: <?= $m->room->floor.'
        '.$m->room->number ?> - Customer: <?= $m->customer-
        >surname.' '.$m->customer->name ?> - Price per day: <?=
        $m->price_per_day ?> - Date from: <?= $m->date_from ?> -
        Date to: <?= $m->date_to ?>
    <?php } ?>
<?php } else { ?>
    There is no summary for the current date
<?php } ?>
```

The command can be executed by launching:

```
$ ./yii reservations/reservations-of-the-day
```

We can also call the pass date parameter to change the date to check, for example, to check the reservations made on 2015-08-05:

```
$ ./yii reservations/reservations-of-the-day "2015-08-05"
```

The last thing to do is to attach that command to a periodic task scheduler according to the operating system, for instance, cron in the Linux or Unix environment.

Summary

In this chapter, we have discussed the third kind of default application installed with Yii's advanced template, the console application.

We have seen the primary differences between console and web applications, and we have learned how to create our first console controller, handling options and parameters to pass to the actions. Then, we have applied a console application with a concrete example, such as making maintenance operation to the reservation table in order to update the status of the reservations to expired.

Then, we focused on how the console application can make pretty outputs, using colors and text formatting features.

Finally, we have mastered how to create a complete periodic task with a console controller action to send a daily summary e-mail containing reservations made in current date.

In the final chapter, we will see the final stage of our development, where we have to make the code reusable but, especially, maintainable.

13
Final Refactoring

This is the final stage of our development. Now that we have written all the working code, we must make it reusable but most importantly, maintainable. This chapter will help you to reuse code by means of widgets and other components. We will see some practical examples on how to use them. Then, we will deal with documentation, an important aspect of app development that allows everyone to quickly learn how a project is structured and built.

For the documentation, we are going to use the two most important tools provided by the framework in order to build API and guide references, making a real-life example. We will cover the following topics:

- Creating widgets
  - Example – creating a widget with a carousel
- Creating components
  - Example – creating a component that creates a backup of the MySQL database and sends an e-mail to the administrator
- Creating modules
- Generating the API documentation
  - Example – using API documentation to generate doc of the app

Creating widgets

A widget is a reusable client-side code (containing JavaScript, CSS, and HTML) with minimal logic wrapped in a `yii\base\Widget` object that we can easily insert and apply in any view.

Building a widget requires you to extend two methods of `yii\base\Widget`:

- The `init()` method initializes the object
- The `run()` method executes the object

In order to instance a widget, it is enough to call the static `widget()` method that accepts just one parameter or better still an array containing values for its public properties.

The following is an example:

```
MyWidget::widget(['prop1' => 'value of prop1', ...])
```

This returns a string containing widget output, passing its value `value of prop1` for its `prop1` public properties.

If we need to insert an extra code in a widget's execution (for example, in the ActiveForm widget), we have a more complex way of instantiating the widget, using the `begin()` and `end()` methods.

The first method, `begin()`, accepts a function parameter with a configuration array to pass to the widget, and it will return the widget object.

When the second method, `end()`, is called, the code between these two methods will be displayed and simultaneously, the `end()` method directly echoes the output of the widget `run()` method:

```
$widget = MyWidget::begin(['prop1' => 'value of prop1', ...]);

..
.. I can use $widget object here  ..
..

MyWidget::end();
```

As for any other views, in the `run()` method, we can refer to a view file, through the `render()` method, in order to display the widget output.

For example, a widget could be a real-time date/time clock. For this purpose, we will build a clock based on a block containing the date/time string updated by the JavaScript code. We can pass to widget construct time some values concerning for example, the color of the border box.

To make an instance, let's start with the basic template app (but this is obviously also valid for the advanced template app). Create a new folder (if it does not exist) named components in the root of the project at the same level of controllers, models, views, and so on, which will contain all the widgets we want to build.

Then, in this folder, we will create a new file named ClockWidget.php with the complete path basic/components/ClockWidget.php:

```php
<?php

namespace app\components;

use yii\base\Widget;

class ClockWidget extends Widget
{

    public function init()
    {
        \yii\web\JqueryAsset::register($this->getView());
    }

    public function run()
    {
        return $this->render('clock');
    }

}
```

In the init() method, we have also made references to the jQuery asset to request the framework to load the jQuery plugin, since we need it in the view file.

In the run() method, we have rendered the clock view, whose content will be discussed in next rows.

So, create a new folder at `basic/components/views` and, within it, a new file named `clock.php` with the following code:

```php
<?php

$this->registerJs( <<< EOT_JS

    function ClockWidget_refresh_datetime()
    {
        var dateTimeString = new Date().toString();
        $('#ClockWidget_realtime_clock').html(dateTimeString);
    }

    setInterval(ClockWidget_refresh_datetime,1000);

    ClockWidget_refresh_datetime();
EOT_JS
);

?>

<div style="border:1px solid black;padding:5px;width:200px;text-
align:center">
    <span id="ClockWidget_realtime_clock"></span>
</div>
```

This code simply displays a box with a string containing real-time values of the current date and time, updated every second.

Finally, we can use our widget in any view using this code:

```php
<?= \app\components\ClockWidget::widget(); ?>
```

Example – creating a widget with a carousel

In this example, we will create a widget that consists of a carousel with some rooms (we can choose which one to display by passing them to the widget with the public property). Again, we will use a basic template application; however, everything is equally applicable to the advanced template apps.

For this example, we will create a new controller to use its view as a widget container.

So, let's create this new controller named `TestCarouselController` at `basic/controller/TestCarouselController.php`. From here, we will pass the `models` property, consisting of a list of maximum three rooms:

```php
<?php

namespace app\controllers;

use yii\web\Controller;
use app\models\Room;

class TestCarouselController extends Controller
{
    public function actionIndex()
    {
        $models = Room::find()->limit(3)->all();

        return $this->render('index', ['models' => $models]);
    }
}
```

Next, we will create the view at `basic/views/test-carousel/index.php` with the widget output as follows:

```
This is a carousel widget with some rooms:
<?=
\app\components\CarouselWidget\CarouselWidget::widget(['models' =>
$models, 'options' => ['style' => 'border:1px solid black;text-
align:center;padding:5px;']]); ?>
```

This builds the widget filling and its public properties `models` and `options`.

Now it is time to create our widget. To isolate the widget from another code as much as possible, we create a specific widget folder at the `basic/components` folder, under a subfolder named `CarouselWidget` inside of which we will create the widget file named `CarouselWidget.php`.

This widget includes a public property, `models` that contains the room's model that has been passed from the container view. It is necessary to pass these models to the Carousel widget at `\yii\bootstrap\Carousel` as an array of this kind:

```
items => [
['content' => '...', 'caption' => '...'],
['content' => '...', 'caption' => '...'],
['content' => '...', 'caption' => '...'],
...
];
```

In this way, in the `init()` method, we will create an internal representation of the models according to the Bootstrap Yii2 widget expectation.

Finally, in the `run()` method, we will output the view now in the views folder at `basic/components/CarouselWidget/views`. This is the widget content; remember that it is stored in `CarouselWidget.php` at `basic/components/CarouselWidget`:

```php
<?php

namespace app\components\CarouselWidget;

use yii\base\Widget;

class CarouselWidget extends Widget
{
    public $carouselId = 'carouselWidget_0';
    public $options = [];
    public $models = [];


    private $carouselItemsContent;

    public function init()
    {
        // It is not necessary because yii bootstrap Carousel
        widget will load it automatically
        // \yii\jui\JuiAsset::register($this->getView());

        $this->carouselItemsContent = [];
        foreach($this->models as $model)
        {
            $caption = sprintf('<h1>Room #%d</h1>', $model->id);
            $content = sprintf('This is room #%d at floor %d with
            %0.2f€ price per day', $model->id, $model->floor,
            $model->price_per_day);
            $itemContent = ['content' => $content, 'caption' =>
            $caption];
            $this->carouselItemsContent[] = $itemContent;
        }

    }

    public function run()
    {
```

```
        return $this->render('carousel', ['carouselItemsContent'
        => $this->carouselItemsContent]);
    }

}
```

The widget view, called in the `run()` method, will be stored in the `carousel.php` file at `basic/components/CarouselWidget/views`:

```php
<?php $styleOption = isset($this->context->options['style'])?$this-
>context->options['style']:''; ?>
<div id="<?php echo $this->context->id ?>" style="<?php echo
$styleOption ?>">
    <?php
    echo \yii\bootstrap\Carousel::widget([
        'id' => $this->context->carouselId,
        'items' => $carouselItemsContent

    ]);
    ?>

</div>
```

Browsing to `http://hostname/basic/web/test-carousel/index`, we will see the carousel widget (only text, but we can also insert some images within).

Creating components

A component is a reusable object that should contain only logic, and it is callable from every point of the app. In a component, we put all the functions that are usable in more than one place of the app.

Technically, a component extends `yii\base\Component` that implements the property, event and behavior features. We can have two kinds of component: component and application component. The only difference between them is that the second has to be also configured in the configuration file of the app in the `components` property and it is available as a property from the `Yii::$app` object. Examples of application components are `db`, `user`, and so on.

Usually, components are stored in the `components` folder starting from the root folder of the project.

Let's see how to create a simple custom component:

```
namespace app\components;

use Yii;
use yii\base\Component;

class MyComponent extends Component
{
..
..
}
```

We can instantiate this component as follows:

```
$myCmp = new \app\components\MyComponent();
```

Then, we will have a new instance of the MyComponent object.

If we want to render this component into the application component and access to it through Yii::$app->myComponent, we must update the configuration file, web.php, at basic/config:

```
'components' => [
    ..
    ..
        'myComponent' => [
            'class' => '\app\components\MyComponent'
        ],
]
```

At this point, we can call myComponent using:

```
Yii:$app->myComponent
```

> Remember that an application component is a single and shared instance of the same object.

We can make custom initializations when a component is instantiated by overriding the init() method of the component.

A concrete example of the component (or the application component, according to our needs) could be sending an SMS to the SMS gateway for the app.

The component could be:

```
namespace app\components;

use Yii;
use yii\base\Component;

class SmsGateway extends Component
{
    public function send($to, $text)
    {
        ..
        ..
        ..
    }
}
```

This example is suitable to use this component as an application component:

```
'components' => [
    ..
    ..
        'smsgw' => [
            'class' => '\app\components\SmsGateway
        ],
]
```

That is usable directly from:

```
Yii:$app->smsgw->send('+3913456789', 'hello world!');
```

Another common example for an application component could be an object to send push notifications to mobile devices, which is made in the same way as the previous SMS gateway object.

Example – creating a component that creates a backup of the MySQL database and sends an e-mail to the administrator

This example will show a common task concerning the creation of backup copies for the main database and the alert messages that the administrator receives once complete.

A backup will be taken using the command line MySQL tool.

Maintenance operations should be executed in a console environment since they can be scheduled (every day, every week, two days a week, and so on), and they could cause a web server timeout (usually, if an operation is not finished, the web server will return a timeout error after 30 seconds) if this operation takes longer than the maximum time available. So we will start by creating a console controller in the advanced template that we previously installed.

Remember that the project root folder for the advanced template is yiiadv.

Create a new component in Maintenance.php at yiiadv/common/components with this content:

```php
<?php
namespace common\components;

use Yii;
use yii\base\Component;

class Maintenance extends Component
{
    public function launchBackup($database, $username, $password,
    $pathDestSqlFile)
    {
        $cmd = sprintf('mysqldump -u %s -p%s %s > %s', $username,
        $password, $database, $pathDestSqlFile);
        $outputLines = [];
        exec($cmd, $outputLines, $exitCode);

        return ['cmd' => $cmd, 'exitCode' => $exitCode,
        'outputLines' => $outputLines];
    }
}
?>
```

The `launchBackup()` method will launch `mysqldump` (which should be installed in the system) by passing the username, password, database, and the destination file path where the SQL output of this command is to be stored.

Then, it will return an array with these values: command, exit code of command, and its possible output text. Now let's create the console controller that we will use to launch the command. We could also launch it from a web controller, for example after clicking on a button.

Let's create the console controller in `MaintenanceController.php` at `yiiadv/console/controllers`:

```php
<?php

namespace console\controllers;

use \yii\console\Controller;
use \yii\helpers\Console;
use \common\components\Maintenance;

class MaintenanceController extends Controller
{
    public function actionBackupDatabase()
    {
        $tmpfname = tempnam(sys_get_temp_dir(), 'FOO');
        $obj = new Maintenance();
        $ret = $obj->launchBackup('username', 'password',
        'database_name', $tmpfname);

        if($ret['exitCode'] == 0)
        {
            $this->stdOut("OK\n");
            $this->stdOut(sprintf("Backup successfully stored in:
            %s\n", $tmpfname));
        }
        else
        {
            $this->stdOut("ERR\n");
        }

        // equivalent to return 0;
        return $ret['exitCode'];
    }

}

?>
```

Let's make some considerations:

- We could set the `launchBackup()` method of the maintenance component as static by avoiding to create an instance of the object; however, if we keep it nonstatic, we could also use it as application component. Otherwise, if we mark the method as static, and then use it as application component when calling the static method `launchBackup()` from the object, we will receive a warning from PHP.

- We could move the file creation inside the `launchBackup()` method because in this case it is a temporary file, but generally we could use a specific file path.

- We could avoid passing database info and get it from Yii parameters, if we store them in the parameters file.

A more complete action is to back up and send an e-mail to the administrator, containing the backup result and eventually, if needed, also the backup file:

```php
public function actionBackupDatabaseAndSendEmail()
{
    $tmpfname = tempnam(sys_get_temp_dir(), 'FOO'); // good
    $obj = new Maintenance();
    $ret = $obj->launchBackup('username', 'password',
    'database_name', $tmpfname);

    $emailAttachment = null;
    if($ret['exitCode'] == 0)
    {
        $this->stdOut("OK\n");
        $this->stdOut(sprintf("Backup successfully stored in:
        %s\n", $tmpfname));

        $textEmail = 'Backup database successful! Find it in
        attachment';
        $emailAttachment = $tmpfname;
    }
    else
    {
        $this->stdOut("ERR\n");

        $textEmail = 'Error in backup database! Check it!';
    }

    $emailMsg = Yii::$app->mailer->compose()
```

```
                      ->setFrom('from@example.com')
                      ->setTo('to@example.com')
                      ->setSubject('Backup database')
                      ->setTextBody($textEmail);

            if($emailAttachment!=null) $emailMsg-
            >attach($emailAttachment, ['fileName' =>
            'backup_db.sql']);
            $emailMsg->send();

            // equivalent to return 0;
            return $ret['exitCode'];
    }
```

Creating modules

A module is practically an application inside the main application. In fact, it is organized as a directory that is called the base path of the module. Within the directory, there are folders containing its controllers, models, views, and other code, just like in an application.

Follow the typical structure of a module:

```
myCustomModule/
    Module.php                    the module class file
    controllers/                  containing controller class files
        DefaultController.php     the default controller class file
    models/                       containing model class files
    views/                        containing controller view and
                                  layout files
        layouts/                  containing layout view files
        default/                  containing view files for
                                  DefaultController
            index.php             the index view file
```

The module class file is instanced when a module is being accessed and it is used to share data and components for code, such as application instances.

The module class file has these characteristics:

- It is by default named Module.php
- It is instanced once during the code execution
- It is located directly under the module's base path
- It extends from yii\base\Module

Let's look at an example of a module class for `myCustomModule` (under the `app\modules\myCustomModule` namespace):

```
namespace app\modules\myCustomModule;

class Module extends \yii\base\Module
{
    public function init()
    {
        parent::init();

        $this->params['foo'] = 'bar';
        // ...   other initialization code ...
    }
}
```

As a standard application, a module can have its own configuration based on a config file that has the same contents of a standard application:

```
<?php
return [
    'components' => [
        // list of component configurations
    ],
    'params' => [
        // list of parameters
    ],
    ..
    ..
    ..
];
```

We load this in the `init()` method of the module:

```
public function init()
{
    parent::init();
    // initialize the module with the configuration loaded from
config.php
    \Yii::configure($this, require(__DIR__ . '/config.php'));
}
```

Then, we create and use controllers, models, and views in the same way we do with a normal application.

We always have to take care to specify the right namespace at the top of every file.

Finally, to use a module in an application, we simply configure the application by listing the module in the module's property of the application. The following code in the application configuration uses the forum module:

```
[
    'modules' => [
        'myCustomModule' => [
            'class' => 'app\modules\myCustomModule\Module',
            // ... other configurations for the module ...
        ],
    ],
]
```

Generating an API documentation

Documentation is definitely one of the most important aspects of an app, since it provides information about its flows and structures. Unfortunately, it is often omitted due to lack of time.

Yii give us a powerful tool to automatically generate a pretty documentation. Basically, it uses all the documentation comments present in the app, those starting with /** instead of the classic /*.

Therefore, we have the advantage that comments in the code are used to produce a complete documentation.

Inside these comments, there are few keywords that are usable according to the context—file, class, or function/method.

In case of a file, the most common keywords to put on top are:

- @link url, where url is the reference URL linked to the file
- @copyright text, where text is the content of copyright
- @license url, where url is the reference to license content

In case of a class, the most common keywords to put on top are:

- @author name, where name is the name of the author
- @since version, where version is the version of the project in which this class has been included

In case of a function/method, the most common keywords to put on top are:

- `@param type name`, where type is the type of parameter and name is the name of the parameter passed as an argument of the function
- `@return type`, where type is the returned type
- `@throws class`, where class is the exception class thrown by the exception

Besides API documentation, Yii provides tools to create pretty guide files that are in the `.md` format (typical of GitHub). It is easy to find information on formatting a `.md` file by surfing the Internet.

Example – using an API documentation to generate a doc of app and services

Let's now see which commands automatically produce a documentation from the Yii app.

There are two kinds of documentation:

- API documentation, which is a reference of each `.php` file in the project, completed with doc comments referred to a single file, class, or function
- Guide, which is a pretty manual for the app, created using the `.md` files that Yii renders in pretty `.html` files

The first step is to install `api-doc`, if it is not already present.

Point to the project root folder and launch this command:

```
$ php composer.phar require --prefer-dist yiisoft/yii2-apidoc
```

This will install the `yii2-apidoc` extension.

 If this command is not properly complete, launch also a Composer update as follows:
```
$ php composer.phar update
```

Now we can launch the command to produce an API documentation starting from the project root folder:

```
$ vendor/bin/apidoc api ./ ../app-doc
```

The parameters are as follows:

- The first parameter, api, identifies the command to execute
- The second parameter, ./, identifies the path of the source files to scan
- The third parameter, ../app-doc, identifies the destination folder of the created documentation

After launching the command, going to the ../app-doc folder on a browser will show us the API documentation created by the framework.

When we make any changes in the source file, it is necessary to relaunch the command to update the API documentation. The second kind of documentation is the guide, a set of .html files produced by .md files.

So we need to create a folder, starting from the project root folder, for example, the folder named guide, where we will put all the .md files that we want to convert into .html pretty files from the command guide.

Now we are ready to launch the command to create our guide, which is totally similar to the previously made API command:

```
$ vendor/bin/apidoc guide ./guide ../app-doc
```

This command will convert all the .md files present in the ./guide folder into .html files, storing them in the ../app-doc folder (together with the API documentation files).

Let's make a concrete example. Starting with the basic template project, create a new controller named TestDocController in TestDocController.php at basic/controllers:

```php
<?php

/**
 * This file contains a controller to demonstrate api documentation
tool.
 *
 * @link http://www.example.com/
 * @copyright Copyright (c) 2015
 * @license http://www.example.com/license/
 */

namespace app\controllers;
```

```php
use Yii;
use yii\web\Controller;


/**
 * This is a controller class to demonstrate api documentation tool.
 *
 * @author Fabrizio Caldarelli
 * @since 1.0
 */
class TestDocController extends Controller
{
    /**
     * Make sum of the operands
     *
     * @param float $a first operand
     * @param float $b second operand
     * @return float sum of parameters
     * @author
     */
    public function makeSum(float $a, float $b)
    {
        return $a+$b;
    }
}
```

Now open a shell console on host, and from the project root folder, launch the command to generate the API documentation:

```
$ vendor/bin/apidoc api ./ ../app-doc
```

This will create the documentation for all files starting with the root folder (./) and storing the HTML result files in ../app-doc.

Now, on your browser, go to http://hostname/app-doc and we will display the API documentation index page. Search for TestDocController.php in the side menu and click on it. This should be the output:

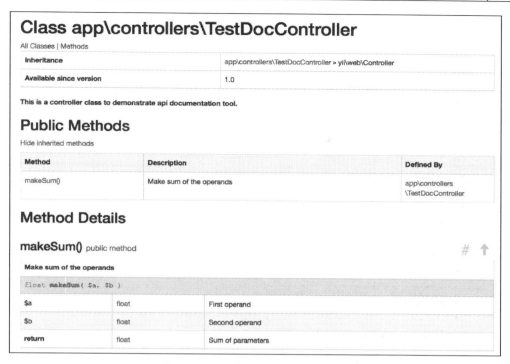

TestDocController API documentation

Now, we want to demonstrate the second kind of documentation—guide documentation.

Create a folder from the project root folder named `app-guide`. In it, put a new file named `test-doc-controller.md` with the following content:

```
## TestDoc Controller

This is the guide for TestDoc Controller.

## Functionalities

It is provided makeSum function, that makes a sum of two values passed
as parameter

```
$a = 10;
$b = 20;
$c = $this->makeSum(float $a, float $b)   // $c = 30;
```
```

Go to the shell console of the hosting and from the project root folder, launch the command to generate the guide documentation:

```
$ vendor/bin/apidoc guide ./app-guide ../app-doc
```

This will create the guide documentation for all `.md` files in the `./app-guide` folder and will store `.html` results in `../app-doc`.

On your browser go to `http://hostname/app-doc/guide-test-doc-controller.html`, you should see the following screen:

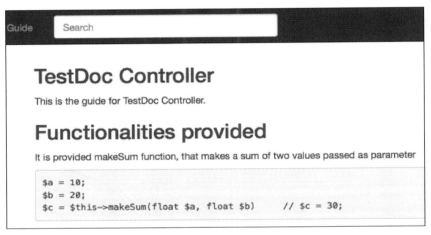

TestDocController guide documentation

Summary

In this final chapter, you learned how to make reusable and easily maintainable code, using widgets and components. Talking about reusable view code (HTML, JavaScript, and CSS), we introduced widgets, defined and focused on the benefits they add to the project. Next, you learned to build and use them, and finally, we did a practical example by building a new widget from scratch. Talking of reusable logic code, we discovered its components, distinguished between components and application components, and also did some practical examples by building useful components for real-life problems.

Then we mastered the documentation generator, specifically API and guide documentation. You learned how to launch and use the tools provided by Yii. Finally, we built a controller class to explain, with a practical example, how to build the API reference and the guide reference for that controller.

Index

B

backend
splitting, advanced template used 212, 213
basic folder, Yii2's application structure
assets 3
commands 3
config 3
mail 3
models 3
runtime 4
tests 4
vendor 4
views 4
web 4
bootstrap template
used, for creating controller 25-28
Bootstrap widget
using 169

C

cache component 7
carousel
widget, creating with 300-303
commands, for retrieving data
query() 78
queryAll() 78
queryOne() 78
queryScalar() 78
common view content
splitting, into reusable views 29
components
creating 303-308
Composer
about 2
URL 3
Yii2, installing with 2, 3
console
output, formatting from 289-291
console applications
interacting with 282, 283
console controller
creating 284-287
contact page
adding 32, 33

content negotiation 248
controller
creating 20-22, 247-250
creating, for room management 250-253
creating, for static news items list
display 25-28
data, sending to view 24, 25
createUrl() method
reference link 28
cron jobs
executing 291
implementing 291
CRUD
generating, Gii used 154
used, for managing customers 155-157
used, for managing reservations 155-157
used, for managing rooms 155-157
CSS
used, for displaying advertising
columns 160-163
custom authentication method
creating, for application 264-268
custom columns
displaying, in grid 131
customer and reservation models
creating, in same view 180-182
customers list
obtaining, authentication used 258-260
customize CSS 158-160
customize JavaScript 158-160
custom responses
creating 274
custom URL rules
about 43
example 44-48

D

data
manipulating, ActiveRecord used 88-91
sharing, between views and layout 34
DataProvider, for grids 128, 129
date
formatting 65, 66
datepicker
using 170-174

layout background
  modifying, based on URL parameter 35
lazy loading 97
linked models
  saving, in same view 179
log component 8
logger
  using 14
login form
  creating, example 190-195

M

mailer component 8
message command 231
methods, ActiveRecord
  delete() 91
  save() 91
  validate() 91
methods, identityClass class
  findIdentity() 186
  findIdentityByAccessToken() 186
  getAuthKey() 186
  getId() 186
  validateAuthKey() 186
Model
  creating 57-61
Model base class, features
  attribute declaration 57
  attribute labels 58
  massive attribute assignment 58
  scenario-based validation 58
Model-View-Controller (MVC) design
      pattern, Yii2 10
modules
  creating 309, 310
multiple customers
  saving, at same time 176-178
multiple database connections
  using 120
multiple grids
  displaying, on one page 148, 149
multiple layouts
  example 39, 40
  using 38

multiple models
  finding, in same view 175

N

naming convention 10, 11
numeric fields
  formatting 65, 66

O

OAuth 2 254
objects, Yii2
  Application Components 5
  Components 5
  Controllers 5
  Extensions 5
  Filters 5
  Models 5
  Modules 5
  Views 5
  Widgets 5
output
  formatting, from console 289-291

P

parameters, URL rule
  defaults 49
  encodeParams 49
  host 50
  mode 50
  name 50
  pattern 50
  route 50
  suffix 50
  verb 50
PHP Data Objects (PDO) 74
placeholders formatting 235-237
Pretty URLs
  using 41-43
public access
  frontend, creating for 216

Q

query parameter 254

Y

Thank you for buying
Yii2 By Example

About Packt Publishing

Packt, pronounced 'packed', published its first book, *Mastering phpMyAdmin for Effective MySQL Management*, in April 2004, and subsequently continued to specialize in publishing highly focused books on specific technologies and solutions.

Our books and publications share the experiences of your fellow IT professionals in adapting and customizing today's systems, applications, and frameworks. Our solution-based books give you the knowledge and power to customize the software and technologies you're using to get the job done. Packt books are more specific and less general than the IT books you have seen in the past. Our unique business model allows us to bring you more focused information, giving you more of what you need to know, and less of what you don't.

Packt is a modern yet unique publishing company that focuses on producing quality, cutting-edge books for communities of developers, administrators, and newbies alike. For more information, please visit our website at www.packtpub.com.

About Packt Open Source

In 2010, Packt launched two new brands, Packt Open Source and Packt Enterprise, in order to continue its focus on specialization. This book is part of the Packt Open Source brand, home to books published on software built around open source licenses, and offering information to anybody from advanced developers to budding web designers. The Open Source brand also runs Packt's Open Source Royalty Scheme, by which Packt gives a royalty to each open source project about whose software a book is sold.

Writing for Packt

We welcome all inquiries from people who are interested in authoring. Book proposals should be sent to author@packtpub.com. If your book idea is still at an early stage and you would like to discuss it first before writing a formal book proposal, then please contact us; one of our commissioning editors will get in touch with you.

We're not just looking for published authors; if you have strong technical skills but no writing experience, our experienced editors can help you develop a writing career, or simply get some additional reward for your expertise.

Yii Project Blueprints

ISBN: 978-1-78328-773-4   Paperback: 320 pages

From conception to production, learn how to develop real-world applications with the Yii framework

1. Develop real-world web applications through easy-to-follow, step-by-step processes.

2. Create eight projects from beginning to end to help you explore the full power of Yii.

3. Build a fast, user-based, database-driven content management system with a dashboard and RESTful API.

Web Application Development with Yii 2 and PHP

ISBN: 978-1-78398-188-5   Paperback: 406 pages

Fast-track your web application development using the new generation Yii PHP framework

1. Implement real-world web application features efficiently using the Yii development framework.

2. Each chapter provides micro-examples that build upon each other to create the final macro-example, a basic CRM application.

3. Filled with useful tasks to improve the maintainability of your applications.

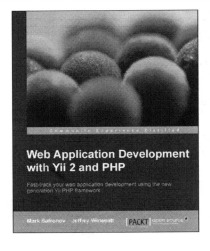

Please check **www.PacktPub.com** for information on our titles

Yii Application Development Cookbook

Second Edition

ISBN: 978-1-78216-310-7   Paperback: 408 pages

A Cookbook covering both practical Yii application development tips and the most important Yii features

1. Learn how to use Yii even more efficiently.

2. Full of practically useful solutions and concepts you can use in your application.

3. Both important Yii concept descriptions and practical recipes are inside.

Beginning Yii [Video]

ISBN: 978-1-78216-448-7   Duration: 02:44 hours

Fast track your web application development by harnessing the power of the Yii PHP framework

1. Develop sophisticated Web 2.0 apps using PHP and Yii.

2. Ideal for PHP developers new to Yii and framework-based development.

3. Build powerful, reliable, and scalable apps fast.

4. Clear and concise video tutorials from an experienced Yii developer.